MW00745094

LITTLE
RED HEN

LITTLE RED HEN

A Collection of Columns from Detroit's Conservative Voice

by

NOLAN FINLEY

Edited by Ingrid Jacques

DG
DUNLAP
GODDARD

A DUNLAP GODDARD ORIGINAL, JANUARY 2016

PUBLISHED IN THE UNITED STATES OF AMERICA
MAUNFACTURED IN THE UNITED STATES OF AMERICA

All the selections in this work were previously published by
The Detroit News, a Digital First Media Newspaper.

ISBN-13: 978-09656040-9-3 (trade paperback)
ISBN-13: 978-09971275-0-8 (mobi)
ISBN-13: 978-09971275-1-5 (epub)
LCCN: 2015959751
A CIP catalog reference for this book is available from the publisher.

Jacket Design by Gus Tyk
Book Design by Graciela Demerath
Author Photograph by Russell Keberly

QUANTITY PURCHASES
Companies, professional groups, clubs and other organizations may qualify for special terms when ordering quantities of this title.
For information, email Special Sales Department at info@dunlap-goddard.com.

To my mother, Mildred Lorena Sells Finley,
the real life Little Red Hen.

Table of Contents

CHAPTER 2
Detroit

CHAPTER 3
Kwame

CHAPTER 4
Michigan

CHAPTER 5
Obama

CHAPTER 6
Politics

CHAPTER 7
Autos

CHAPTER 8
Education

CHAPTER 9
Our Money

CHAPTER 10
Family

CHAPTER II

Terror & War

CHAPTER I2

The Middle East

CHAPTER 13
Holidays

CHAPTER 14
Drugs

CHAPTER 15
The Environment

CHAPTER 16
Farewells

CHAPTER 17
Freedom

CHAPTER 18
Newspapers

Foreword

One of my favorite stories about Coleman Young, Detroit's irascible mayor of the 1970s and 1980s, comes from an encounter he had with Nolan Finley.

At the height of Detroit's budget crisis in the early 1980s, Finley was covering the city for the *Detroit News*. He got a tip that Young, who was busy talking cutbacks and slashing city worker pay, had nonetheless ordered a new mayoral limousine.

Thwarted when he asked if that was so, Nolan went down to city hall, saw a new Cadillac limousine parked outside, and decided to wait to see if Young came out and got in. He stood there a few hours, and started to lean against the car. That's when Young came bounding out the door, flanked by his security detail.

"Somebody get that mother-fucker off my new Cadillac," Young said.

In a flash of Young's classic, profanity-laced exasperation, Nolan had his story.

One of the great things about Nolan's column in the *News* over the past 17 years is how much that life of reporting in Detroit—the characters, the strange and wonderful stories, the city's unrelenting pace and troubles—is reflected in the work.

You read Nolan to see what he's saying—about politics, about finance, about life in the metro area and America. But just as important, it's the historical context and quintessential Detroit outlook and attitude that frame his work, and make it a must-read.

It's even more important, perhaps, that Nolan has been able to cut such a significant profile in a city whose politics and sensibilities are so different from his own.

Detroit's union culture, to Nolan, is part of what led the city to failure. The dominant narrative about the important emphasis on black political leadership? For Nolan, that is a distraction.

But he is respected for the way his classic conservatism is expressed: in clear, discreet arguments that are pointed but fact-based, and avoid personal attack.

As a liberal columnist at a competing newspaper, I rarely agree with Nolan. I read his column, though, because I respect his point of view, his history in this city, and the consistent, critical voice he intones.

And then there's this: the love he so clearly has for Detroit, and Michigan. It's not an immature, fawning unquestioning love, but a seasoned connection with the place he has called home for most of his life.

That love has been best expressed, of late, in the series of columns Nolan has written about the exciting changes emerging in downtown Detroit, and the need for people of every racial background to be part of the progress.

In typical Nolan fashion, the crusade is framed in blunt, explicit terms. "Where are all the black people" was the headline emblazoned on his first missive.

But also, as always, the work reflects a knowing sense of what's right for Detroit, and an affection for the city's future that is abiding, and indelible.

Stephen Henderson
Editorial Page Editor, *Detroit Free Press*

Chapter 1

Culture

October 19, 2008
America should follow The Little Red Hen

If America really is structurally broken, as we've been warned with authority from the campaign trail, then it's not because our fundamental principles have failed us, but because we've strayed so far from them.

I'm not talking about the values defined by Jefferson, Adams, Hamilton and crew; though Lord knows we could certainly use a good refresher course in those.

The principles I miss are the ones voiced so eloquently by *The Little Red Hen*, *The Three Pigs* and *The Little Engine That Could*.

Generations of Americans were raised on these fables and in the process were taught lessons that would be considered harsh on *Sesame Street*. But they reinforced who we were.

From the feisty Little Red Hen we learned the rewards of hard work. We also learned to savor those rewards guilt-free and to understand that what we create belongs to us.

The hen would have flailed the Rainbow Fish had he come sashaying around with his share your crayons silliness.

She planted the wheat and ground the flour and baked the bread and felt no obligation to break off a piece for the shiftless sheep or do-nothing donkey —unless she wanted to. She was my kind of chick.

But she doesn't fit into an America that increasingly questions the fairness of one person having more than another, without weighing sweat or skill.

In the hen's world, if you produced, you ate; if you were able to and didn't, you went hungry. Why is that too sinister a concept to teach tykes today?

This country will become a very dangerous place if the mindset takes hold that the fruit of individual industriousness is a collective asset.

Those house-building pigs drove home the reality that bad choices carry bad consequences. Build your house out of sticks or straw, and your hams will be steaming on the Wicked Wolf's table. Build it out of bricks, and you can safely rest them in a La-Z-Boy in front of your big screen TV.

Compare that lesson to the plea that we have no choice but to open our wallets to the Wall Street tycoons who overplayed their hands or to the home-owners who borrowed too much without reading the fine print.

The Little Engine is my favorite. He huffed and puffed up that hill on his own steam, and kept stubbornly going even when he wasn't sure he could make it to the top. He didn't pull off the tracks to wait for Dora the Explorer to give him a push.

The Engine's breed of self-reliance and determination to overcome obstacles would serve us well as we enter what promises to be the most challenging economic stretch in decades. Will we turn to the government to pull us up the hill, or will we get up a good head of steam and go for it ourselves?

In a couple of weeks, a large number of voters, likely even a majority, will go to the polls to choose a political Pied Piper to lead them to an America where everyone shares and hugs and plays patty cake in equal-size houses.

I'd rather follow that cranky Red Hen.

October 1, 2000
Change the moral, not legal, climate on abortion

Now that abortion is a prescription rather than a procedure, it's time for those warring against Roe v. Wade to give up the fight and turn their efforts in a more productive direction.

If ever there were a genie not about to go back in the bottle, it's the right of a woman to obtain a legal abortion. The decision last week by the Food and Drug Administration to legalize the so-called abortion pill RU-486 makes an already futile fight even more so.

Moving abortions out of the operating room and into the medicine cabinet ends all hope of the pro-life movement to put an end to abortions by making them impossible to obtain. You can shut down a clinic, perhaps, but stemming the flow of pills is another matter.

We've learned that from the drug war, haven't we? More laws and harsher penalties haven't worked to keep people away from illegal drugs. Make surgical abortions illegal and you simply create another staple for the pusher's inventory—RU-486.

The battle is lost, at least on the legal front.

No matter where you stand on the question of choice, bringing an end to the divisive, bitter and unresolvable debate over Roe v. Wade has to be viewed as a positive.

Abortion, for good or ill, has become institutionalized. Prohibition is not likely, no matter who sits in the Oval Office or on the Supreme Court.

Voters motivated by the choice issue are convinced a new Bush administration would bring an end to abortion rights. There's no evidence to support that. It didn't happen during 12 years of Republican rule in Washington during the Reagan-Bush era or, for that matter, during 10 years of the current GOP leadership in Lansing.

The timing of the FDA's announcement, just five weeks before the presidential election, is suspect. Democrats know Bush's more moderate views on abortion cause him trouble with certain wings of his party. Tossing the abortion pill into the campaign is a convenient distraction from the real issues.

But so far, Bush is wisely deflecting the RU-486 question. He has refused to take the bait and pledge to revoke the FDA approval if elected. Instead, he said he would "work to build a culture that respects life."

The message is remarkably significant, and more ardent anti-abortionists should take it to heart: Stop focusing on changing laws and instead concentrate on changing behavior.

The law does nothing but provide the right to choose. It doesn't mean that we as a society advocate abortions or that we encourage them.

In fact, many supporters of choice abhor abortion. But they can't abide the idea of a woman desperate to end a pregnancy turning to dangerous, back-alley alternatives.

The abortion pill should be welcomed in part because it enables earlier termination of pregnancy and hopefully will cut down on the demand for some of the more barbaric late-term procedures.

If the pro-life movement surrenders its attack on the basic law, it might find it has some allies on the other side for efforts to allow states to pass reasonable abortion regulations, including parental notification and a ban on partial-birth abortions.

It also may find common ground with groups like Planned Parenthood in reducing the demand for abortions through better education and contraception.

Bush is right to shift the debate from the legal to the moral. Pro-lifers have been fighting the wrong enemy. There's no victory at the end of the battle against Roe v. Wade.

Changing the law without addressing the demand accomplishes nothing. If the goal is to eliminate abortions, pro-lifers should redirect themselves toward changing hearts and attitudes.

Efforts to encourage adoption, counsel shelter and protect at-risk pregnant women, and foster a frank national discussion about what abortion really is would save more unborn babies than raging against the Supreme Court or clogging the entrances to abortion clinics.

Meanwhile, Bush should continue to keep abortion out of the presidential campaign and resist any attempt to use RU-486 to cloud Tuesday's debate with Vice President Al Gore.

Abortion is a thorny political issue, particularly for Republicans. Bush's theme to change the culture, not the law, may play quite well with the vast number of voters who find themselves somewhere near the middle of this wearisome fight.

August 19, 2001
How should society deal with people who are just too stupid?

The biggest challenge of a democratic government is dealing with stupid people.

That comes to mind again in light of the horrific story of Shaniqua Betty, the 20-year-old single Detroit mother who handed her infant son to a stranger at a bus stop and asked that he hold the baby while she went home for her purse and shoes.

Outraged readers have jammed our mailboxes since the baby was found dead in an abandoned Detroit home. Some are demanding a government solution; others are looking for a government scapegoat.

Those urging state intervention seize on the fact that Betty, who lacks the maternal sense of a trout, is reportedly pregnant with another child. The government, they argue, should do something.

You may feel a little, or even a lot, of sympathy for Betty. You may feel like the system let her down. But by any measure, Betty is just plain stupid. You wouldn't ask a midnight stranger at a bus stop to hold your wallet, let alone your baby.

No one wants to see someone that dumb bring more children into the world. I once interviewed a young prisoner who was about to deliver her sixth child. More than half her life had been spent in various lock-ups, and all her babies were born behind bars—two were conceived in prison. The oldest, barely a teenager, was already in a juvenile home. Why keep having children for her poor mother to raise? "I likes babies," was her answer. Pitifully dumb, but even locking her away didn't stop her procreation.

So what then? Sterilization of the ignorant? Forcing contraception on those who fail a parental IQ test? Mandatory abortions for anyone deemed too sorry to raise children?

Wouldn't that make us a lot like China, which brutally manages the reproductive activity of its citizens?

As much as we'd like to close off this direct route to poverty and misery, we know we can't, at least not by government mandate. It's our frustration talking.

Equally frustrating are those who would make the state the fall guy in baby Isaiah's death. They argue that given Betty's troubled childhood and her history of instability, welfare agencies should have been more pro-active in protecting her baby. They insist she should have been given more help.

Of course she should have.

But Betty's was not simply an isolated case missed by a negligent system. The maternity wards in Detroit are bursting with babies born to too-young mothers, mothers with little or no support, mothers who haven't a clue how to keep their babies safe and healthy.

Seventy percent of the babies in Detroit are born out of wedlock, many to teenage mothers.

The system is overwhelmed. We can point our fingers at social workers whenever a baby Isaiah is abused or killed, but these workers are frazzled. They can't possibly keep up with the avalanche of babies being born to mothers who fail the most basic parental fitness test.

We can't stop mothers like Shaniqua Betty from having children. We can do precious little to protect their babies after they're born.

But we can speak out loudly and honestly against that shocking illegitimacy rate. Until it's brought under control, until women and men approach reproduction with far more responsibility, until contraceptive use is as widespread as casual sex—until people stop being so damn stupid—we should expect more baby Isaiahs.

March 10, 2002

Another birthday starts boomer talking 'bout my generation

Today is my birthday, so indulge me a little self-indulgence.

I'm not yet old, but I'm close enough to old to envy its movie discounts. A friend said recently that I'm "rushing toward 50." Unfortunately, I can't remember which friend said that.

Because along with the hairline and reading vision, age feeds on memory. My face recognition file no longer lines up parallel with my name recognition file. Passing a familiar face now, most often the distance between "Hello…" and "…Judy" is several slabs of sidewalk. And still, there's a better than even chance that Judy is actually Sue.

This happens even when the face is very, very familiar. Sometimes even when the face belongs to one of my children.

So I've taken to using non-committal endearments like Chief, Big Guy and Buddy until I can locate the drawer where I've stashed the real name.

Obviously, I'm a boomer, a member of a generation that has not just celebrated its youth, but wallowed in it. We are extremely reluctant to put away our childish things—witness the too-many stringy, gray ponytails. Growing up has been hard to do; growing old will be even harder.

We are not likely to supplant our parents as the Greatest Generation. We have been way too narcissistic for that. But we did invent rock-and-roll and the Internet, and we are likely to reinvent what it means to be gray in America.

As a group, we are healthier than any previous generation, and will stay fit and active longer. That should also mean that we'll keep producing and contributing much deeper into our senior years than did our parents or grandparents.

Given our obsession with youth, we are not likely to give up and go quietly to the sidelines. We love the stage too much.

That's good, because our numbers are staggering. There are 82.8 million boomers in America, compared with 39.9 million in Generation X. The worry is that our mass retirement will sink Social Security and drain wealth from our children and grandchildren.

But that's only if we think of aging and retirement in traditional terms. Rather than worrying so much about propping up Social Security and building individual retirement funds to last for decades, we should be encouraging Boomers to stay on the job well beyond age 65.

That will require motivating older workers and redefining the career arc. It will also mean purging the workplace of age bias. Careers that haven't caught fire by age 40 shouldn't be written off automatically. Workers in their 50s and even 60s should still be considered for promotions and new challenges.

Mothers who left the workforce for a decade or more should be welcomed back to pick up their careers where they left off. Instead of looking toward the pasture at age 55, we should still be striving for the executive suite.

Longer lives should naturally mean longer careers that remain rewarding and productive.

Of course, that will take some tolerance and understanding from our younger colleagues. Jason will have to shrug it off when we call him Scott.

It will be annoying for them at times, I'm sure. But it is better than the alternative of reaching deeper into their own wallets to keep us fat and frisky in Florida.

June 30, 2002

America has big ol' butt; are we to blame, or are we marketing victims?

Having just returned from a week at the beach, I can say with authority that America doesn't look so good in a bathing suit.

Our nation is porky. Porky but proud, judging from the blushingly scant amount of material covering its enormity.

America's flabby middle prompted an admirably fit President George W. Bush last week to prod his fellow citizens to eat less and exercise more.

Bush noted that 61 percent of the nation is overweight, a condition that adds $117 billion a year to health care costs. Checking the insurance industry's recommended height-to-weight ratios, and even fibbing my body frame into the jumbo category, I have to say, "me too."

But our collective chubbiness may not be entirely our fault.

Fresh from vanquishing the tobacco companies, those who believe in better health through litigation, regulation and taxation are now taking aim at jelly rolls. The Wall Street Journal reported recently that trial lawyers are gearing up to haul food manufacturers into court to answer for America's obesity.

Meanwhile, the food industry is lobbying Congress for liability protection and reworking product labels to make sure no one in America is unaware that washing down a dozen doughnuts with a six-pack of cola will clog the arteries and double the chin.

The obesity lawsuits will likely follow the same model as the tobacco litigation. First step, relieve the individual of all responsibility.

Already, some researchers argue that fatness is a disease, perhaps caused by a virus. The food industry, the case will go, exploits the ailment by larding up their goodies with sugar, fat and artificial flavorings, making them irresistible to the afflicted.

Irresponsible marketing, not poor self-control, explains those thunderous thighs.

You can imagine the end result of all this, based on the tobacco experience. A Twinkie Tax on snack cakes. Candy and soda machines banned from public places. Sign a waiver before you order a Big Mac.

Absurd, perhaps. But we might have said the same thing 25 years ago of predictions that smokers would someday have to stand out in the cold to enjoy a cigarette at work and would be unwelcome in many bars and restaurants.

Once a case can be made that our bad habits affect others, whether through second-hand smoke or the higher insurance premiums caused by obesity-related illnesses, our health is no longer a personal matter. Pro-choice ends with abortion and doesn't apply to the choice to smoke, overeat or abuse drugs and alcohol. Then, our bodies enter the public domain, and someone else—everyone else—has a right to tell us what to do with them.

Those who facilitate our excesses with their tempting products will, as with the tobacco industry, be required to fork over their profits to those who can't control their appetites and to the government bodies that use the courts to impose a back-door tax.

We started down this path with the tobacco lawsuits. It will be harder now to turn back the opportunists who see a chance to blame suppliers of chocolate, sugar and ice cream for our big national butt.

As someone who gets most of his daily calorie intake from dessert, this is quite distressing. I'm hoarding Ho-Hos and stocking the freezer with Drumsticks. With apologies to Charlton Heston, they can have my apple fritter when they pry it from my cold, dead fingers.

December 28, 2003

A hardware store junkie bemoans the passing of nails by the pound

A bona fide hardware store is a marvelous thing. And rare.

I can march through a shopping mall like Sherman through Georgia, knocking items off my list and spending at a per-hour rate that would make the best congressional porkers proud.

But in hardware stores, I luxuriate, moving along the shelves slowly, reading labels and daydreaming about actually finishing a home improvement project or two.

When the Home Depot store near the house was open 24 hours, I'd find myself wandering the aisles on sleepless nights, sighting along 2x4s I had no intention of buying and sorting through bins of plumbing parts, even though I swore off all plumbing after a simple faucet drip repair ended with the entire kitchen counter upside down on the floor.

So I welcomed the opportunity to take a break from Christmas errands for an emergency hardware run. The opportunity was presented by my snowblower, which has an aversion to cold weather, an unfortunate condition given its career choice.

With the broadcast news reporters in near hysterics over the predicted blizzard of the century, I decided to try once again to get the snowblower running. I headed off to the hardware store for a spark plug and starter fluid.

Although their numbers are shrinking, there remain in Metro Detroit a few true-blue hardware stores, unaffiliated with the franchise chains, where you can get nails by the pound, window glass cut and tools that aren't held captive in shrink wrapped packaging.

And no food. Real hardware stores don't sell food.

Count among the faithful Duke's Hardware in Dearborn, Pointe Hardware in Grosse Pointe Park, Brooks Lumber downtown and a small handful of others.

Murray's Hardware in Redford used to be my happy place, even though it added a jewelry counter years ago and now has home decorating stuff squeezing out the electrical and plumbing supplies. But it has balanced its dual missions well. You can still get all the ingredients for an engine tune-up, and if it added a rack of ladies lingerie, a guy could do all his Christmas shopping in one place.

Sadly, I didn't pick any of these hardware stores for my shopping task.

I opted instead for one of the chain stores where everyone wears the same brightly colored vest, and which deep down dreams of being a grocery.

Worse, I picked the same store that once gave me the heave-ho for pitching a fit in the middle of the peanuts/chips/cereal/auto parts aisle because it stocked enough nabs to stuff an office party, but no two-cycle oil.

They still keep an eye on me when I walk through the door. This time, I moved quietly through the stacks of cereal boxes, canned beans and assorted holiday candy, past the teensy packages of screws and finish nails, and found the small space in the back where the starting fluid ought to be. It wasn't.

"I don't think we carry that," the vested young clerk said. "Or maybe the shipment is coming tomorrow."

Not wanting to risk banishment again, I bore my indignation silently, and simply turned and stomped out of the store muttering, "Maybe I'll try the Farmer Jack for starter fluid."

But not before picking up a couple packages of chocolate-covered peanuts and some Corn Flakes. I just couldn't beat the price.

April 11, 2004

Why protect privacy?
Because Lary Howard's story could be yours

Those who wonder why average, law-abiding Americans should worry about the government grabbing more power to poke into the private corners of our lives should consider the case of Lary Howard.

Howard, 56, of Canton Township, is a Livonia middle school teacher whose professional record is unblemished and whose public personal conduct is above reproach.

Not the kind of guy who should ever have to worry about peeping through the wrong side of jail cell bars.

Except that Howard has a bit of a pornography fetish. He's a sucker for those disgusting XXX Horny Housewives and Debbie Does Donkeys emails that pop up unsolicited on computer screens. Most people cringe and kill the file without looking.

Howard opened them and went looking for more. Lots more. Thousands of images of naked people doing what naked people do found their way to his computer hard drive.

That may make Howard a perv, but one with plenty of company. Snoop around the attics, basements and garages of any household that has at least one male resident and likely or not you'll find a porn stash.

Howard isn't proud of his predilection—who would be?—but he practiced it in the privacy of his own home.

"It certainly isn't something I'd want my students to know about."

But now they do.

On Feb. 26, Canton police kicked down Howard's door and with guns drawn arrested him and hauled him off to jail. They also seized his computer with its dirty little secrets.

The charge: Child endangerment and possession of child pornography; six counts, each carrying a potential 20-year sentence. You can imagine what those charges will do for the career of a school teacher.

The evidence against Howard was delivered to police on a computer disc by his ex-wife at the end of a very bitter divorce. Canton police enlisted an expert, who initially decided that among the images on Howard's computer were some that might be children.

Howard swears on a stack of Playboys that he has no interest in kiddie porn and only visited adult sites that guaranteed their models were of legal age. After 26 days of hell, prosecutors agreed and dropped the charges.

It's a lot easier to dismiss a criminal case than it is to restore a reputation.

Howard remains under suspension with pay; Livonia school officials are concerned about a confession he allegedly made when first interviewed.

Howard says the confession was coerced during a panic attack and without an attorney present. He also blames a panic attack for not opening the door when police knocked.

Canton Police Capt. Alex Wilson says the handling of the case is under review in response to a complaint Howard filed.

"My privacy was invaded," says Howard. "My life was laid bare. It's a private matter that's now very public."

You might think Howard should be locked up for indulging his appetite for trash. If so, better build more jail cells.

The crime here is not Howard's creepy fancies. But rather that the most private places of a person's life can be unlocked for public review on the barest suspicion of a crime.

Think about that when you consider how much access the government should have to the keys to those places.

June 13, 2004

Region needs more two-sided talks about race, fewer lectures

Channel 4's Devin Scillian and Emery King scored a breakthrough when they staged a public discussion about race relations during the Detroit Regional Chamber's policy session.

Scillian says the taping on Mackinac Island opened a floodgate; everywhere he went afterward people stopped him to talk about race.

"I could barely get through the Grand Hotel," he says.

The "Flashpoint" show sprang out of personal conversations between Scillian, who is white, and King who is black. The two, Scillian says, have reached a comfort level where they can express any opinion, ask any question of each other.

But asked whether he feels equally comfortable talking candidly about race in a more formal setting, or to answer the call of one panelist to hold confrontational conversations about race, Scillian says no.

"Definitely not," he says. "And I would say most white people would be uncomfortable doing that in many situations."

Conversations about race still tend to be more one-sided lecture than dialogue. Whites, as Scillian notes, still pull punches, are still too politically correct.

For good reason. The consequences of making a mistake are great. Say the wrong thing and you risk the racist label. From there, you're on a street corner with a tin cup and a sign saying, "Will Never Work Again."

To reach the point as a people that Scillian and King are as individuals will mean lowering the racism antennae considerably. For sure, whites must understand that racism is real and has a powerful impact on the lives of African-Americans. But blacks have a responsibility, too. They have to stop searching for the racist bogeyman in every shadow, to accept that not every slight is rooted in racism.

A friend who helps tend the trains at Greenfield Village has to lower the crossing gate before the locomotive starts rolling. Being a retired engineer, he is extremely precise. If the book says lower the gate at 12:10, that's when it goes down.

On a recent weekend, he lowered the gate as a group of Boy Scouts, all African-American, approached. One of the leaders took offense and loudly accused him of blocking their way because they we're black. The leader called the worker a racist and threatened to complain.

The gate tender, a decent man, went home heartsick. And a group of young Scouts went home convinced they were victimized by racism.

Yes, we have to talk about race and find real answers. But coming to the middle means both sides have a journey ahead.

Mayor Kwame Kilpatrick perfectly illustrated that when he stunned a Mackinac audience still basking in the positive glow of the "Flashpoint" session with this gem: "What is it with you white people? You love your drug wars."

Imagine if the mayor's fellow panelist, L. Brooks Patterson, had made a similar remark. Sensitivity trainers would now be stopping off at Lexus dealers on their way to Oakland County.

Double standards breed resentment. Good, honest talk is the only way to defeat this region's shameful segregation. But we have to do more than lecture rich, white people about black history over creme brulee. We have to create a forum where both blacks and whites are willing to not just complain about each other, but also hear hard things about themselves.

March 6, 2005
Paddles might work better in classrooms than Commandments

Best I can recall, the Ten Commandments were not posted in any of the schools I attended while growing up. But there were paddles hanging from the wall of every classroom—that I remember very well.

There was no standard-issue model. The paddles reflected the individual tastes of their wielders. Some were long and skinny, for those who favored velocity over heft. Others were wide, for maximum coverage. Some had holes drilled through the surface to cut down on wind resistance, and many were personalized with war colors or the signatures of their victims.

A few even had notches along the edges.

These were not ceremonial artifacts. They were working tools, kept within easy reach and pulled down with regularity to enforce the only commandment that mattered in our world then: Thou shalt not push the teacher over the edge.

We also knew well the formula for escalating punishment—for every stroke you got at school, you got two more at home. Nobody filed a lawsuit against a teacher in those days for making a kid mind.

Paddles have long been vanquished from America's classrooms and most homes. Perhaps for the best. But I suspect that at least some of the decline in our schools can be traced to the inability of teachers to maintain classroom order with a good, strong forehand.

There are some who think the answer to restoring discipline and moral behavior is to display the Ten Commandments in schools and other public spaces.

Advocates went before the U.S. Supreme Court last week to make their case.

It's a waste of effort, even if they prevail. Simply carving words in marble won't guarantee children will read them, or that they'll buy the idea that life should be lived by a specific moral rule set.

They won't get that from words set in stone. For the commandments to have any impact on children, they have to see adults living by them.

In the house I grew up in, a plaque of the Ten Commandments, the words embossed on a gold background, hung in the hallway. There was another one in my grandmother's living room and in the homes of most of my friends and relatives.

But I can't say I ever bothered to read to the bottom of any of those tablets.

I didn't really need to. I was raised by people who knew the commandments by heart and who darn sure wouldn't spare the rod when I got crossways of a few of them.

Maybe everyone, school children included, would act better if everywhere they went they bumped into a list of the "Thou shalts." But I doubt it.

After the first few encounters, the words would blur into the wallpaper. Nobody would notice, let alone stop to read them.

You can't say that about paddles, though.

Hang a paddle on the wall, and it's hard to take your eyes off of it. Take it from someone who remembers the sting of wood hitting the sweet spot.

Maybe there's a better idea here.

Forget the plaques. Carve the Ten Commandments on paddles, and hang those in classrooms.

At least there'd be a passing chance they'll get read.

August 12, 2007

New religions are as stifling as the old

Modern man has shucked off most of the restraints of traditional religion. While a majority of people still say they believe in God, or at least in some form of higher being, they have rationalized their belief system so as to owe no real tribute to their ill-defined deity.

No longer are they bound by the sanctions and rules dictated by the old-time religions.

But instead of enjoying their liberation, their freedom from the inconvenient "thou shall nots," they're embracing a different sort of puritanism and welcoming equally suffocating restrictions in deference to the new gods of health and the environment.

These new faiths, in practice, are amazingly similar to the old.

They have their own schedule of sins and vices and are just as intolerant and judgmental of those who stray from the path of righteousness. They also will go to extremes to impose their doctrines—witness New York City's just-passed law forbidding city hospitals from sending new mothers home with baby formula, to push breast-feeding.

Skeptics are demonized as heretics. To question the causes and impact of global warming, for example, is blasphemous, and many in the scientific community are finding the price for expressing doubt is banishment.

The new religions are no more tolerant of non-conformity—smokers are shunned the way libertines once were. And they are equally instilled with an evangelical zeal to spread the faith.

Like their predecessors, the obsession of the new religions is controlling the behavior of the flock. The real agenda of the campaign against global warming is to achieve the longstanding goals of environmentalists to force people onto mass transit, draw them back from far-flung suburbs and minimize their ability to profit from the earth.

The new religions give new interpretations to several of Catholicism's seven deadly sins, including:

- Pride.

  The vanity of individualism is discouraged as a threat to the collective good. Lifestyle choices must conform to the standards of propriety set by all-knowing spiritual leaders (think Al Gore).

- Gluttony.

  Consumerism and overconsumption are the great evils. Frugality is a virtue, and piety is attained by the Carteresque measure of living a smaller life, accepting less. Traditional religions reward sacrifice and self-denial with immortality; it's not yet clear how the new faiths will incentivize deprivation.

• Greed.

The notion that American ingenuity and productivity entitle this country to a bigger piece of the pie is unholy. We're expected to feel guilty about our prosperity, pressured to give away our wealth.

• Lust.

While the new faiths don't meddle so much in your sex life—nearly any sexual practice is OK, as long as it's "safe" and consensual—if you hunger for big trucks, big houses, big cigars, your wages are damnation.

Unfortunately, there is no separation of church and state to protect non-believers from being pressed into observance. Canonical law is written by secular legislatures and enforced by public agents.

An agnostic—or Mother Earth forbid, an atheist—living in this new religious environment may find life as uncomfortable as did the witches of Salem.

April 27, 2008

Our Lady of GPS has changed my life

I once was lost—hopelessly and nearly all the time. But now I'm found.

Ever since I accepted Our Lady of Global Positioning Satellite as my personal navigator, my wheels are set on the path of right direction-ness.

Suction-cupped to my windshield, Our Lady of GPS leads me not into the temptation of shortcuts that go nowhere, but delivers me from the evil of having to stop to ask the teenaged gas station attendant for directions.

Until she came into my life, I was a technology agnostic, tapping into just 10 percent of my Blackberry's brain and using my laptop as a TV tray.

But I've given myself over completely to Our Lady. And the rewards are immense.

She acquires the heavenly satellites on my behalf and guides my journey with simple yet confident commandments. She accepts me just as I am, without one plea other than faith.

Trusting was not easy at first. I questioned her infallibility, rebelled against her omnipotence and cursed the persistence of her demands. Sometimes, we got into quite a racket.

But in time, I learned to submit my free will to her wisdom.

Now, when Our Lady says continue straight, then straight, it must be, even if every fiber of my being is screaming right, and old Beelzebub in the passenger seat is tempting me left.

When I stray, as I will, she calmly recalculates my route without questioning my IQ or thumping me over the head with a rolled-up Rand McNally, a marked improvement over my previous navigation system.

I have grown from an uncertain convert to a proselytizing zealot.

If I leave the office and am asked if I want to take along a printout of directions for the trip, I shout: "Get thee behind me MapQuest!" Our Lady is my co-pilot.

As happens anytime you go from wanton wandering to the straight and narrow, life is less stressful, but not nearly as exciting.

I no longer take wrong turns into unexpected neighborhoods or accidentally pass landmarks I promise to come back to, if I can ever find them again.

On the other hand, I don't wind up in Ann Arbor when I'd set out for Mount Clemens, either.

Our Lady is proof that it doesn't take a village to drive a car. She and I can get along just fine on our own. (That would be even truer if she were programmed to scream "RED LIGHT! RED LIGHT!" at just the critical moment).

It has been suggested, somewhat maliciously I suspect, that it's a shame Our Lady's guidance ends in the driveway. That it might be useful if she could be stuck to my forehead and follow me into the house, where she'd continue to offer helpful instructions. "Close the toilet seat," "Load the dishwasher" and "Cough up the clicker," perhaps.

That's a level of directional redundancy I'm not sure I'm ready for.

But on the road, at least, I've turned the wheel over to a higher power.

Now when the inner voice speaks, it says, "In point-three miles, turn right, then stay right." How could I possibly lose my way?

October 12, 2008
No room in America for class warfare

The odds were steeply stacked against my dad ever striking it rich. Born deep in the Kentucky hills, he traded high school for work and war, tried to scratch a living out of poor dirt and finally moved his family to Detroit, whose factories were wide open for cheap, unskilled labor.

He worked his way up to working class, managing to pay the monthly bills with a little help from the local loan office. But he had bigger dreams. He borrowed enough money to buy a laundromat near Wayne State University, and then a second in Delray, and when he punched out of the chemical plant he spent another long shift patching up washing machines.

His vision was of a laundromat empire. And if he hadn't died young he might have got there. But keeping the doors of those two stores open consumed most of what he made at his day job, and in the end, he was worse off than when he started.

Still, when he looked in the mirror he saw a potential rich guy. In his mind, no rungs on the economic ladder were beyond reach. That belief is what has kept generations of Americans striving and climbing; it's the energy that's powered all of our innovation and prosperity.

That's why it's distressing to endure a political season that's made class warfare a central campaign theme.

Populism usually falls flat with American voters. Witness the failure of Al Gore's "people versus the powerful" or John Edwards' "two Americas." We don't identify ourselves by economic class because we hold economic mobility as a core value.

But there's something different about this year. The Wall Street debacle has turned "CEO" into a dirty word and branded anyone in an executive suite as a robber baron. Hefty salaries aren't the pay-off for long hours and personal sacrifice, but ill-gotten gains lifted from the pockets of working people.

Democratic presidential candidate Barack Obama has found his treasure in this attitude shift. The wealth redistribution schemes that form the heart of his economic plan—once red flags for Americans who understood that when they became rich, it would be their money that was being confiscated—are now embraced as the change we need.

Equalizing income based on need saturates Obama's platform. Nearly every bullet point involves—paraphrasing the candidate—giving less to those at the top and more to those at the bottom.

It sets my teeth on edge when I hear him say that because it reveals a belief system that views wealth as a collective asset to be parceled out by the government, not the property of the individuals who earned it.

The obvious outcome of penalizing success is that it destroys the incentive to succeed. Adopting European-style socialism will turn us into France, sluggish and unambitious, with productivity and growth falling as taxes and handouts grow.

My father, were he alive, would be a major beneficiary of Obama's Robin Hood plots. But he'd have rather taken a beating than a government check.

America risks its identity if it tells folks like him to stop reaching for their own reward and instead pick the pockets of those who've already made it.

December 7, 2008
Vive le CEO? Not in today's America

The building hostility toward the executive class is starting to take on a French Revolution feel.

Expect the mobs at any moment to break through the boardroom doors and carry away to the guillotine all the chairmen, directors and chief executives.

CEOs have been made the scapegoats of America's distress, and politicians are more than willing to deflect the blame for the misery away from themselves.

"It's horrible," says David Brandon, CEO of Domino's Pizza in Ann Arbor and chairman of Detroit Renaissance, the civic group made up of the region's most powerful executives. "The image of the CEO has been thoroughly trashed—it's as if we're sub-humans. I don't want anyone to recognize me in the grocery store."

Brandon faults, in part, a political season in which Republicans and Democrats used "CEO" as a pejorative. Then came the Wall Street collapse, and the subsequent bailout at taxpayer expense of financial firms that paid their executives as if they were New York Yankee shortstops.

The pizza chief admits there were compensation abuses, and that CEOs have to shoulder some of the blame for their status. But he says it's wrong to paint all executives as overpaid elitists who would sell their workers' souls for a profit.

He's right. And it's dangerous. Business leaders are the dollar signs behind efforts to rebuild communities like Detroit. They write the checks for symphonies and museums, build the hospitals and bankroll the do-gooder work of the nonprofit world.

They also create the jobs that keep the rest of us in paychecks. It's a 24-7 responsibility. Heads of national companies are on the road much of the time.

When they climb on a corporate jet, it's not for the luxury; it's to save a few precious hours they can pour back into their work.

Most didn't inherit their seat in the corporate suite. Again like Brandon, they worked their way up from the bottom by being better at what they do than everyone else.

The danger of turning them all into Simon LeGrees—or Ken Lays—is that it emboldens the anti-business forces and makes the public less sympathetic to improving the business climate. In Michigan, that means little support for fixing the suffocating state business tax surcharge, which is driving investment out of the state.

Once you convince Americans that business is the problem and government is the solution, you build a constituency for excessive regulation and punitive taxes.

And you soften them up for accepting that massive government spending programs make more sense than a long-term economic strategy built on encouraging private investment and job creation.

Brandon is already seeing that in California, where Dominos sold off its corporate franchises because it couldn't deliver enough pizzas to cover the regulatory costs.

"It's easier to do business in France than in California," he says.

Perhaps easier to be a business executive in France, too, even with the guillotines.

June 18, 2009

In RenCen, CEOs tilt at windmills

My favorite joke has two Jehovah's Witnesses working a neighborhood when they finally happen upon a homeowner who responds to their plea, "Can I tell you about Jesus?"

"Sure," the homeowner says. "Come on in." Once they're settled on the couch, the homeowner asks, "OK, what now?" The Witnesses look at each other and shrug, "We don't know. We never got this far before."

I thought about those startled missionaries this week when I wandered to the "People's Summit" in Grand Circus Park, set up to protest the National Summit on the economy a mile away in the Renaissance Center.

As I walked up, a speaker was railing against "the corporate community that is responsible for the crisis in this country. What they're doing in the RenCen right now is an affront to all of us."

So I asked what they wanted. The answer: national health care; more spending on welfare programs; an end to free trade; punish the corporations; re-educate CEOs and slash their pay; nationalize industry; take from the rich and give to the poor.

They've won, and they don't have a clue how to handle victory.

The agenda espoused by these dreadlock-wearing, sign-carrying, slogan-shouting habitual protesters was once a quixotic quest, but now reflects mainstream thinking in Washington. The pinstriped set at the summit, asking for freer markets and regulatory relief, are the impossible dreamers.

President Barack Obama has spent far more time marching with the likes of the People's Summiteers than he has sitting across the table from CEOs, and his vision of America's future better aligns with the former than the latter.

Since January, corporate America has been a pariah in Washington. Business executives are saddled with the blame for the nation's collapse, and no one in charge is much interested in hearing their ideas for fixing things. Corporate chiefs are the new disenfranchised class.

"They've been steamrolled by the popular express," says Lou Anna Simon, president of Michigan State University.

And that's a tragedy. Because there were some solid, common-sense solutions for reviving America put on the table this week in Detroit. The brain power gathered in the RenCen's silos could have moved a mountain, if anyone had been listening.

In normal times, this line-up of CEOs would have drawn overflowing crowds of wisdom seekers. But many of the sessions were sparsely attended, despite featuring some of the nation's top corporate bosses.

Business doesn't matter in the upside-down world in which we live. Government has all the answers, all the money and all the muscle. Critical decisions are being made about the future of industry without the input of industrialists.

In a heartbeat we've moved from a nation that worships entrepreneurship, innovation and the freedom to succeed to one that craves the false security of an economy carefully contained by the government.

The CEOs acknowledged their diminished status and the danger of making the word "corporate" as pejorative as communist was 60 years ago,—particularly for a nation that must encourage its youth to become engineers, entrepreneurs and executives if it hopes to avoid becoming the servant of more enlightened economies.

"We're got to make it cool again to be in business," Ford CEO Alan Mulally said. "Industry is the source of all wealth creation for everybody."

The power really is to the people. But it's not the people, at least not the sign toters in Grand Circus Park, who will rebuild businesses, create jobs and return America to a level of prosperity that lifts all boats.

Those people were in the RenCen tilting at windmills.

July 19, 2009

Space defined my generation

Growing up, if one of my parents was in the school building, chances were good that I was in trouble.

A rare exception came on a February morning in 1962, when I looked up to see my mother stumbling into my second grade classroom, her arms wrapped around the bulky black-and-white television set that normally sat in our living room.

She plopped it on a desk, adjusted the rabbit ears and soon my classmates and I were watching as the seconds ticked down and astronaut John Glenn rocketed across the screen and into space as the first American to orbit the Earth. Watching TV at school was unheard of then, and I couldn't have been prouder of my mom.

For baby boomers, the space program is a common thread that runs through our lives. We were young children when John F. Kennedy made the race to the moon a national mission, and teenagers seven years later when the mission was accomplished. We watched the Sunday night lunar landing with our families, and by then some of us had color TV sets.

We watched every launch and every splashdown on television, molded rockets out of clay for school art projects and dreamed of following our Apollo gods into space.

The new Space Age dulled us to the marvels of technology—the inventions and innovations came so fast that that we stopped thinking about them as miraculous and absorbed them as a matter of course.

Those advances enabled our generation's break with traditions. Space-age electronics fed our obsession with music; discoveries in everything from food processing to fabrics loosened our ties to home and family; the arrival of high-tech plastics made the essentials of our lives more portable and more disposable.

The space program helped make us the first truly modern American generation, the first whose growing-up experience was different in nearly every way from that of our parents'.

Pride in what America's astronauts and scientists were accomplishing should have fueled our nationalism. But while man was walking on the moon, Americans were marching in the streets.

Just three months after the lunar landing, the Days of Rage student riots erupted in Chicago, an angry reminder that a nation capable of taking man to the moon still had some work to do back on Earth.

As adults, our fascination with space ebbed somewhat. The shuttle program didn't thrill in the way those Apollo shots did. The drama was gone. But not for long.

I was working the city desk at The News in 1986 when the Challenger exploded, killing teacher Christa McAuliffe and her crewmates. Once again, I found myself huddled with my peers, eyes glued to a television screen, watching history.

The footprints Neil Armstrong and Buzz Aldrin left on the moon's surface 40 years ago tomorrow are expected to last forever. For sure, the imprint the space program made on my generation also will endure.

April 30, 2009

Detroit's entitlement culture withers a bright, blue dream

I remember when Dick Dauch bought American Axle Manufacturing from General Motors and poured tanker truckloads of bright blue paint over what was then a dreary complex of parts plants sprawling across Hamtramck and Detroit.

Dauch, the quintessential factory man, was hell-bent on proving heavy manufacturing could still be done here, with a union work force, and with the Big 3 automakers as the customer base. That eye-catching paint job was the symbol of his hopes.

Now, 15 years later, Dauch is cutting the Detroit work force sharply and consolidating the work in Three Rivers, Michigan, and Mexico. He isn't mealy-mouthed about the reasons.

"This isn't a North America problem, or a Michigan problem. It isn't a union problem. It's a Detroit problem," says Dauch, who has headed manufacturing for GM, Chrysler and Volkswagen North America. "Detroit has an entitlement culture—'You owe me this job.'

"Detroit can compete on quality, but it can't compete on costs. And the difference in the global economy is cost structure."

Dauch is still obviously angry over the 87-day strike by the United Auto Workers union against AAM last year in response to demands for concessions. In the end, the new contract reduced wage and benefit costs, but that was only part of the answer.

"The No. 1 disadvantage to being in Detroit is labor costs," Dauch says. "No. 2 is reliability."

Detroit has the highest absenteeism rate of any AAM facility. In Mexico, Three Rivers, Indiana and elsewhere, absenteeism is barely a blip. Many days, the Mexican plant—also unionized—has no workers absent.

But in Detroit, absenteeism runs at least twice as high, and on some days it can approach nearly one-third of the workforce in parts of the plant. Lines have been shut down because not enough employees show up.

"I've been working since Aug. 24, 1964, and I've taken three-and-a-half sick days," says Dauch. "I've got employees who miss two or three days a week."

Maybe that would have flown 30 years ago when Detroit was still fat and happy. But jobs are fungible today. Employers like Dauch have a fiduciary responsibility to take work where it will be done most efficiently.

It isn't just about hourly wages. Dauch's employees in Three Rivers, also UAW members, make about the same hourly rate. But they've agreed to a contract that gives the company more operating flexibility, and they show up for work.

Dauch says he hasn't given up on North America. In fact, he's opened four plants in the United States, including one in Indiana. He hasn't even given up on Detroit. He's keeping the equipment here and, if business picks up, may bring back work.

But he offers fair warning to this job-starved city. We aren't entitled to anything, least of all a job that someone someplace else is willing to do not just cheaper, but also better.

Wednesday, I listened to several autoworkers complain on the radio about union-busting corporations, unfair trade policies and the loss of middle-class manufacturing jobs.

But not one mentioned that on the same day, there were places in Dauch's now-faded blue Detroit factory where nearly one in three workers were AWOL.

April 4, 2010
You reach out, I'll circle back

I've been sitting through a lot of meetings lately, both inside and outside the office, which means there's been a lot of opportunity for my mind to go wandering.

My fascination during the ongoing yak-yak is with how the vocabulary of business has changed.

I'm over the annoyance that we share instead of talk. But now we don't contact each other to do so, we reach out, as in, "I'll reach out to Jennifer to see if she has anything to share."

Frankly, I find the expression creepy. It's too intimate. I get an image of hands and arms reaching out from everywhere, perhaps even trying to hug me, and I'm not much of a hugger.

After we've reached out and shared, we no longer follow up to make sure all the boxes are checked. We circle back. Don't like this one either. It's a little too meandering, lacking any sense of urgency.

By the time someone gets back to your point in the circle, you may no longer be in the same place. Having everyone in the same place is vital to producing results.

What am I saying? We don't get results anymore, we generate deliverables. I can't shake the image of a big truck backing up to our front door and dumping a load of deliverables.

We need them, because we are all about transparency. We are keeping score after all, and we intend to issue a report card on our future progress once all our deliverables are in place. That's how you know we're accountable.

Uh-oh—let's back up. Future is no good, either. We have to forget about the future and focus on sustainability going forward.

Our worry today isn't about making our product profitable. We have to all step up to monetize it. Seems like there ought to be a machine we could put our product in to facilitate that transformation, except that we don't transform, we morph.

We are still customer-focused, and now we know exactly where we can touch them. They're on the ground. That's where the real organic business gets done, not floating around in the air somewhere.

Unless you're an airline, in which case having your customers on the ground for too long would make it difficult to create the synergy for monetizing your operation.

At one time we dealt with issues and areas, now they're spaces: "Let's invite Dr. Smith to speak, he's an expert in that space."

It sounds sort of confining. If you get bored sitting at the same table with all the stakeholders in your space, I'm not sure whether you're empowered to reach out to someone in another space. I'll find out and circle back.

Language is constantly morphing. Every generation has its own business clichés.

Today's vocabulary stresses interactivity. If something is not interactive, forget about it. And it's more user-friendly than the cut-to-the-chase verbiage it replaces.

But I still find myself missing the old paradigm.

May 13, 2010
Welfare surge kills initiative to prosper

America is rapidly turning its safety net into a comfortable cocoon.

President Barack Obama's 2011 budget contains a welfare surge that will raise social spending by 42 percent above 2009 levels, according to an analysis by the Heritage Foundation. State and local welfare spending will total $953 billions.

The goal is to close the quality of life gap, so that nobody in America is too prosperous or too poor.

In the process, the federal government risks making the dependent class even larger by destroying the basic incentive to work.

Already, landscapers say they can't compete with unemployment checks to fill jobs that pay $10 to $12 an hour. Jobless benefits now stretch to nearly two years, allowing some laid-off workers the luxury to refuse job offers. Similar generosity in Europe has institutionalized the jobless rate at twice the average U.S. level.

You can defend extended unemployment benefits in an economy that isn't creating jobs. But having established two years as the high water mark, it's unlikely Congress will pull it back as the jobs outlook improves.

Washington is much better at creating new entitlements than trimming existing ones. The War on Poverty launched by President Lyndon Johnson in 1964 has grown 13-fold in terms of spending, and yet the enemy is still alive and well.

So now we're trying new weapons. Like cell phones.

You may have seen the commercials on television advertising free cell phones and 200 minutes of service a month to those on public assistance. The program, which you pay for through a fee on your phone bill, was approved by Congress years ago, but is only now being broadly activated.

The justification is that poor people need phones to search for jobs so they can get off welfare.

But if you can make a case for free cell phones as a necessity of life, why not free cable television? Some cities have, requiring cable operators to offer free or reduced rates for low-income residents. Some demand free Internet and computers as well.

Government checks to help pay your rent, stock your pantry, cover your health insurance, lower your utility bills and keep you fully wired may not be enough to satisfy you. You probably want more out of life.

But for some people, having their basic needs covered by someone else is all they could ask for. The larger that group gets, the more likely it is that you'll be working harder to get less, while they work less to get more.

It's unfashionable to call that set-up socialism. You're bound to get eye rolls when you use that word to describe what's happening in America today. But there it is.

November 25, 2010

Editing God out of history distorts truth

Ask any grade school kid who the Pilgrims were giving thanks to on the first Thanksgiving and I'll lay you three-to-one odds that the answer you get is, "the Indians."

Public education is so obsessed with separation and so uncomfortable with discussions of religion that it has sanitized the unbreakable link between faith and America's founding. Now children are taught that the Pilgrims set the first Thanksgiving dinner for the Native Americans who helped keep them alive during their first harsh year in the New World.

This is more than just a small distortion in the name of political correctness. And it's not one of those Merry Christmas versus Happy Holidays issues. Whether you're a believer or non-believer, you should be concerned that God is being written out of this nation's history because doing so will limit our understanding of who we are as a people.

Faith was the driving force in the lives of the Pilgrims. Certainly the Indians helped them through the deprivations of that first year. But the settlers believed it was their prayers that accounted for their survival. And despite the starvation and sickness, they saw this new land as a great gift from God, a place where they were free to practice their religion.

The freedom to worship sparked a hunger for other liberties and created a culture that chafed at submission to arbitrary authority.

The words they used matter. When you edit out "endowed by their Creator with certain unalienable rights" from the Declaration of Independence, as President Barack Obama has been doing lately, you lose the understanding that the early Americans were able to take the extraordinary risk of breaking way from their king and taking responsibility for their own governance because they believed God was the only sovereign they were answerable to.

It was a remarkable proposition at a time when the entire rest of the world was under the rule of monarchs.

The belief in America's divine destiny and its providential partnership fueled the nation's sea-to-sea expansion and sparked a missionary zeal for spreading freedom. It gave rise to the notion of America's large and unique place in the world and the theory of American exceptionalism that is also now considered quaint in many quarters.

The irony here is that schools have no problem exposing our flaws in the name of getting history right. It almost relishes defrocking our heroes—Jefferson owned slaves, and so did Washington; Jackson practiced genocide; the pioneers ravaged the land.

They do so even to the point of challenging the nation's legitimacy.

But when it comes to discussing the very complex and integral ways religion shaped our history, educators lose their nerve.

So they invent more convenient scenarios, such as Pilgrims cooking up the idea of a huge Thanksgiving dinner to honor their Indian benefactors, instead of the God whom they ardently believed led them to this New World and controlled every aspect of their fate.

There's both good and bad in the nation's religious history. Americans have done some noble things in the name of serving God, and they've made some tragic mistakes doing the same.

It's not proselytizing to explore that relationship between God and country. It's just telling the truth.

≺ ≺ ≺

February 6, 2011

We need another Reagan

I was still a young man when Ronald Reagan became president, just starting a career and a family.

My first mortgage carried an interest rate north of 11 percent, and after years of unchecked inflation, my paycheck from what should have been a good job barely covered the bills.

It wasn't the financial struggle that bothered me; it was the message from Washington that I'd better get used to this new reality, that America's good times were over for good, and that the country's diminished status demanded Americans live smaller, accept less.

Jimmy Carter made me gag with his vision of a humbler America. I couldn't stomach the prospect that my ambitions and possibilities would be stifled by a country on the wane.

And then along came Reagan, a genuine Yankee Doodle Dandy, ready to jerk the nation up by its bootstraps and get it back to fulfilling its destiny. There was a little cornpone in him, but when he talked of America as a shining city on the hill, I could see its lights.

Where Carter was a collectivist, convinced that less for everyone meant more to go around, Reagan was a man of the West, imbued with the spirit of the cowboys he played on the big screen. His vision was expansive. He understood America's future depended on recapturing the values of its past—independence and individualism.

His belief was that if individual Americans strive to succeed and are allowed to reap the rewards of their success, the nation as a whole will prosper. And he was validated by 25 years of prosperity.

America was still in the era of self-loathing that grew out of the Vietnam protests and the Nixon scandal when Reagan arrived. It was easy to believe we had lost our greatness, especially since we were being bullied about by every raggedy band of misfits that could swap a barrel of oil for a gun.

Reagan ended that nonsense, too, and in recognizing America's unique place in the world, brought freedom to millions of people who never dreamed they'd be free.

Our current president is compared to Reagan for his mastery of the spoken word. Although Barack Obama can channel Reagan's rhetorical gifts, he speaks in Carter's voice.

Today's marking of the 100th anniversary of Reagan's birth finds the country once again in a debilitating malaise. A new generation of young people worry they'll be denied their shot at the brass ring.

Our leaders are again trying to force us to sacrifice individual aspirations and choices for the greater good. Wealth and ambition are demonized.

And we're hearing again that America has no rightful claim to its brilliantly beaming hilltop and should settle in the valley with everyone else.

We need another Ronald Reagan. We'll always need another Ronald Reagan. I hope the United States in the 21st century is still a place that can spawn his kind of American.

May 8, 2011

Mom beat the devil, and me

My mother believed she was locked in a to-the-death war with the devil for control of my soul and was not about to lose.

She went into battle armed with hair brushes, fly swatters, coat hangers, willow switches, belts and the wooden paddles that came in Easter baskets. I dreaded that toy.

As you might suspect, I was a difficult child. And yet her patience for hammering me into a model citizen never waned. An otherwise charming and well-loved person, she did not care to count her three children among her "friends."

Her job was mother, and she craved our respect first, love second. She was the boss. We didn't sass—at least not and remain upright. Even when I was a grown man, she could make me flinch.

I think about my mom's parenting techniques whenever I read a story of a child gone wild. A few months ago, a 13-year-old Detroit girl claimed to have been kidnapped and chained to a bathroom pipe by a man who repeatedly raped her.

During the six weeks she was missing, she called her mother several times to describe her ordeal. She finally broke free and ran home, and her tormentor killed himself.

If true, her account is astounding. How could a girl be held for six weeks by a pervert, with her mother getting a daily play-by-play, and this not raise a national response?

More astonishing, though, was the mother's explanation for not alerting police when her daughter went missing. "I thought she was just out having a good time," the mother said.

Good time? No good time was worth my mother's wrath if I missed a curfew. She expected to know where her kids were and what they were doing, and if she didn't, she'd go on the hunt of us locked and loaded.

I was also struck by a column about a mother who was at wit's end because her 10-year-old son had been expelled from school and was hanging out with older gang members.

"I don't know what to do with him," she lamented.

My advice—cut a switch. My mom would have striped our legs before making such an admission.

Corporal punishment is out of favor. Sparing the rod is now a mandate, not a failing. A few years ago, I wrote a column suggesting children might behave better in school if classrooms still had paddles hanging on the walls.

I was pummeled for it. An entire class from Grosse Pointe wrote me letters decrying the barbarity of my idea. Some of the kids' notes were so impertinent they would have merited a good thrashing in the day.

I confess I wasn't much of a spanker with my own children, and yet all three managed to get to honorable adulthood.

But I never begrudge my mother's more hands-on approach. To her, good mothering meant not just loving, nurturing and protecting, but also knocking off our rough edges and training us to be respectful, responsible individuals. She'd rather endure our resentment than to see us stray from the straight and narrow.

I'm grateful for it. I'd hate to think where I might be today had my mom surrendered before Old Scratch did.

October 9, 2011
Can't wait for Occupy Detroit

I can't wait for the menagerie of malcontents who call themselves Occupy Wall Street to arrive in Detroit and other mainstream American cities.

It will be good for real Americans to get a look at the folks President Barack Obama says represent their frustration with the condition of the country.

The protest movement that started in New York's financial district several weeks ago with a couple hundred enthusiastic and unfocused shouters has grown to a few thousand, and now is vowing to take its show on the road.

They're expected in Detroit near month's end.

Occupy Wall Street's main objective, from what I can make out from the inchoate signage, is the destruction of capitalism (a goal to which Obama can relate), although on a whim they can switch to global warming, medical marijuana or any number of other pet causes dear to the disaffected Left.

Clearly, they're angry with America, resent its founding values and would like to see the fat cats who run the place boiled in oil.

Or at least that's what they're Twittering.

Obama, asked about the budding movement last week, said he "sympathized" with Occupy Wall Street—not surprising, since they share a donor base.

And he opined that they are speaking for the great body of Americans who resent that some people have nice stuff and others don't, and are counting on him to play Robin Hood.

It's odd that such a small and predictable group could grab the president's attention.

He didn't seem to hear anything of value when tens of thousands of tea partiers were pouring into the streets to protest exploding deficits and Washington's fiscal recklessness.

He certainly didn't sympathize with those Americans. Nor did he accept that they represented the country's broader discontent.

And while the president and his media horde heard every whisper from a tea party rally that sounded like a threat or suggested racist undertones, they seem blissfully ignorant of the vicious and hateful side of Occupy Wall Street.

This is far from a peaceful protest. Cops in New York are arresting the increasingly violent activists by the hundreds.

Videos have caught incidents of Jewish passers-by being taunted by the protesters—of course, it's a quick step from attacking financial institutions to indulging anti-Semitism.

State lawmakers in New York have received emails reportedly connected to Occupy Wall Street containing this cheery call to action: "It's time to kill the wealthy."

I haven't taken a poll, but my hunch is more Americans relate to "cut the spending" than to "kill the wealthy."

That's why I'm eager to see this freak show arrive in Detroit.

It'll be informative for voters to compare the American protesters Barack Obama sympathizes with to those he despises.

Feb. 5, 2012

If life's cheap, murder's not news

Everybody agrees that there's something wrong when the horrific murder of a 12-year-old black girl in Detroit gets far less newspaper ink and television footage than the slaying of a white Grosse Pointe matron.

But there's little agreement on the reason for the unequal coverage.

The default answer is race, and I don't discount that. I've wondered how the media will react when it's a Kerry instead of a Tamika whose bloody body is found discarded in the weeds, when murder touches the hip young suburbanites who are filling Detroit's lofts.

I also can't ignore the whodunit aspect of the Jane Bashara case, the suspicions surrounding her husband and the salacious details, from a hidden girlfriend to a basement S&M club. You don't get to write about sex dungeons every day.

But I suspect the real reason has more to do with the nature of news. By definition, news is the unusual. Grosse Pointe Park hadn't had a murder in roughly 20 years before Bashara was beaten and strangled, apparently in the garage of her tony home.

There's nothing unusual about a homicide in Detroit. In the first 30 days of the New Year, the city had 27 slayings.

Even child killings have become commonplace. Even when a child is killed on the front porch of her own home by bullets intended for her mother, it doesn't shock us as much as it should because it's not all that outside the norm.

When bodies are accumulating at the rate of nearly one a day, it gets harder to work up an outrage, even at the most outrageous crimes.

The danger of becoming desensitized to bloodshed is that the raging homicide rate falls down the priority list. While bullets are flying all over the city, the City Council is debating an austerity budget that could lay off up to 1,000 police officers.

How that reins in violence, I don't see.

But as Police Chief Ralph Godbee has said, a cop on every street corner won't help if citizens won't police their own behavior.

It's not a law enforcement challenge when adults don't have the good sense not to blast away over a missing cellphone; it's a cultural one.

Instead of counting camera time, we ought to have a deep discussion about the disintegration of civilized society.

Why is life so cheap in Detroit? Is it poverty? Drugs? Ignorance? Illegitimacy? Hopelessness?

All of the above?

Until we can answer that question, we're not going to stop the bloodbath.

Go ahead and accuse the media of not valuing black life as much as it does white life. That could even be true. But Detroiters obviously don't value black life, either. If they did, they wouldn't be taking so many.

The issue isn't that the media found a bigger story in the Grosse Pointe garage than it did on the Detroit porch. It's that Detroit has allowed slaughter to become so common it's no longer newsworthy.

February 12, 2012

Michigan is breeding poverty

Since the national attention is on birth control, here's my idea: If we want to fight poverty, reduce violent crime and bring down our embarrassing drop-out rate, we should swap contraceptives for fluoride in Michigan's drinking water.

We've got a baby problem in Michigan. Too many babies are born to immature parents who don't have the skills to raise them, too many are delivered by poor women who can't afford them, and too many are fathered by sorry layabouts who spread their seed like dandelions and then wander away from the consequences.

Michigan's social problems and the huge costs attached to them won't recede until we embrace reproductive responsibility.

Last year, 43 percent of the babies born in Michigan were to single mothers. And even though Medicaid pays for birth control, half of the babies born here were to mothers on welfare. Eighteen percent were born to teenagers who already had at least one child. And nearly 1-in-5 new babies had mothers with no high school diploma.

In Michigan, poverty is as much a cultural problem as it is an economic one.

I spoke with an educator who is dealing with a single mother, mid-30s, with 12 children and a 13th on the way. The kids have an assortment of fathers with one thing in common—none married their mother. This woman's womb is a poverty factory.

It wouldn't matter if Michigan's economy were bursting with jobs, the woman and her children would still be poor.

Who's supporting these kids? If you're a taxpayer, you are. The roughly 45,000 children a year born onto the welfare rolls is a major reason Medicaid will consume 25 percent of next year's state budget.

Those kids are more likely to grow up to be a strain on Corrections spending or welfare recipients themselves. And they'll drain money from the schools and universities that could help break this cycle.

In the 1990s, Michigan considered penalizing women who had more babies while on welfare, but pro-life groups killed the idea out of fear it would lead to more abortions.

Now, says state Human Services Director Maura Corrigan, the state is trying other measures, including attacking school truancy and the new four-year limit on welfare benefits, which she says is already increasing participation in work training programs.

"We are trying to get at generational poverty," she says. "We're studying positive incentives to change."

But she says the cultural breakdown is a strong tide to row against.

"We're watching marriage move from being part of the social fabric to being merely optional," says Corrigan, who devotes her personal time to working with disadvantaged children. "The kids I mentor don't know people who are married."

They do know people whose irresponsible behavior is being subsidized by their neighbors.

And as long as the taxpayers of Michigan keep paying for them, those babies will keep on coming.

January 24, 2013
Save the prison cells for those who scare us

Two unrelated conversations this week started me thinking about crime and punishment.

The first was with members of Business Leaders for Michigan, the CEO group committed to pushing reforms that will make this a top 10 state for economic growth and opportunity.

The business leaders want the state to set spending priorities that favor higher education and transportation infrastructure.

Recognizing that there's no new pot of money to tap to reach these goals, the group suggests Michigan cut spending on prisons.

Corrections is a good target. Michigan spends $2 billion a year to keep 50,000 inmates locked up. Its incarceration rate is 31 percent higher than the Midwest average, and it holds on to inmates far longer than most other states.

The thinking is that if Michigan could slash prison spending it could invest more in higher education, lower tuition costs and increase the number of college graduates.

It's a great objective. But who gets locked up and who remains free? The state is continually roiled by parolees who commit horrible crimes.

The latest was the rampage by Eric Ramsey, who raped a Central Michigan student last week before being killed by cops. Keeping him locked away would have been a good investment.

That leads to the second conversation, with a local judge and concerning Diane Hathaway, the Supreme Court justice who pleaded guilty to bank fraud and resigned this week.

Hathaway stole a lot of money—$600,000 in a mortgage swindle. But she presents no physical danger to her fellow citizens. She faces hefty financial penalties. She'll lose her law license, and thus her livelihood.

Should she also go to prison, where she'll take a cell that could be occupied by a violent criminal like Ramsey?

"Absolutely," my judge friend answered. She then explained the four pillars of punishment—to deter others, to discourage the criminal from repeating the offense, to protect society, and to rehabilitate the offender. Not imprisoning Hathaway, she said, would send a message to other potential criminals that her crime—essentially bank robbery—is taken lightly. It would fail to convey to her the severity of her offense.

I get it. Former Detroit Mayor Kwame Kilpatrick, on trial now for racketeering, is proof some non-violent criminals are as incorrigible as street thugs, and won't stop their wicked ways as long as they're exposed to opportunity.

But I also believe that there are many non-violent criminals idling in prisons because of one-time mistakes they'd never repeat.

They let greed get the better of them. They were momentarily negligent. They walked off the dock.

We aren't afraid of them. We're angry with them. And they do deserve punishment.

But does it have to be prison? At one time, we preferred brutal but expedient penalties. Forty lashes. A few days in the stocks. Hanging.

We're more humane today—we just slam the iron bars on what otherwise might be productive years.

If we've reached a point where we are setting spending priorities that mean fewer of our residents will be in prison cells, then we should also make the best decisions about who should occupy those cells.

November 7 2013
From one Bubba to another

Damon Keith is the only person who can call me Bubba without the risk of raising my temper.

The legendary Detroit federal judge tagged me with that handle a dozen years ago, after I wrote a column about why America couldn't stay mad at then-President Bill Clinton. He called me to talk about it, and that led to lunch, then to a fast friendship, and also to something I'd managed to avoid my whole life—a nickname.

He's called me Bubba from the start, based on a reference to Clinton in that column. When we're together, he introduces me as Bubba Finley, and I have to whisper to my new acquaintance, "That's not really my name," lest the moniker take hold.

The judge always starts his notes to me with "Dear Bubba," and signs off as "Judge Bubba Keith."

It amuses him, and as long as that's true, I'll gladly be Bubba.

If you're looking for someone to admire and emulate, a role model if you will, it's hard to beat Damon Keith.

He's the most gentle and genteel person I know. The judge takes a genuine interest in his friends, always asking about your life and loved ones before you get a chance to ask about his.

Dozens, or more likely hundreds, of people in this community count him as their mentor, a group ranging from Tigers great Willie Horton to former Gov. Jennifer Granholm, with lots of very well-known folks in between.

But he also has time and energy for lesser lights. I've watched him sit in his chambers softly and earnestly counseling a young boy at risk of taking the wrong path.

I'll hear from him now and then when he likes something I've written, but I understand our politics are vastly different, and that he disagrees with much, if not most, of what I write. He's kind enough not to mention those columns.

When we're together, we don't talk about what separates us, but rather what we have in common: Fathers who worked themselves into the ground, the family farms we each feel obliged to preserve for the next generation, a shared love for the history of this city.

I'm happiest when he's talking about his most ardent passion, the United States Constitution, and am always moved by Keith's deep faith in the power of that document to protect individual liberties. He lived through an era when this country tried to deny those protections to folks like him. But instead of bitterness, he's triumphant that his trust in the Constitution was ultimately affirmed. DK has a pure sense of fairness, and a determination that America will live up to its promise.

That comes through in the newly released biography, "Crusader for Justice." I've heard many of the stories first-hand, but am eager to learn more. At first look, it appears to be wonderfully written and richly detailed.

Still, the book doesn't seem quite fat enough to encompass nine decades of such an eventful life. Hopefully, there are a few more chapters left to be written about Damon Keith.

Congratulations, Judge Bubba. Love, Bubba.

February 2, 2014
America still mobile—for now

Lots of things President Barack Obama said in his State of the Union speech made my hair curl. But nothing as much as his assertion that the rungs have fallen off the ladder to success in today's America.

The president, after touting his own rise from a single-parent home to the White House, told all those young people living in humble households that they're stuck, the door to opportunity is shutting, that they may not be able to do what he did.

What a tragic message from a man whose rags to riches story ought to inspire all children to dream, strive and achieve.

And the worst part is that his claim, used to justify a new round of entitlement programs destined to make the poor even poorer and more dependent, is just not true.

The path from bottom to top today is no narrower than it was decades ago when Obama was traveling it.

In a new study, researchers at Harvard University and the University of California-Berkley—hardly right wing bastions—examined the income tax data of those born into poverty in the 1970s and assessed their ability to rise financially beyond the conditions of their birth.

"What we found is that mobility has remained remarkably stable," Harvard's Nathaniel Hendren, a co-author of the study, told National Public Radio. "The chance in which kids can climb up or down the income ladder has remained pretty stable over the last 20 to 25 years."

While the study does confirm Obama's other assertion—that the income gap between rich and poor is greater—it has not slowed upward mobility.

But the opportunity to climb the economic ladder is not automatic, and never was. The study says poor children who were born in regions of the country with a higher percentage of two-parent families and better schools were twice as likely to rise.

That's common sense stuff. Obama, like many of us, owes his success to a mother who insisted he get an education and envisioned a better life for her child than she was able to live herself.

I keep on my office wall a photograph of a small, three-room house—shack, really—that sits in the Appalachian foothills. No running water. No central heat. It was my first home, and the photograph reminds me that it might still be my home today had my parents not made every sacrifice imaginable to give their children an opportunity.

Whatever dreams they may have had for themselves, they set them aside to dream for us.

That's not some secret formula. Strong families that stress education, smart choices, personal responsibility and an understanding of what it really means to work hard are how successful children have been raised for generations in this country.

Obama didn't talk about those values. He'd rather us think that we must stand on the shoulders of a benevolent government to reach the top rung, that getting ahead depends on getting a hand-out, and that our shortfalls can be blamed on the success of others.

The route to prosperity isn't closed off yet. But if the president's message takes hold, it soon will be.

⅓ ⅓ ⅓

April 13, 2014

Don't charge mob with hate

I've been hearing from lots of folks—mostly white folks—who find some sort of vindication in the likelihood that hate crime charges will be filed against the suspects in the mob beating of Steven Utash.

After seeing the racism accusation applied so liberally, they get satisfaction when the shoe is on the other foot.

But I don't think these suspects should be charged with hate crimes.

It's not that I doubt the dozen thugs who swarmed the Clinton Township man when he stopped to aid a child he'd struck with his pick-up truck on Detroit's east side were racially motivated—Utash is white, the gang was black.

It just doesn't matter. No one should ever be charged with a hate crime.

For one thing, layering on the hate crime charge creates unequal classes of victims.

If you get murdered by a junkie who wants your wallet, or a jealous husband, or a maniac on a killing spree, you're just as dead as someone who gets offed by a racist.

Your family's loss is just as great, you're cheated of the same right to life. Why should your justice be less?

What matters is the crime. The motive is irrelevant, except to establish premeditation or support circumstantial evidence.

In the Utash case, the suspects already face the deadly serious charge of assault with attempt to commit murder, which could land them in prison for up to life. In determining a sentence, the judge is free to take into account whether he believes they are dangerous racists who merit a harsher penalty without the prosecutor having to prove this was a hate crime.

Hate crime charges are also a back-door assault on the First Amendment in that they criminalize thoughts, attitudes and speech.

Americans have a constitutional right to hate. We have the right to be racist, anti-Semitic, homophobic and all manner of other despicable things.

The hate only becomes criminal if we act on it. And when we do, there are laws in place to cover every offense, whether it's murder, assault, vandalism or harassment. But the hate itself should not be a prosecuted.

In most cases, what decides whether the hate crime charge is levied is what the suspect says while committing a crime. Utter a racial epithet, and it's evidence of hate, even if the prevailing motive is actually greed, jealousy or just plain meanness.

That runs contrary to the guarantee that even the most offensive speech is protected by the First Amendment. Nasty name-calling ought to get you punched in the nose, perhaps, but it shouldn't make you a criminal, even if the slurs occur during the commission of a crime. And even if the insults are racially infused.

The hate crime charge also is used to undermine double jeopardy protections. A defendant cleared in a state court can be charged with a hate crime and prosecuted again by the federal government for the exact same incident.

We can punish criminals for what they do, and not what they think or say, while still delivering justice for their victims—and without weakening the Constitution.

November 23, 2014
What *Daily Show* didn't show

A colleague who watched the taping of my interview with Comedy Central's *The Daily Show* said afterward, "Well, you were 95 percent good."

Right then, I knew the 5 percent of the 90-minute session that wasn't so good would be where the editors found excerpts for the TV show.

I was mostly right, although, in fairness, I felt I got off easy. Jon Stewart's schtick is slaying conservatives, and I expected the worst. So why do it in the first place? Why not? I enjoyed the sparring, had fun with the reporter and crew, and knew exactly what I was getting into.

I just wish it had been funnier.

The hilarity typical of the faux news program was missing. That may be because there's not much humor in what's happening in Detroit, particularly when it comes to water shutoffs.

Like every other outsider who has come to Detroit to report on the water shutoffs, *The Daily Show* seized the narrative of a heartless city closing the taps of the desperately poor. But the issue is much more complex, and Stewart's crew was certainly not alone in missing the layers.

During the interview, I repeated the unfairness of singling out Detroit—every city in America cuts off water service to those who don't pay their bills. The difference here is that a dysfunctional government allowed people to get away with not paying for so long the delinquent tab was too much for a lot of customers to handle when the city finally called the debt.

I spent at least a third of the time talking about Detroit's culpability, but that didn't make the cut either. The last thing I wanted was to appear as the defender of the city's incompetence.

Still, fairness demanded an explanation that after its ham-handed initial round of shutoffs, Detroit did pause, regroup and put in place subsidies and payment programs to aid those who truly can't handle their bills. Today, most service cutoffs are restored within 48 hours.

What I wanted most to convey is that in Detroit, soaking the rich is not an option, because there are so few wealthy residents and the corporate community is too thin. If you don't pay your bill here, your neighbor, who may be just as bad off as you are, has to cover it. A major reason the poorest residents in Metro Detroit pay the highest water rates is that 50 percent of the customers in the city were delinquent on their bills, in the amount of $91 million.

Weeding out those who are gaming the system from those who truly need help is a messy but essential step in restoring functionality to city government. That's true whether we're talking about water or property taxes. The no-pay culture has to end.

Yes, the city screwed up in every humanly possible way. And yes, some business customers are among the scofflaws—though two cited by the program, Palmer Park golf course and Joe Louis Arena, are city-owned facilities.

It doesn't change the reality that Detroit will not recover from its financial collapse if people take services and don't pay for them. *The Daily Show* felt it scored its gotcha moment when I said, "Nothing's free." But I'll stick by that. The free ride is over; now, everybody has to pay. Not funny, but true. 🦌

Chapter 2

Detroit

November 11, 2004

Only tough choices will save Detroit from bankruptcy

Pardon me for piddling on the parade during what is a grand week for Detroit.

The beautiful Campus Martius park opened downtown just in time to greet the hundreds of thousands of visitors who come to the city for the annual Thanksgiving festivities. It's one of dozens of upgrades parade visitors will notice this year, including new shops and restaurants and freshly paved streets.

With all the construction and repair work going on in preparation for the 2006 Super Bowl, downtown exudes the feel of a city finally finding its feet.

But in truth, Detroit is riding a rocket toward bankruptcy and may hit that target before the NFL hits town.

Having ignored for decades warnings that it must restructure city operations to reflect sharp population and revenue declines, the day of reckoning has arrived for Detroit. The city budget will be $214 million short next year. All the one-time gimmicks for closing the budget gap have been exhausted.

That means tough choices can't be postponed again.

Between 2000 and 2003, Detroit's population dropped by nearly 30,000 people. But its payroll grew by more than 400 workers. Over the past 10 years, employee salaries and benefits have grown by $370 million, while revenues have increased just $165 million—most of that from the casinos.

Employee ranks and population loss shouldn't necessarily be proportionate. The city still covers the same geographic area as when it had 2 million residents, with the same number of street lights, roads and other infrastructure to maintain.

But there's no justification beyond the political for allowing the payroll to balloon.

"The city has never contracted to reality," says Finance Director Sean Werdlow. "If we don't make these decisions, I think you know where we're headed."

Laying off workers is the third rail of Detroit politics. It's never been done.

When Mayor Kwame Kilpatrick proposed a meager 377 layoffs this year, the City Council erupted in protest, and some joined ranks with the city's labor unions to fight the cutbacks.

Next year, the number of layoffs will have to grow to somewhere between 2,000 and 4,000 of the 18,700-person work force if the city is to finally address its structural problems.

Kilpatrick indicates he'll fight for those layoffs, even though it's an election year, and even though one of his likely opponents, Councilwoman Sharon McPhail, has pledged no layoffs, no how.

Staying the course will test Kilpatrick's leadership and political will. Following his lead will test the council's commitment to act in the best interests of the city.

Detroit doesn't exist to provide jobs. It exists to provide services. If it does that well, the private sector will create the jobs.

Changing the way the city sees its role requires strong leadership. If the leadership isn't there, there's no way Detroit can avoid receivership. A state-appointed receiver will be free of politics and will cut without mercy until the budget balances.

Detroit's leaders have one last chance to avoid that. But it means they have to make the tough choices themselves.

March 13, 2005

Urban farming may well hold the key to the future of Detroit

What do you do with a city after most of its people leave? That's not a question that gets asked often in Detroit.

Instead, we keep posing the more hopeful questions.

How do we restore Detroit's neighborhoods to their 1950s heyday? How do we draw residents back to refill the schools and revitalize the business districts? How do we recreate a meaningful downtown?

But what if the answer to those questions is, "It ain't gonna happen"?

Then what? What do you do with a city that's been all but abandoned? Do you let it become a ghost town?

As Detroit's residents drain away, they leave behind gap-toothed neighborhoods. Residential blocks with only one or two viable homes. Vast expanses of vacant land.

A city built to hold 2 million people now contains less than half that number. Thousands of acres sit idle within the city borders.

Recently, teams of urban planning students from the University of Michigan swarmed over Eastern Market to brainstorm ways of pumping new energy into that part of downtown.

The teams looked at fresh designs for the market, as well as how to better use it to energize the surrounding community.

One of the more intriguing ideas posted by several of the teams was urban agriculture.

Farms in the city. Truck patches to grow produce to be sold in Eastern Market's stalls.

A terrific idea, and one that should be considered citywide.

Suburban sprawl is a reality in Metro Detroit. People keep pushing outward, and nothing seems to deter them.

Urban decline is also a reality. City residents keep leaving, and neighborhoods continue to fall into neglect, and so far, we haven't found the answer to stop the slide.

We may reach a point where struggling against the inevitable is pointless. Then, the challenge will be putting all that empty land to use.

City farming might be an option.

Rather than a strong urban core with rural outskirts, Metro Detroit may evolve into a suburban ring around a re-ruralized core.

It's one way to counter the negative affects of sprawl. As a region, we'd replace the open spaces that are being gobbled up on the outer edges with new farmland and forests where the city used to be.

"It may be that the future of Detroit lies in a series of viable communities linked by open spaces, parks, forests and farms," says professor Roy Strickland, director of the Masters of Urban Design program at U-M. "That will require some tough political decision-making about the future direction of the city."

Farming fits Detroit's history. The city started as an agricultural settlement, with long narrow farms stretching inland from the river.

Then as now, Detroit is built on good, fertile ground.

And while nobody's suggesting turning downtown's skyscrapers into grain silos, we may eventually face the choice of letting that empty land continue to sprout weeds and tumble-down houses, or putting it back to work growing tomatoes and grazing cattle.

That wouldn't necessarily mean giving up on Detroit's future, but rather making the vision of the future better fit the reality.

June 16, 2006

Tear down Tiger Stadium and let's all move on

One of my favorite memories of my father is sitting with him in the green, wooden bleacher boxes atop Tiger Stadium. Bat Day. Fifty thousand people in the seats. Most of them kids banging their Al Kalines and Willie Hortons on the concrete in deafening unison. And dad with his fingers deep in his ears.

Years later, I took my own son to his first Tigers game. Barely old enough to walk, he had no clue why we were there. But when the players ran out onto the field in their crisp, white uniforms, he froze, whispering a reverent "Wow."

My nostalgia for Tiger Stadium runs as deep as anyone's.

But still, if they let me, I'll be on the corner of Michigan and Trumbull cheering as the wrecking ball crashes into my old friend.

Tear it down and let's all move on.

Tiger Stadium did its duty with honor for a good, long time. But it was made for baseball, and forcing it to do something else just to keep it standing would be a humiliation.

Allowing it to continue to shamefully decay is also a disservice to the stadium's proud legacy and to the city that loved it.

Our memories of Tiger Stadium will be no less precious when it's gone. We won't forget '68 and '84, and doing the wave with thousands of other sweaty, ecstatic fans. We won't forget the narrow seats, the narrower walkways, the obstructed views, the sounds and the smells. We'll always have those.

But we have to let go. Tiger Stadium is hallowed ground for a lot of people. So was the downtown Hudson's store.

For more than 20 years, we wrung our hands as that glorious building rotted, and much of downtown along with it, because die-hard preservationists insisted it be saved.

Once it finally came down and the Compuware headquarters went up, downtown finally began its slow rebirth. But it was too long in coming.

We are at risk of repeating that tragedy with Tiger Stadium. Other towns, when new stadiums were built, paid their respects to the old parks and gave them a proper burial. Cincinnati has said goodbye to two baseball stadiums.

But Detroit can never seem to let go.

We've allowed our downtown skyline to remain filled with dozens of abandoned hotels and office buildings, beautiful for sure, but unsuited for renovation.

We pretend that someday, someone will find a use for the soaring Michigan Central train depot, so we let it stand as a ghoulish gateway to a blighted city.

Warehouses that have been empty since before World War II still stand on the edge of downtown. Abandoned homes poison our neighborhoods. Idle factories stretch out for miles.

What are we holding on to?

Tear them all down. And start with Tiger Stadium. Let whatever replaces it become the next Compuware, the next catalyst for revival.

The old ballpark gave us too many memories, thrilled us too many times, for us to let it suffer the indignity of becoming yet one more monument to hopelessness and despair.

July 20, 2008
Don't let Detroit die without a fight

A city must be awfully hard to kill. How else do you explain that Detroit is still breathing?

Detroit is down with a fatal case of chaos. The structure of government has dissolved, with every public institution in dysfunction and disarray. Last week's shouting match between City Council members and mayoral appointees looked a lot like anarchy.

And it was brought on by public officials who are all about serving themselves, rather than their people.

Kwame Kilpatrick once promised to leave a legacy as the boy wonder who gave Detroit back its dream. Now, his stubborn refusal to step aside despite facing perjury and corruption charges has assured he will be remembered as the man who strangled a city.

In other places, the City Council might be counted on to offer stability when a mayor stumbles. But this is Detroit, and the Detroit City Council on its best day barely rises above inept.

Instead of putting out the fire, the council poured on fuel by getting itself entangled in a federal bribery probe. The council can't very well yank the mayor for corruption when some of its members may be heading to the courthouse with him.

While City Hall is burning, no one seems to notice that the Detroit school board is at war with its newly hired superintendent. The school district has mismanaged its finances so thoroughly that it is just a bounced check or two away from insolvency.

Try packaging all that into a two-minute elevator pitch to sell Detroit to investors, job creators or new residents.

Can Detroit be cured? Maybe. But you're kidding yourself if you think a return to health will require anything short of a miracle.

The prescribed miracle is for Detroiters to get mad as hell and declare they're not going to take it anymore.

But instead, Detroiters are sitting on the rooftops like the pitiful Katrina victims waiting for a rescue boat to float by.

That boat's not coming.

If Detroit survives Hurricane Kwame, it only will be because its residents decided to step up and save themselves.

Detroiters need to march down to City Hall and drag the rascals out. It's maddening that six months into this unnatural disaster there's still no credible recall drive underway to get rid of the mayor quickly and cleanly. Start one today. And leave spaces open on the petition to add any council member whose name shows up on a federal indictment.

You're not helpless Detroit. And you don't have to be a victim. Get angry. Get loud.

Shout down the parasitic preachers who have a pocketbook stake in protecting their political partners. Wave off the excuse makers who urge you to let the legal process play itself out. You may be six feet under by then.

This is your city. You can't wait for the business community to do something. It's got no vote. You can't wait for Gov. Jennifer Granholm to do something. She's got no spine.

As a city, you've got to lift yourself out of your deathbed.

Come on, Detroit, don't die without a fight.

March 1, 2009

Elect a crazy council, get crazy results

Nowhere is Michigan's brain drain on greater display than in the Detroit City Council chambers.

My hopes for Detroit's future faded as I watched the tape of last Tuesday's council meeting, the one that considered the Cobo Center expansion deal.

It was a tragic circus, a festival of ignorance that confirmed the No. 1 obstacle to Detroit's progress is the bargain basement leaders that city voters elect. The black nationalism that is now the dominant ideology of the council was on proud display, both at the table and in the audience.

Speakers advocating for the deal were taunted by the crowd and cut short by Council President Monica Conyers, who presided over the hearing like an angry bulldog; whites were advised by the citizens to, "Go home."

Opponents were allowed to rant and ramble on uninterrupted about "those people" who want to steal Detroit's assets and profit from the city's labors.

A pitiful Teamster official who practically crawled to the table on his knees expressing profuse respect for this disrespectful body was battered by both the crowd and the council.

When he dared suggest that an improved Cobo Center would create more good-paying jobs for union workers, Conyers reminded him, "Those workers look like you; they don't look like me."

Desperate, he invoked President Barack Obama's message of unity and was angrily warned, "Don't you say his name here."

Juxtapose the place and the faces and imagine a white Livonia City Council treating a black union representative with such overt racial hostility. The Justice Department would swoop down like a hawk, and the Rev. Al Sharpton would clog Five Mile Road with protesters.

But in Detroit, dealing with the council's bigotry is part of the cost of doing business. As is dealing with its incompetence.

Emmet Moten, the developer who just opened the Fort Shelby Hotel downtown, was at the meeting and found it appalling. Moten went to Lansing in 1983 on behalf of Mayor Coleman Young to successfully lobby for a regional tax to support Cobo.

"And now we're saying, 'We don't want your money,'" Moten says. "If Coleman were alive today, he'd be outraged. It hurts, it really hurts."

Now, Moten says, "we Detroiters gotta be outraged."

Outraged enough to go to the polls in November and elect a brighter, more responsible council. Moten and others I talked with this week are encouraged that mayoral primary voters picked Dave Bing and Ken Cockrel Jr., the two most rational candidates on the ballot.

The test now will be whether it's those primary voters or the angry council crowd who represent the real Detroit.

As Moten notes, "You can't fix this for us. We have to fix it ourselves."

Nobody can help Detroit if voters again elect a City Council composed of separatists, clueless dowagers and the apparently insane.

September 19, 2010
The three I's of Detroit's decline

Detroit used to make cars. Now it makes poor people. The city pumps out poverty on a three-shift, seven-day-a-week cycle.

The raw materials in this factory are ignorance, illegitimacy and isolation.

Ignorance is by far the main ingredient. Citizens came to Mayor Dave Bing's town halls on right-sizing last week shouting for jobs. Let's get real.

Two-thirds of Detroit residents don't have a high school diploma. Half are functionally illiterate. Only about 10 percent graduated from college.

What kind of jobs do residents expect Detroit to attract with a work force that ill-prepared? Certainly not the technical jobs that are driving the 21st century economy. And the city can only support so many fast-food joints.

Emergency Manager Robert Bobb came to town hell-bent on reinventing a school system that fails two out of three children. And yet some elements of the city are fighting him as if he carried the plague.

Unless Detroit commits to making its people smarter in a red-hot hurry, Bing's land use plan will amount to little more than moving poor people out of already blighted neighborhoods and into neighborhoods soon to be blighted.

Illegitimacy is a direct by-product of ignorance. More than 70 percent of the city's babies are born to unwed mothers, and more than half to teen-agers. There's no greater predictor of poverty. Most Detroit babies are added to the welfare rolls before they leave the delivery room.

Some rise above the circumstance of their birth, either through determined mothering or the strength of their own character. But many more have no hope of beating the long odds against them.

Under-parenting is a scourge of Detroit, and yet few are willing to take up a crusade against illegitimacy.

Isolation is the most dangerous element in this poverty plant. The more dire Detroit's circumstances become, the more suspicious its citizens are of "outsiders." Bing found that out at his community meetings. A shockingly high percentage of the audience believed he was really crafting a sinister plan to let suburban rich guys take over the city.

A possible solution to Detroit's troubles would be to make the city part of a regional government. The outflow of the city's black middle class, which accelerated after the housing crash made suburban homes more affordable, is leaving Detroit a single race, single economic class city.

That creates a lot of social needs, while stripping the city of the tax base to meet them. A regional government would spread the costs over a wider area, and possibly bring Detroit more economic and racial diversity. But does anyone think Detroiters would grab onto that lifeline, let alone that suburbanites would throw it to them?

A plan to make Detroit's footprint match its population is an urgent necessity. But it won't fix the core problems.

Poverty will wear a "Made in Detroit" label as long as the city wallows in ignorance and illegitimacy and isolates itself from those who might help.

December 19, 2010
Detroit? It's Bing, not Kwame

Something important to keep in mind in assessing the impact of federal racketeering indictments against former Mayor Kwame Kilpatrick and his posse: That was then, this is now.

The Detroit mayor's office doesn't operate as an organized crime outfit under new Mayor Dave Bing. And for that matter, it didn't under Mayor Dennis Archer.

Archer and Bing are bookends of integrity, with the wretchedly corrupt Kilpatrick years in between.

Much of Bing's mission has been to send the message that the pay-to-play culture is gone from City Hall. And he's done a pretty good job. Those who do business with the city today say there isn't a whiff of impropriety in dealing with the Bing administration. The shakedown days are done.

And yet every time Bing gains some traction in polishing Detroit's image, another episode of the Kilpatrick crime drama is released. It's like that rash you picked up in the service; it just won't go away.

Making the rounds of holiday events this past week, I found a business community that was once again back on its heels, disgusted and discouraged about the latest Kilpatrick headlines. Many of these folks have been touched by the scandal, simply by doing business with the city during the Kilpatrick years.

They've been called before a grand jury, had FBI agents show up at their front doors, and have had what they thought were legitimate business deals tainted by the scent of payoffs. They now have to worry not only about the image of the city, but also about the reputation of their own companies. Who could blame them if they gave up and got out?

This is Kilpatrick's legacy to Detroit. By now, there should be no doubt that Kilpatrick was a pox on this city. For crying out loud, he shook down a homeless shelter for $10,000 to pay for his Las Vegas jaunts, according to the indictments. Money that should have gone to caring for the city's most vulnerable was tossed instead on craps tables.

And yet there are still too many Detroiters who believe "y'all's boy" got the shaft. And there are too many who view Bing as an interloper and his efforts at rebuilding a shattered city as illegitimate.

This mayor hasn't got anywhere near the support he deserves for stepping in to keep Detroit from collapsing under Kilpatrick's corruption.

The Detroit you've been reading about the past few days? It doesn't exist anymore, thanks to Bing.

Disagree with Bing's policies and proposals if you like. That's fair game. And those are the conversations we should be having, instead of whispering about how much money a mayor is stuffing into his pockets.

Bing is showing the world that crooked dealing and thuggery are an aberration, and not endemic. Like Archer before him, Bing is proving that you can be mayor of Detroit and also be honest and ethical.

After the things we've heard this past week, it's hard to place a value on that.

⇜ ⇜ ⇜

June 26, 2011

We love Detroit despite its flaws

William Faulkner wrote of the South, you don't love it because, you love it despite.

Doesn't that also capture our relationship with Detroit?

We love this city despite all the things that should be right by now, but are still wrong.

We love it despite its stubborn self destruction, its frustrating habit of missing opportunities, its abusive outbursts, its broken promises.

We love Detroit despite the relentless blight and deterioration that makes it often seem as if decline and revival are running neck-and-neck, with no way to pick a winner.

We love it even when loving it requires us to squint so we don't see the blemishes.

We love it even when it can't quite love itself.

It's a wearying kind of love, hardened by heartbreak and conditioned to disappointment. It's also a love we feel the need to explain, if not apologize for.

Last week, out-of-town journalists were here to participate in Transformation Detroit, an annual singing of the city's praises. There's a desperate quality to these sorts of events.

We work ourselves into a sweat to convince our visitors that beneath Detroit's pock-marked exterior beats a heart of gold. We want so badly for them to understand the complexity of our feelings for Detroit.

I attended some of the sessions, and the organizers did a good job of selling the city's present and potential. It's a useful reinforcement of what we know but sometimes forget—Detroit has some awfully good qualities and some extraordinarily talented people. I'm sure most of the journalists were impressed, and perhaps surprised.

Still, I always wonder if they don't get on the plane asking themselves what we see in a city with so much baggage.

We must seem like gluttons for punishment. There are certainly easier places to live; fresh, sparkling cities that we could experience with the giddiness and romance of a new relationship. Why stay here?

It's not always easy to put into words why we stick it out.

Except on days like today, when thousands of us will be downtown for the River Days festival, enjoying a riverfront that isn't quite as fabulous as it could be, but is a whole lot better than it once was.

The work done by the Riverfront Conservancy to revive the riverfront is an example of the huge returns you can reap in Detroit when you invest a bit of hope.

Polish one piece of this jewel and it makes you eager to shine another. In a landscape so devastated, everything you do makes a noticeable difference.

So maybe we love Detroit because it needs us so much.

Or maybe it's enough to just say there's a lid for every pot, and we're Detroit's.

April 26, 2012

Want to save Detroit? Help tear it down

We should take a break from our excitement about rebuilding Detroit and turn our focus instead to tearing it down.

Not the whole city, but those parts of it that are already caved in, rotting and burned out.

That's a big piece of Detroit. Charitable estimates place the number of abandoned dwellings between 30,000 and 40,000, though some believe the number to be twice that large.

In any case, it's a mountain of blight to move, a cancer that is raging through the entire body of the city.

And until it's gone, there's no hope that Detroit's revival will ever outpace its decline.

Blight breeds blight. People who look out the windows of well-tended homes onto a landscape of scorched and tumble-down houses eventually get fed up and leave, too. It's all but impossible to sell a home, even in better neighborhoods, if there are vacant and neglected buildings on the same block.

And the empty structures also are a major contributor to the city's crime troubles.

Getting rid of them must be high on the priority list of a city that has so many needs fighting for top billing. Until the abandoned houses are gone, it's difficult to judge which neighborhoods are viable and which should be surrendered.

But the cost is numbing. At roughly $10,000 per house for demolition, clearing away the abandonment would cost $300 million to $400 million—enough to triple the length of the proposed Woodward Avenue light rail line.

Detroit doesn't have that money; neither does the state. The federal government could be tapped, but it already sends the city $20 million a year in neighborhood stabilization funds that Detroit hasn't managed to spend, and is unlikely to throw good money after bad.

Mayor Dave Bing pledged to tear down 10,000 abandoned houses in his first term. So far, he's only managed to bulldoze about 4,300, despite having the unspent federal bucks and another $20 million in the state Fire Insurance Escrow fund that's available for demolition. At this rate, even if not another home is deserted, it will take two decades to clear away the current inventory.

And that doesn't account for the thousands of commercial buildings that are devolving to rubble, or the 50 or so abandoned structures downtown. Bringing them down could easily double the tab.

Kurt Metzger of Data Driven Detroit, which did the Detroit Parcel Survey in 2009, says efforts must be targeted at neighborhoods that are still fairly healthy to attack blight before it takes root.

"Even the best neighborhoods are on the edge," Metzger says. "Vacancies lead to squatters, which lead to fires, which lead to the need for demolition. If you have limited resources, you have to prioritize them to get the best results."

Bing's Detroit Works project is supposed to do that, but it is slow in launching.

The mayor clearly needs help, both in developing a strategy and in executing it.

On any project, the remodeling work is more rewarding than the demolition phase. But you can't rebuild until you tear down. All those who are so energized about Detroit's revival should target their funds and sweat to get the nasty knock-down work out of the way first.

February 3, 2013

Detroit's 'Super' lost chance

New Orleans will show off its post-Katrina face today, using the Super Bowl exposure to give the world a look at how it's come back from one of the worst natural disasters in American history.

Although it's been a tough seven-year struggle, there seems now to be consensus that New Orleans is emerging from the devastation of the hurricane as a city being rebuilt in the right way and poised to soar.

Entrepreneurs have brought new energy and investment to the city. Its infrastructure has been rebuilt, and its government institutions, particularly its schools, are operating more efficiently and more honestly than they were before Katrina hit.

Today's football championship is the revitalized city's coming-out party. Meanwhile, in Detroit...

The 2006 Super Bowl, held five months after Katrina struck, was supposed to affirm the beginning of something big for the Motor City.

Detroit had a bright, enthusiastic young mayor with the charisma and potential to rally his city to greatness. Its business community was stepping up to not only fund the Super Bowl, but also to invest in the city's long-term success.

The national media ended its three-decade disparagement of Detroit and was saying nice things about our city.

It felt like a jumping-off point to something grand.

Instead, Detroit hit a wall. The mayoral wunderkind was brought down by his appetites. The business community, particularly the automakers who bankrolled much of the Super Bowl, were ransacked by the recession.

In those seven years, 150,000 more residents packed up and left, leaving behind ruined houses and neighborhoods.

The news about Detroit today is mostly focused on the financial collapse of city government, and the speculation centers on the timing of its inevitable bankruptcy.

In terms of lost opportunities, Super Bowl XL was a doozy for Detroit.

Detroit was never able to fully leverage the positive vibe it produced to draw the kind of investment, jobs and new residents needed for a broad stabilization.

While the event did birth the enthusiasm for downtown that is now filling lofts and offices with a new sort of Detroiter, it didn't change the overall trajectory of the city.

Too soon after the fans from Pittsburgh and Seattle went home and the Rolling Stones packed up their guitars, Detroit was tripped by the same obstacles that always seem to thwart progress—tough economic breaks, weak leadership, abandonment.

Events both within and beyond its control brought the city too quickly crashing down from the euphoria of that super weekend.

New Orleans is climbing back from its natural disaster and will trumpet that today.

The rolling disaster that is destroying Detroit goes on.

That will take something much bigger than a Super Bowl to fix.

≺ ≺ ≺

March 3, 2013

Gov. Snyder, Mayor Bing never clicked

Detroit is getting an emergency manager in large part because two business-men-turned-politicians could not forge a working partnership.

Mayor Dave Bing and Gov. Rick Snyder came from the same fraternity of CEOs who thought applying business principles was the way to fix government. They should have been natural allies.

But the two never clicked, never built the sort of relationship that was expected when they took office. Worse, they never quite trusted each other.

Snyder is careful in describing the relationship, and why it was not as effective as perhaps it could have been: "We both have other parties that we have to deal with. In his case, he has the City Council, and I have the Legislature. I would have to say the Legislature has been a pretty good partner. I think he's had more challenges with the City Council."

While both hailed from business, they are vastly different executive types. The distinction is primarily pace.

When Snyder speaks of dog years, he means it. He wants a problem solved and off his desk as soon as possible.

Bing is more deliberate in his approach to decision making, perhaps because he came out of the world of heavy manufacturing, where change evolves slowly. Snyder played in the high-tech, dotcom arenas, where, if you wait too long to act, you're out of business.

Where Snyder was energized by the mess he inherited, Bing was over-whelmed by City Hall's dysfunction. The governor boasts of relentless positive action; the mayor complains about long hours and poor help.

Their personal communications were mostly cordial, but there has been animosity between their staffs. Snyder's team often complains that deals agreed to by Bing are consistently undone by his aides.

The biggest issue, though, is trust.

The governor felt badly burned by Bing when the state intervention began in late fall of 2011. The mayor joined the Detroit for Detroiters chorus, fuel-ing fear and resentment and setting back the process. There have been other incidents. Asked if he is at times frustrated with the mayor, Snyder said, "there are things that one would have to describe as challenging to understand. Belle Isle would probably be the easiest illustration."

I asked Snyder a few times in recent days whether Bing had been a good partner, and he always gave some variation of this answer: "I don't go into areas like that because I view that as potentially blaming or fighting with someone, and I don't do that."

Now Snyder is sitting Bing on the sidelines, a place where the Hall of Fame guard isn't used to finding himself.

"I hope he's engaged in this," Snyder said, outlining a ceremonial role that would have the mayor serving as liaison to the community and continuing to work on special projects.

In the parlance of business, what's happened here can't be described as a hostile takeover, but nor is it a merger of equals.

March 17, 2013

Kevyn Orr just might get the job done

It's hard to bring myself to say I'm optimistic about the city of Detroit, even though I'm extremely encouraged by Gov. Rick Snyder's appointment of Kevyn Orr as the city's emergency manager.

Sit down with Orr, as I had a chance to do last week, and you start to believe there's a path back to functionality and financial stability.

But I've seen too many fresh starts turn into false starts to break out my cheerleader pom poms.

Orr arrives in Detroit as perhaps the most competent person ever to walk through the doors of City Hall. He's got an impressive turnaround pedigree, as well as a tanker full of hubris. If the job can be done, I believe he's the one who can do it.

But that's the big question: Can the job be done? Detroit looks for all the world like a city that has already slipped past the tipping point.

Operationally, everything is broken in Detroit. Residents don't pay their taxes. Cops can't keep the streets safe. The lights are still out. Technology is out of date. Orr and his team can develop strategies for making city departments more efficient. But can they change the culture of incompetence that has been allowed to steep at City Hall for decades?

While he promises to be a consensus builder and weigh the human impact of his decisions, in reality Orr is going to have to march through the bureaucracy like Sherman through Georgia.

He'll have to once and for all establish that city government is a service provider, not a job provider.

Orr says that restructuring Detroit without a bankruptcy can be done, and quickly, if everyone cooperates and acts in good faith. But this is Detroit. Can anyone remember the last time everyone worked together for the good of the city?

Snyder said something similar nearly a year ago when he signed the consent agreement with Mayor Dave Bing and the City Council. It will work, he said then, if everyone does what they've promised to do. They didn't, and now it's on Orr to get it right.

He's got the skills, for sure. But there are several things outside Orr's control that can trigger a bankruptcy. He'll have to artfully use the bankruptcy lever to bring in line both creditors and unions.

Orr shows a toughness honed during 30 years of bare-knuckled negotiations in the private and public sectors. He'll need it to get deals done with interests that up to now have not seen any reason to bargain.

I'm impressed by Orr's confidence, intellect and affability. He comes off as a guy eager to get to work. His mind seems to be constantly turning over problems and kicking out ideas. He promises frequent communication with Detroiters, and if he carries through, he'll charm their pants off.

He's done tough jobs before, and will be backed by Snyder's team and the best consultants money can buy.

So while there are lots of reasons this new beginning won't work any better than the previous ones, it just might.

April 28, 2013

Let's stop trashing Detroit

What is it about Detroit that makes people so comfortable trashing it?

Driving along Jefferson Avenue last week, a guy in front of me rolled down his window and tossed out a fast-food bag that landed on the curb, where it likely still rests.

Opening day of the baseball season was a festival. Downtown was packed with people loving baseball and loving Detroit. That night, the streets around the ballpark were covered with a carpet of blue and red beer cups, left there for someone else to pick up.

Downtown restaurant owner restaurant owner Larry Mongo was beaten the other night when he tried to stop a gang of punks from tagging the Downtown Synagogue.

Detroit may as well be a designated garbage dump for the way we treat it. Nobody's innocent. Detroiters blame suburbanites for coming into the city for fireworks, boat races and the like and leaving behind mountains of trash. And that's true.

But it's also true that litter is ankle deep along almost any Detroit street, thrown there by residents who have to live among it.

It reflects a lack of respect for a city that is struggling so hard to regain some grandeur.

The Downtown Detroit Partnership picks up more than 500 tons of trash each year in the central business district. It's why downtown manages to look relatively spic-and-span so quickly after major events.

If the folks who profess to love partying downtown would put their junk in receptacles or bag it up and take it home, the partnership could devote those resources to other projects. I can't believe the suburban visitors treat their own neighborhoods this way, nor would they tolerate Detroiters coming there to build a Solo mound.

But Detroiters do treat the places where they live this way, and that confounds me. Littering is as common as jay-walking. People who live with so much blight are likely desensitized to fields of paper wrappers and plastic bottles. But there's no excuse for making ugly even uglier.

As for the jerks Mongo encountered, they make a mockery of a Creative Detroit. Perhaps the garish scrawlings are considered art in certain places, but on the side of downtown buildings, it's vandalism.

Downtown business owners should pool their money for an anti-graffiti effort to catch and prosecute the vandals. Graffiti makes it look as if no one cares about a city, and there's nothing hip about that.

When I was a kid, the Don't be a Litterbug campaign created both peer pressure and a conscience that worked to limit littering. Today, global warming gets most of the attention in classrooms. We need to make room for a strong anti-littering message as well.

Detroit has a littering ordinance that's rarely enforced. It could divert some of the vigilance it gives parking meters to writing citations for littering.

Education and enforcement will help keep Detroit clean. But so would a lot more respect for the place where we live, play and work.

≮ ≮ ≮

August 11, 2013

Everything must change in Detroit

Fixing Detroit is the comparatively easy job.

With the dictatorial powers he possesses, and an assist from bankruptcy court, emergency manager Kevyn Orr ought to have the city solvent and clicking like a sewing machine by the time he leaves late next year.

Then what?

Unless Detroit changes nearly everything it was doing before it went bankrupt, the return to fiscal health Orr orchestrates will be just a brief respite from the city's long deterioration.

Detroit is not a victim of circumstance. Its financial collapse was not imposed upon it by forces beyond its control. Bad things happened, certainly. There was white flight. There was the meltdown of the domestic auto industry. There was shrinking support from the state and federal governments.

But the failure to respond to those things, the stubborn refusal to change policies and practices to head off disaster, the corruption, dismal leadership, entitlement attitude, denial—they all belong to Detroit.

The question is whether becoming the largest municipality to file for bankruptcy and having their democratic rights suspended is enough to jar Detroiters into the reality that the city has to change.

It's too early to say with certainty.

You can read from Mike Duggan's remarkable write-in victory in Tuesday's mayoral primary a seismic shift toward change—a white candidate hasn't been on the general election mayoral ballot in 40 years, and he's a businessman to boot.

But it was a very low turnout that may not be representative of the broader electorate. During the primary, the racial divisiveness that remains at the root of so many of Detroit's ills was a major theme. Benny Napoleon spoke of being the candidate for the neighborhoods, not downtown. That code is simple to decipher: Neighborhoods mean black Detroit, downtown means the white business community. Same old us vs. them.

Separatism hasn't worked all that well for Detroit. Coming out of bankruptcy, it has to open itself up to the help that so many of the so-called "outsiders" are willing to give.

It has to look at business as an essential ingredient for restoring the city. It has to concentrate on keeping what's left of its middle class and attracting more residents with the ability to pay taxes. It has to elect leaders who don't see their duty as providing jobs and contracts to their political supporters, but providing services to residents.

Detroit is bankrupt, but not broken, or at least it won't be when Orr gets done. The good news is that when it starts governing itself again, the city will have a road map to follow to prosperity.

It must commit to doing whatever it takes to stay on that course.

Dec. 14, 2014

Where are the black people?

Near the top of the list of the challenges Detroit faces as it starts its post-bankruptcy era is avoiding becoming

Two cities—one for the upwardly mobile young and white denizens of an increasingly happening downtown, and the other for the struggling and frustrated black residents trapped in neighborhoods that are crumbling around them.

Nobody wants to inject race into the marvelous story of downtown's rebound, driven largely by young creatives who grew up in the suburbs and are now fiercely Detroiters. I don't either. It's a downer, and the last thing I want to be involved in is another conversation about race.

But with racial tension simmering across the country, Detroit must heed obvious warning signs.

It's a clear red flag when you can sit in a hot new downtown restaurant and nine out of 10 tables are filled with white diners, a proportion almost exactly opposite of the city's racial make-up.

It's a warning signal when you go to holiday events for major Detroit cultural institutions and charities, and you can count the number of African-American revelers on both hands.

It should stop us in our tracks—as it did me the other day—when a group of 50 young professionals being groomed for future leadership shows up to hear advice from a senior executive, and there's only one black member among them.

Pay attention to the stories about the cool kids who are leading the Detroit revival by starting businesses, social groups and nonprofits. Overwhelmingly, the subjects are white.

I'm not disparaging the newcomers. Detroit was an opportunity sitting there for the taking, and they seized it. And what they're doing is miraculous. We can talk all day about why more African-Americans didn't do the same thing. It doesn't matter. We have to understand that we're buying trouble if we don't encourage more black participation.

This isn't about handouts or set-asides or affirmative action. Nor is it about gentrification, an absolutely ridiculous concern in a city that needs so much rebuilding. I don't even believe it's about racism.

Rather, it's about downtown employers making sure they're truly cognizant of the diversity of their workforces, and stretching a bit more to recruit and train native Detroiters, who will then help fill the lofts and nightspots.

It's about encouraging black entrepreneurs to come to or stay in the city, and recognizing there are cultural and opportunity gaps that have to be closed to create a vibrant base of small business started by people drawn from the city's neighborhoods.

And it's about the African-Americans who've already made it showing up in Detroit, putting their money and time into the city's civic, cultural and charitable organizations. Drawing affluent blacks back from the suburbs is also a key step.

Detroit is now the city of opportunity. Fairness demands that those who were here when no one else wanted to be share in the fruits of the comeback.

It's like playing with dynamite to have black Detroiters looking out of devastated neighborhoods at a downtown bustling with hope and hopeful young people, and not seeing their own children among that hip crowd. ✒

Chapter 3

Kwame

January 30, 2005

Kilpatrick channels the worst of Young's personality

David Eberhard slipped out of his chair at the Detroit City Council table, crossed the room to press row and tapped me on the shoulder. "Check out the parking lot," he whispered.

So I did. There in the VIP spaces adjacent to the City-County Building was a long and gleaming, baby blue Cadillac limousine.

It was the summer of 1980 and Detroit was in the midst of a budget crisis, asking its employees for concessions and its residents for sacrifice. Surely Coleman Young hadn't ordered himself these expensive new wheels.

There was only one way to find out for sure. I hopped up on the hood of the limo and waited. After an hour or two of enjoying the sunshine, Young finally pushed through the doors flanked by his usual contingent of bodyguards. He froze when he saw me perched on the Caddy.

"Get that (*&%$*&) off my car," he growled to his muscle. They did and not gently. But I had the confirmation I needed that the mayor, who had advised senior citizens struggling with property tax bills to "eat more beans," was still reserving for himself a steak and champagne lifestyle.

The then and now parallels are obvious. Young had his limo; Kwame Kilpatrick has his shiny red Navigator.

And both had the mistaken notion that the mayor's chair is a royal throne that lifts its occupants above the rules that apply to everyone else in the city.

The late Walt Stecher, who was Young's budget director, waved me into his office one day during that same period, visibly mad as hell.

"He's ordered me to give Joyce Garrett a raise," Stecher fumed. Garrett was a city department head and Young's longtime romantic interest.

At the time, there was a pay freeze on all city employees, and Stecher reminded Young of that, to no avail.

"He said, 'She's my (x#%$&#) girlfriend and I'll give her a (#$@%*) raise if I want to,' " Stecher quoted the mayor.

Not all that different from Kilpatrick's defense of a chauffered ride and two security officers for his wife's shopping trips to Somerset and Sunday brunches in Grosse Pointe.

There is a difference in stature, though. Young was the city's first black mayor, and many saw him as a Moses.

The more we in the press banged away at him, the more the people worshipped him.

Young knew his audience, and it wasn't suburbanites or the business community. He played to those who loved to see him flip off The Man.

Kilpatrick doesn't have that luxury. His success depends on building regional confidence and alliances. And his most fervent critics come from the city's African-American establishment. That makes it useless for him to throw the race card on the table.

Kilpatrick says Young is his hero. Many in Detroit feel the same way.

But Detroit was a bleaker place after 20 years of Young's reign, and much of the blame goes to the divisive tactics he used to maintain political power.

If Kilpatrick really wants to fulfill the vision he has for Detroit, he might want to think about getting a different role model.

October 30, 2005
Forced to choose, business picks the race baiter

I've been trying to work up a hot dose of outrage about the racist ad that ran in the Michigan Chronicle on behalf of the Kwame Kilpatrick mayoral campaign, but I can't get my mad on.

And it's not just because the mug shot under the headline "The Media Lynch Mob" makes me look a lot less bald.

It's just too absurd to fester over. For one thing, my fellow media mobsters, Jack

Lessenberry, Brian Dickerson and Mildred Gaddis, would make a more menacing book club than a lynching party. Mildred's the muscle of that group, for sure.

But mostly, I believe the genius of the First Amendment is that it encourages even the most despicable ideas to be brought into the sunlight, where they can be debated and discredited. Otherwise, they'd percolate in the shadows, becoming even more poisonous.

There's a strong undercurrent of black racism in the city of Detroit, and this full-page ad puts it on the street where it can't be denied.

Rooted in black nationalism, the latest racial scourge to devastate Detroit feeds off the twisted theory that a legion of white, suburban power brokers are poised to swoop in and take back a city that is the birthright of African-Americans.

Only a strong, tough talking, truly black leader can turn them away. Kilpatrick has positioned himself as that leader, fanning the irrational fears as he desperately tries to hang on to his office.

No surprise there. Kilpatrick will do whatever it takes to win, even if it means keeping his city in the dark ages.

What's puzzling is that the very white businessmen whom the lynching ad degrades will gather this week at a major fund-raiser for the mayor.

Ask these business leaders to identify the biggest obstacle facing Metro Detroit, and they'll inevitably say the region's horrible race relations.

And yet they are writing checks to a race baiter. Most of them are employers, and if their workers were associated with anything as racially obscene as the lynching ad, they'd fire them.

But freshly seduced by Kilpatrick's potential, they pretend not to see his destructiveness.

In condescending acquiescence to Detroit's worst nature, they accept the wisdom that exploiting the racial divide is the only way a politician can get elected here, and hope the damage can be repaired later.

But I believe that the majority of Detroiters are better than this, and that they'll repudiate the hate mongers on Election Day.

They understand that the region's challenges are so immense that they'll only be met by city and suburbs, black and white, pulling together. We simply don't have the luxury of hating each other any longer. Kilpatrick denounced the image of the lynch mob ad, but supported its sentiment.

That sentiment of divisiveness and hatred is a millstone around Detroit's neck.

Kilpatrick has no interest in removing it. My bet is that Detroiters will choose someone who will.

January 25, 2008

Nothing to LOL about in Kilpatrick's latest stumble

Few in Detroit are LOL-ing today, especially not the business and civic leaders who placed their bets on the rehabilitation of Mayor Kwame Kilpatrick when they rallied to his re-election bid in 2005.

They had begun to breathe easier after more than two years without a serious personal misstep by the Detroit mayor. Now, in the words of one business group chief, they feel "like we've been kicked in the stomach."

That's the story of Kilpatrick's mayoral career so far. He's a flawed hero, capable of moving mountains of decay with his faith and determination, and yet susceptible to his appetite for the high life and seemingly oblivious to the possibility that he could ever get caught.

And once again, the people who banked on him are weighing the fact that Kilpatrick is capable of doing as much damage to his city as he is good for it.

"This is a terrible story, there's no getting around that," says Al Glancy, retired chairman of DTE Energy, of the publication of salacious text messages that reveal Kilpatrick's love affair with his chief of staff. "We were all hopeful for the second term and believed his personal behavior would improve."

The frustration with Kilpatrick is his Clintonesque penchant for squandering his potential. The public mayor and the private mayor are such starkly different performers.

I can look out my window and see the impact of the public mayor. Workers are scrambling all over the once-rotting Fort-Shelby Hotel, which just a year ago was a roost for urban buzzards.

A few blocks over, the Book-Cadillac renovation is moving ahead full steam. The development activity in downtown Detroit defies the economic troubles of the region. And there's also hope for revival in Detroit's neighborhoods, thanks to various initiatives from the mayor's office.

Kilpatrick, who just last Friday gave a rousing speech to the Detroit Economic Club extolling his city's comeback, is a dynamic leader, the type Detroit must have to overcome the obstacles to its renaissance.

In his speech, Kilpatrick reminded the audience that just a couple of years ago, receivership seemed inevitable for Detroit. Through sheer will and deft political skill, Kilpatrick guided his city past that abyss.

But the private mayor is the public mayor's worst enemy.

From the beginning, Kilpatrick has considered himself above the rules. He couldn't resist the spoils of office, indulging himself during his first term with an expense account fit for a king.

The rumors of his first-term tom-catting were legendary. Radio talk show call-in lines buzzed with reports that the mayor was spotted carousing at one club or another. And, of course, there was the infamous Manoogian party. Did it really happen? Does it even matter now, given the abuses of office that have been documented?

Still, my phone calls Thursday revealed a business community desperate for Kilpatrick to survive this latest self-inflicted wound. The people whose money, time and energy are so heavily invested in Detroit's turnaround still see him as the guy best equipped to get the job done.

"He can work his way through this," says S. Martin Taylor, chairman of the Detroit Economic Growth Corp. "The momentum doesn't have to stop. It may be that this prompts others to step up and work a little harder to keep things going."

The great fear is that if this latest scandal distracts Kilpatrick from his work, efforts to attract new investment to Detroit, provide more education options and bring life back to the city's suffering neighborhoods will wither. There's also very real concern that the national conversation about Detroit will move away from the city's successes and back to the mayor's foibles.

That's why people who should feel severely burned today are once again trying to work up the energy to ride to the mayor's defense.

They know he's far from a perfect savior. But at this moment, he's still the only savior they've got.

January 27, 2008
Sex won't ruin mayor, but money might

It's not the sex or the lies. It's the money.

If it turns out all Detroit Mayor Kwame Kilpatrick has to worry about is a sex scandal and the excruciating humiliation of seeing his randy text messages to Christine Beatty in print, he can survive.

Plenty of other politicians have. Look at Rudy Giuliani. He once had an outgoing wife and an incoming wife fighting for the same bed in the New York City mayoral mansion, and he emerged not only with all of his private parts intact, but also poised to run for president.

Kilpatrick wisely chose the Bill Clinton strategy to deflect the fall-out from revelations that he did the hula with his chief of staff and then lied about it under oath.

In his brief statement after the text messages were published, Kilpatrick cast the incident as a private matter that occurred at a difficult time in his life, and one that he and his wife had already worked through.

By focusing on the sex and not on the perjury, Clinton turned an initially disgusted nation sympathetic to a poor couple forced to watch their most intimate interactions played out on TV.

Nearly everyone today accepts that sex, even extramarital sex, is a private matter, and that politicians should have the same right to sexual privacy as everyone else.

There is also growing acquiescence to the notion that when backed into a bad corner, nearly everyone will lie about sex, particularly to protect the innocent from getting hurt. Even if Kilpatrick gets nicked on perjury charges—not as certain as everyone seems to think—it won't necessarily mean the tide of public opinion will turn against him.

Particularly if he manages his image carefully.

Like Clinton, expect the mayor to emerge publicly contrite, apologetic to his family and constituents, and with a minister at his side. And like Clinton, expect him to eventually turn righteously indignant. The Clintons' vast right-wing conspiracy will be played out locally as an attack by the exploitive white media.

Don't underestimate Kilpatrick's charm, another trait he shares with Clinton. Voters have a soft spot for their kind of bad boy.

So Kilpatrick has reason to be optimistic about his prospects. The sex alone won't bring him down.

But the money is the wild card.

Detroit has paid out more than $9 million to resolve lawsuits filed by police officers who say their careers were ruined by Kilpatrick and Beatty for investigating mayoral misconduct.

If it can be proven the officers were targeted because their questions were getting too close to revealing the pair were slipping around, it takes the scandal to a different place.

Taxpayers might be willing to excuse their politicians having some dangerous sex. They may forgive the lying about that sex.

But if they find out they're the ones who paid for the sex, this could get uglier.

Kilpatrick's hopes for riding out the storm hinge on whether Wayne County

Prosecutor Kym Worthy can connect the dots between the sex, the lies and the money.

March 16, 2008

Is Kwame Kilpatrick irreplaceable?

Say Detroit Mayor Kwame Kilpatrick dodges this bullet and manages to keep himself out of a criminal court or, worse, jail.

Should he keep his job?

To forgive Kilpatrick of transgressions that undeniably cost Detroit taxpayers $8.4 million, you have to first believe he is irreplaceable, that no potential successor could match the progress he's brought to the city's turnaround. And second, you must have faith that he can survive this scandal in sound enough shape to rebuild the broken trust with the community and restore himself as an effective leader.

Kilpatrick argued his irreplaceability in a speech to Metro Detroit's business leaders Thursday. This group has been his most loyal supporter and is most concerned with the question, "If not Kilpatrick, who?"

The mayor told the executives that without him, Detroit runs off the tracks. The investment pouring into downtown dries up. The confidence of Wall Street fades. The revitalization of the neighborhoods ends. The reform of government is over.

Earlier, Kilpatrick said that if his shenanigans cost the city millions, he's worth the money.

While his defense is incredibly egotistical, it's not without supporters. The business community in particular is well aware of the shallowness of Detroit's leadership pool.

Comparisons have been drawn between the scandal engulfing Kilpatrick and that of New York Gov. Eliot Spitzer. When Spitzer's misdeeds were revealed, the calls for his resignation were immediate and from all quarters. Why isn't that the case in Detroit?

One reason is that in New York, there's no sense that the state would falter without Spitzer, that his resignation would leave a huge void. The institution of New York is stronger than its leader.

That same confidence doesn't exist here. Detroit is more fragile, its survivability less certain. That explains why some seem willing to overlook behavior in Kilpatrick that they wouldn't tolerate in their own organizations, nor could get away with themselves.

The question of effectiveness is stickier. Kilpatrick was able to overcome the bad-boy escapades of his first term and win re-election despite being written off as politically dead. He convinced his wary backers that he'd learned a lesson, addressed his personal flaws and would be a grown-up.

He emerged stronger; self-assured, energized and with an aura of invincibility. The past two years have been the most productive of his tenure. But this time Kilpatrick has dug an even deeper grave. Can he play Lazarus once more? Is the city ready to believe again his reassurances of rehabilitation?

The answer is crucial. If Kilpatrick survives but as irreparably damaged goods, he's Bill Clinton post-Monica Lewinsky. He will have his office, but not his agenda.

And if that's the case, if there's no trust, no cooperation, no enthusiasm for his vision, the question becomes: Is the harm done to Detroit already so great that the city has a better chance without Kwame Kilpatrick than with him?

July 26, 2008
Remove Detroit Mayor Kwame Kilpatrick before city falls

Enough, already. The escalating disaster that is the Kwame Kilpatrick administration must end now. One more day is one too many.

The Detroit mayor placed what should be the final stamp on his ruinous tenure when he got himself involved in a physical dust-up with a Wayne County Sheriff's detective trying to serve paper on Kilpatrick's favorite city contractor, Bobby Ferguson.

It doesn't matter whether the mayor's belly bumping rises to criminal assault. He had no business interfering with an officer of the law, and his city-paid bodyguards certainly had no justification for screening a county process server.

Kilpatrick acts like a thug, hangs out with convicted thugs like Ferguson and has projected an image of thuggery on the city of Detroit.

His street scrapping follows his pronouncement earlier in the week that Prosecutor Kym Worthy is trying to use what Kilpatrick called the racism of the region to poison the jury pool that will ultimately be called on to decide his felony perjury and corruption charges.

The mayor is setting back regional race relations 20 years with bluster like that and a racially offensive remark aimed at the detective.

Kilpatrick has made Detroit a national joke. It will take years of excruciating work for the next mayor to restore Detroit's reputation and credibility.

He has to go. But he clings to his office entirely for personal gain, caring nothing for the damage his continued presence is doing. He stays so he can leverage his job to mitigate the consequences of a criminal conviction and to shake down city vendors for donations to his defense fund.

Until now, I've thought it would be a horrible move for Gov. Jennifer Granholm to use her authority to remove the mayor. My fear has been, and still is, that an outsider taking down a black Detroit mayor would spark a racial firestorm.

But Detroit is under mob rule; something has to be done and soon. The governor might be encouraged to act if the people of Detroit made it clear that they are ready for Kilpatrick to go.

A fledgling recall effort is ongoing, but it is way under-staffed and underfunded. It needs 58,000 valid signatures by the end of August.

But it also needs a lot more volunteers and a lot more vocal support from the so-called leaders of this community. And it needs money.

The business community has had little recourse during this scandal but to watch from the sidelines as their investment in Detroit dissolves. They've got something they can do now. They and others can write checks to give this recall movement the money it needs to succeed.

The recallers are so short of cash that they don't have phone lines. But they've got a Web site—www. recallkilpatrick.com. Go there, and turn a struggling effort into a groundswell for tossing out this embarrassment.

Even if they get enough signatures, the earliest the recall can go to voters is early February.

By the time he cleans out his office, there may not be anything left of Detroit to save.

August 17, 2008
Red lights couldn't slow Kilpatrick

A pickup truck pulled alongside me at a red light in Detroit the other day, paused for just a second and then sailed on through the intersection without waiting for the signal to turn green.

I couldn't help it—I craned my neck to see if Kwame Kilpatrick was behind the wheel.

The driver of the truck knew there'd be no consequence for blowing off the red light; traffic laws are rarely enforced in Detroit.

That's the same attitude Kilpatrick brought to City Hall. Yes, there are rules. But why should they slow me down when I can get away with breaking them?

Even now that he's been pulled to the curb, Kilpatrick is convinced he can get the ticket fixed.

For months, he's been urging community leaders to intercede on his behalf with Wayne County Prosecutor Kym Worthy.

All he wanted, the mayor claimed, was to stay out of prison and be able to support his family, but he couldn't get Worthy to talk turkey.

A lot of folks, including myself, thought a reasonable plea bargain would be the most efficient way to clean up this mess and let Detroit move on.

Compuware Chairman Peter Karamanos even led a delegation for a sit-down with the prosecutor to lobby for settlement of the charges.

But Kilpatrick didn't want a reasonable deal. That's why he never sent his lawyers in to meet with Worthy, at least not until recently.

He wanted off the hook. He wanted to plead guilty to a misdemeanor, keep his law license and finish out his term as mayor. And he thought he could use community pressure to get Worthy to go along.

She was never going to make that deal, no matter who carried it into her office. And she certainly won't now, with Kiplatrick teetering on his last legs.

Yet the mayor is still trying to avoid taking his licks. Last week he begged Gov. Jennifer Granholm for a pardon, something she likely can't give if she wanted to.

And you can bet she doesn't. Granholm can salvage her governorship by taking down Kilpatrick. She's not going to let that gift horse slip away.

Rewind this drama and you can pause it in so many places where the outcome would have been different had the mayor accepted that there's nothing so special about Kwame Kilpatrick that places him above the law. Even now, with his life collapsing and nearly every voice in Detroit pleading with him to go, Kilpatrick doesn't seem to understand or accept that he's not a rock star anymore.

What level of extreme denial must he be in to think he'll be welcome in Denver next week as a superdelegate to the Democratic National Convention?

Obama operatives right now are shopping for fat chains to wrap around the convention center in case he shows up.

Kilpatrick is desperate to manipulate a soft landing for himself and put things back the way they were. But this tragic car wreck will be over soon. And when it ends, Kwame Kilpatrick will be just another guy who ignored the red lights and got crushed.

March 12, 2013

Tragedy of Kilpatrick is the waste of potential

The last time I talked with Kwame Kilpatrick was just a short while before he stepped down as mayor of Detroit. I'd come to his office to sit in on a meeting of education reformers who were hoping he'd help them accelerate the opening of charter schools in the city.

Everyone at the table knew the clock was ticking on Kilpatrick. The lurid text messages between him and Christine Beatty were opening door after door into his sordid dealings, and that brought an awkwardness to the session. No one asked about his troubles, and he didn't mention them.

What he did do was warm to the immediate task. Within just a few minutes he was in command of the meeting, tossing out suggestions, outlining plans, shaping a vision that charged the room with energy.

It was nuts. We all knew that Kilpatrick wouldn't be around to bring any of this to fruition, and yet he had us believing. That ability to sell an idea, to sell Kwame Kilpatrick, really, never failed to amaze me.

He was waiting in the hallway as I walked out, and pulled me aside, out of earshot of the others.

'Look," he said. "I know everyone wants me to resign. I want to go. I'm done with this. But I've got to be able to take care of my family. Could you talk to the business guys and see if they can put together some walking away money?"

That was Kwame Kilpatrick in a nutshell: Natural born leader, natural born con man. A man who could one minute thrill an audience with the rich future he painted of his city, and the next be angling how to cut himself in on a payoff.

The jury that sealed his fate Monday heard a lot about the latter Kilpatrick. Federal prosecutors wove a trail of greed and corruption worthy of any organized crime family. They presented a solid case, and the jurors made the right call.

What we'll remember from here on out is Kwame the Crook. We've heard too much about shakedown money moving from stuffed bras to his pockets. Read too many text messages directing the extortion of contractors by his cronies. Got too deep into the inner mind of an entitled man, a man without a conscience, who viewed public service as the road to personal enrichment.

But there's a Kwame Kilpatrick the jury didn't see.

That's the brilliant Kwame, and he is that, accept it or not. He came to office as a man whose political skills belied his youth. He could stand before a room of the state's most powerful people and completely seduce them to his vision for his city.

For awhile, he was Detroit's savior. The hip-hop mayor who could rally the city's talented young people and channel their energy into building a better city. The risk-taker not afraid of dreaming big. The kid with a large future.

That was why we forgave him so much, and for too long, writing off his missteps to the learning process. It's why those who should have known better stood by him even as the evidence of his dark side mounted.

And it's what makes what happened Monday so tragic.

There was so much potential still to be developed, so much good that might have been done, such soaring heights that could have been reached.

Instead, Kilpatrick allowed his insatiable appetites to destroy it all. And now he almost certainly will spend the remainder of his best years in prison, away from the children who need him, away from the spotlight he so craved, away from the city he loved—but not more than he loved himself. He deserves to be behind bars.

But what a waste.

October 11, 2013

Kilpatrick fulfills his destiny

For those of you old enough to do so, think back over the past 28 years. Remember all of the things that fill that space.

The people you've welcomed into your life and those you've said goodbye to. The love you shared and the tears you shed. The places you've been to and the people you met; the many milestones you marked along the way. All the events and experiences that shaped and changed you. So much happens during such a lengthy span that it's hard to remember it all.

Think, too, of the many mornings you woke up with the blessed freedom to do anything you chose.

The next 28 years will pass for Kwame Kilpatrick with little of that everyday memory making.

He will fill his time counting minutes, hours and days. He'll miss graduations, weddings and funerals. His schedule will be penned by someone else. The food he eats will be selected by someone else. He'll sleep where someone else tells him to sleep. He'll hug his children and grandchildren when they come, only when someone else says it's OK. He'll be absent from three decades of family photographs.

That's a lot of missed life. A lot of time. And it comes in exchange for a lot of damage.

Federal Judge Nancy Edmunds detailed the destruction in explaining the long sentence, noting the former Detroit mayor had filched at least $4.6 million from taxpayers and others, had put minority contractors out of business so he could enrich his pal Bobby Ferguson, and had exacerbated Detroit's financial crisis.

Kilpatrick, in a self-serving courtroom speech intended to project an aura of contrition he doesn't possess, added to the tally himself, noting he had killed the career of his mother, "beat down" the spirit of a city, and ruined his marriage and family.

That's the obvious stuff. We'll never know the full extent to which Kilpatrick's preoccupation with his own enrichment contributed to the city's ongoing disaster. Much of that harm is unquantifiable.

For instance, Kilpatrick came into office at age 32 and brought with him his peers, who were at the time some of the brightest young people in the city. Certainly they were elevated before they were ready, but they had a chance to mature into a generation of leaders that truly could have saved Detroit.

Instead, many of them ended up as convicts, like their boss. Some went to prison. Others are untouchable because of the Kilpatrick taint. Their potential was wasted by a man who wasted his own.

I used to fret about what Kilpatrick could have been, thinking of him as a brilliant talent who simply went astray. But now I think he's fulfilled his destiny.

Kilpatrick told the court, "I'm ready to go to prison." Turns out, he was born ready. His corruption trial left no question that every move Kilpatrick made throughout his career was calculated by how it would benefit him. He was never anything more than a crook.

If he ever walks out of prison, it'll be as an old man with nothing more to show for three decades of life than counting time.

He will re-emerge into an unfamiliar world that will likely have forgotten him.

And hopefully he'll have forgotten where he hid the money. ⟍

Chapter 4

Michigan

August 14, 2005

No room in today's Michigan for a guy like Jimmy Boles

Jimmy Boles called the other day to straighten me out, and with a name like that, I should have known what I was in for.

Boles is a Ford retiree. He put in 35 years at local auto plants and has lived in Ypsilanti for more than 50 years. But ask him where home is, and he says Clinton County, Kentucky.

His intent was to fix my politics, but I was more interested in hearing him talk about himself in a soft, slow voice that made me more than a little homesick.

My mother's family is from Clinton County, and as Boles spoke, many of the names and places he mentioned cross-tabbed with my own memories.

Boles tells a story familiar to the thousands of Metro Detroit families who are part of the diaspora that drained rural Kentucky after World War II. Returning soldiers found the pickings too slim in dirt farming and coal mining, so they rushed north to the auto plants, steel mills and chemical factories.

So many came that towns like Taylor, Hazel Park and Ypsilanti earned the mean nicknames Taylor-tucky, Ypsi-tucky, etc.

They came with few saleable skills, but with an appetite for hard work. As much as any other ethnic group, they helped build this town.

"There were jobs everywhere then," Boles says. "You could make yourself a good life."

The noise and dirt of the factory, the traffic and the gray skies were hard for a country boy to get used to, Boles says. So every chance he got, he headed home, driving the 10 hard hours south, and back, often in the span of a weekend.

He never intended to stay in Michigan this long. But over time, the reasons for going home died off, the family farm was sold, and Boles found his roots were deeper in Ypsilanti than in Clinton County.

"I stayed homesick all the time the first few years," he says. "But you couldn't beat the money here, and the people were nice."

Boles never married—"I proposed to a couple of girls, but they didn't have the same feelings for me, I guess"—and now lives alone. A slight man and a bit of a dandy—when I met him for lunch he was wearing a tropical shirt, lemon pants and a pencil mustache—Boles fills his time tap dancing for other seniors in nursing homes.

"I got started dancing in my grandmother's kitchen," he says. "She played Irish jigs on a violin. I dreamed of going to Broadway, but never got past Ypsilanti."

Walk around this town and you will bump into a lot of Jimmy Boleses, men and women who left well-loved homes to come here, put in years of back-breaking factory labor and, in the end, stayed with their children and grandchildren.

It doesn't happen that way anymore. The factories are withering away, and Michigan is no longer a destination point for dreamers. Instead, its young people are following the reverse journey, leaving home for the South and West.

Ask what he'd tell his Clinton County kin about prospects in Michigan, and Boles says, "They needn't come."

The legacy of hope created by Henry Ford and other automotive pioneers has been squandered.

We didn't build on their foundation, we stopped innovating, we never found the next new thing that would keep drawing people across our borders on the hunt of fat paychecks.

And so now, as Boles says, "There's nothing here for people like me anymore."

And that's the real tragedy of Michigan's economic unraveling.

↞ ↞ ↞

December 18, 2005

Out of crisis will come opportunity for Michigan

If Michigan is looking for a new slogan, try this one: Will work for food.

It's been a long time since conditions were so bleak in this state, and the tragic fact is that it will be a long time before things get better.

While Gov. Jennifer Granholm chirps cheerily about 100 new jobs here and 50 there, Michigan is losing jobs at its key employers in increments of 10,000.

The news is bad and getting worse every day, and no amount of political happy talk will cover the cold, hard facts.

Michigan is tied for 48th in unemployment, surpassed only by states ravaged by hurricanes. It's 49th in personal income growth; dead last in job creation, and again at the very bottom of the Index of Economic Momentum, a measure of population, income and employment.

Last week, the Wall Street Journal said Michigan is "busy reclaiming its 1970s title as home of the rust belt," noting that United Van Lines moved more people out of the state last year than in any year since 1982.

And no one seems to have a clue about how to break this free-fall. The best Lansing could do last week was deliver an economic stimulus plan that cuts business taxes by a mere fraction of a percentage point.

That whisper of positive news won't even be heard over the dire economic reports that shout to the nation's investors, "Don't come here!"

Increasingly, there's a sense that Michigan has passed the point of no return. We've waited too long to make the structural changes that would have allowed the state to exploit the global economic transformation, rather than be buried by it.

Nothing policymakers or business leaders can do now will avert the devastation that will almost certainly accelerate in 2006 and 2007.

But out of crisis comes opportunity.

Until now, Michigan has been limited by the politically possible. Neither business nor government could muster the will to take on the formidable special interests that keep the state locked deep in the last century.

They won't have a choice much longer.

Detroit's automakers understand that they have to craft a rational, competitive contract with the United Auto Workers union. Incremental changes won't be enough to pull these companies out of their death spiral. There's no more wiggle room.

Say the same thing about the city of Detroit.

Having failed to deal with the budget crisis in his first term, Mayor Kwame Kilpatrick will start his second term flat broke. He'll have to decide whether to radically restructure city government to cut costs or send his city into receivership. Either way, Detroit will be forced to face fiscal reality.

For the state of Michigan, the excuses have run out. Granholm can keep whining that she's not to blame for these problems, but it doesn't matter anymore. It may not be her fault, but it's her responsibility. She'll have to lead.

All we can see now in Michigan is the bottom racing up to greet us. We'll hit it soon. After that, we can choose to wallow there or start climbing back up.

March 11, 2007
State can't count on business altruism

Why stay? Cindy Pasky struggles with that question every time she looks at the books of her Detroit-based company.

Michigan is not the most dynamic market for Strategic Staffing Solutions, her information technology consulting firm. It's not the place where she expects to find her future growth. And it's not the easiest state in which to do business.

"Whenever I get that question, I say we stay because I own the company and I believe in Detroit," Pasky says. "But I never say it's the best business decision."

Pasky understands the financial pressures the directors of Comerica Bank faced when they decided to move their headquarters to Dallas from Detroit.

Staying in Michigan was costing the bank money, and a public company can't justify that sacrifice to its shareholders.

Privately owned Strategic Staffing has more leeway in mixing business with philanthropy. But Pasky warns that Michigan can't count on altruism to sustain its economic base.

"If we were starting this company from scratch, we wouldn't choose Michigan for our headquarters," Pasky says. "It wouldn't make sense."

Pasky is not among those who see Michigan as the victim of circumstance, helpless to revive itself as long as the domestic automakers are down and out. She says there's a direct link between the state's tax and regulatory policies and its inability to diversify its economy.

Those policies favor old-line manufacturers over growing service industries.

And Gov. Jennifer Granholm is about to make things worse.

"Should her tax policy stand, Michigan will be the most costly of the 18 states where S3 does business," Pasky says.

Granholm, she says, doesn't seem to understand that different businesses have different needs and require different policies from the state to thrive.

Michigan's executive corps is bristling this week over the lectures from Granholm and her husband, Dan Mulhern, on balancing money-making with civic responsibility. Philanthropy starts with profits.

"I tell my people that our ability to support the community depends on us driving strong profits for S3," she says. "That gives us the resources to do charitable things."

Because Strategic Staffing Solutions is headquartered in Detroit, Pasky does the bulk of her charitable work here. If she were to move to Charlotte or Austin, where the economic grass is greener, those cities would reap the benefit of her largesse.

And her business, plenty successful as it is, would likely grow at a much faster clip. "If we were living and working everyday in a place that was growing, we'd have a better opportunity to tap into that growth," Pasky says. "At this point, you stay for reasons other than business and look to make your money elsewhere to support that decision.

"How many companies will do that and for how long?"

That's the life-and-death question facing Michigan as it stands on the edge of adopting a tax structure that will cause many job providers to answer, "No longer."

December 13, 2012
Right to work returns Michigan to the people

Union chants echoed off the Capitol dome before the Republican-controlled state Legislature's courageous vote on the right-to-work bill: "Whose house?" "Our house!"

Not anymore. The Capitol now belongs to all the people of Michigan.

For 60 years or so, labor unions have dominated policymaking and politics in this state. Even as their membership dwindled to a sliver of the work force—17 percent—their stifling influence over Lansing kept Michigan from adopting the common-sense reforms that would have made it more competitive for jobs and investment.

Competitiveness is what Gov. Rick Snyder is all about. His decision to lead the right-to-work push stemmed from his desire to give Michigan every advantage possible in competing with other states for economic development. It was not, as his critics charge, a capitulation to big money GOP interests or a hypocritical betrayal of his commitment to relentless positive action.

The only hypocrisy at work is labor's wailing that Snyder broke his pledge to avoid divisive issues.

For two years, Snyder has been trying to raise Michigan from the ruins of the union-backed Granholm administration. He's put in place policies to improve the state's attractiveness to job creators and made better use of precious taxpayer dollars. He's fought to keep the burden of today's spending from breaking the backs of future generations.

And the unions have fought him every inch of the way. They've sued him when he tried to save Detroit from fiscal oblivion. They sued him when he sought to bring public employee benefits in line with those of private-sector taxpayers. They hit him with a costly referendum to undo his agenda. They've instructed their Democratic puppets in the Legislature and on the Detroit City Council to oppose him on every significant measure he's offered.

Yet now they claim it's Snyder who is dividing Michigan. Labor and Democrats had a chance to work with the least partisan Michigan governor ever to fix the state, and instead they chose to fight. And they lost.

They lost in large part because they no longer have the hearts of Michigan's citizens. Those 83 percent who don't belong to unions, but have had to live under their political dictates, handed the union's power-grabbing Prop 2 a huge defeat in November, paving the way for right-to-work.

Michigan residents have watched for decades as union intransigence drove jobs from this state and kept new jobs out. They bear the unfairness of having to sacrifice public safety and other services to pay for absurd public employee pensions that they'll never enjoy themselves. They see through the hysterical, false claims that this bill will destroy unions and end collective bargaining and wonder why unions are so afraid of giving their members a choice.

And they don't buy that unions hold the key to the middle class.

In recent years, the labor movement has been a primary force in killing middle-class jobs. Yet we're supposed to maintain fealty to the movement because it supposedly created the middle class. Well, a Republican president freed the slaves. But in the last election, 93 percent of African American voters cast their ballots for a Democrat.

Times change. Right to work will allow Michigan to change, too—into a state that works for all its citizens.

January 16, 2014

Just bury me in a pothole

The winter I was an intern, the *Detroit News* dispatched its reporters and photographers to find the region's most grisly potholes. Then we'd run photos with a superimposed cartoon character—Chucky Chuckhole, a sort of *Where's Waldo?* precursor—planted inside the giant cavities.

Sometimes he'd be floating in a hub cab. Sometimes he'd have a ladder. It was a hokey way to bring levity to an aggravating situation.

Nearly 40 years later, there's no humor in Michigan's still disintegrating roads. The early January snow and ice storms, followed by arctic temperatures, have pretty much finished the destruction of the state's driving surfaces.

All week, I've been plunging into potholes big enough for Chucky to do laps in. The snowbanks are littered with busted tires and other parts that have jarred off cars. I lost a passenger side mirror. I feel lucky it wasn't a molar.

I've also spent the week wandering through the North American International Auto Show at Cobo Center, with it's dazzling assortment of new vehicles screaming "Buy me!" But it would be cruel to take one of those beauties out on Michigan's car-eating highways.

We've been griping about Michigan's roads for too long. How about we finally fix them?

Gov. Rick Snyder in his State of the State address tonight is expected to again ask the Legislature to find a funding source that would raise $1.2 billion annually to rebuild Michigan's roads and bridges. He will make the case that maintaining good highways will enhance Michigan's economic competitiveness. He'll ask for new taxes or fees, or both.

And since it's an election year, he won't get it.

Instead, lawmakers are clamoring for a tax cut to dispense with nearly $1 billion in surplus revenues resulting from an improving economy. Republicans want to lower the income tax rate; Democrats want to restore the tax exemption for pensions.

I do love a tax cut. But it would be derelict for the Legislature to cut taxes while our roads are in such outrageous condition.

Besides, the horrid roads are a hidden tax of sorts. All those folks who busted tires this week, or had their suspensions compromised, or lost mirrors or other parts are paying the price for Michigan's longtime neglect of its infrastructure.

That $1 billion should not be considered mad money. It should be viewed as the cavalry arriving just in time to keep us from being overwhelmed by an army of potholes.

Even if this surplus is just a one-year windfall, the extra funding will make a big difference in road conditions. And if the excess revenue turns out to be chronic, then instead of rolling back the tax rate, we should dedicate that portion of the income tax to fund highway work. That would be easier for lawmakers to swallow then passing or raising another tax.

I'd like for once to drive to work without wearing a life vest and mouthguard. Let's fix our roads and bury Chucky in his favorite chuckhole. ✍

Chapter 5

Obama

March 15, 2009

Obama opens new era of recklessness

The miraculous marketing machine that carried a junior senator into the White House is now at work trying to convince Americans that writing fat checks from an empty Treasury represents a giant step toward fiscal responsibility.

President Barack Obama has sent Congress a $3.6 trillion federal spending plan that outlines his administration's priorities.

It starts out $1.75 trillion in the red, the largest deficit by any measure in the nation's history. But because he's Barack Obama and everything he does must be chiseled in stone and handed down from the mountaintop, he's proclaimed this first budget as ringing in a "New Era of Responsibility."

Call it the Audacity of Hype. The president, casting himself as the somber task master of a frivolous people, is demanding sacrifice of every American. But there's little sacrifice in his budget.

His entire claim to responsibility rests on raising taxes on the wealthy, an action that is as ideologically driven as anything George W. Bush put on the table and will likely do severe harm to the economy.

Lower and middle-income earners will see tax cuts, even while spending soars, the same sort of financial recklessness that was condemned when Bush was the one going into hock to buy political points.

The Obama budget perpetuates the have-it-now, pay-for-it-later mentality that has brought us to the brink of financial ruin. He isn't going to let the economic crisis deter him from enacting his hugely expensive social agenda.

Nor will he heed warnings that his energy and health initiatives may place additional financial hardships on struggling taxpayers.

In his weekly radio address, the president explained, "like every family going through hard times, our country must make tough choices." But few families in tight financial straits can choose to borrow to accelerate household spending.

Instead of tightening the national belt, Obama is taking out another mortgage on America's future. The loans will come largely from China, a nation that hardly shares our world vision.

Rather than exalting personal responsibility, Obama is encouraging dependency. His plan will turn more Americans from contributors to the system to recipients of government handouts.

Cutting the tax credit for charitable donations made by the wealthy will take an estimated $9 billion away from nonprofits and send it to Washington, where it will be redistributed as Obama sees fit. The idea of taking care of your own—your own families, your own communities—will become a quaint notion.

Obama will spend less of the budget on defense than any president since Jimmy Carter, a dangerous choice in a world that is increasingly unsettled and where those hostile to America's interests remain unsubdued.

Overall, the Obama budget will make Americans more dependent on government, explode the federal deficit, risk further crippling of the economy and leave the nation more exposed to its enemies.

If this is what responsibility now looks like, then we have for sure entered a new era.

November 1, 2009
Obama looks for union label

Workers in Barack Obama's new economic order fall into two categories—those who are worthy of the president's energies, and those who aren't. You may be surprised to learn where you rank.

Obama doesn't weigh the value of workers based on their paychecks, what they do or whether they slip their feet into wingtips or steel-toed boots in the morning. His sole interest is in whether they have a union card in their wallet.

If they do, the president is in their corner, working hard to make sure they don't get the short end of any stick. But if they are among the 88 percent of American workers who don't belong to a union? Ask Delphi's salaried employees what Obama thinks of them.

As part of Delphi's restructuring in bankruptcy court, the Troy-based auto parts maker dumped its pension plan onto the federal Pension Benefit Guarantee Corp.

That usually means a continued pension check, but one that is much smaller. And for Delphi's salaried workers, that's what they can expect.

Delphi's union-represented workers, however, will dodge that bullet. The Obama administration swooped in and, in an extraordinary deal, is forcing General Motors to make the 46,000 union workers and retirees whole. GM used to own Delphi, and relies on the supplier for much of its parts.

"The U.S. government is taking care of a select group of people and tossing the rest of us under the bus," Peter Beiter, a retired financial manager for a Delphi plant in Rochester, N.Y., told the *New York Times*.

And it's doing so with the tax dollars of those like Beiter who aren't in the favored class of workers. GM is operating with more than $50 billion in government bailout money.

That gives Obama the freedom to force GM to subsidize the pensions of union workers it has no legal obligation to, and who are employed by an entirely different company.

Perhaps the administration, in ignoring the nonunion Delphi employees, assumes they all are fat cats who can fund their own retirements.

But among those 21,000 salaried Delphi employees and retirees are clerks, secretaries and others who earn far less than the overtime-eligible blue collar workers.

It isn't about money, it's about membership. Obama protects union members with the fervor of a shop steward. Obama forgot all about the GM and Chrysler salaried staffs during the automakers' White House-directed bankruptcies. They lost more of their benefits than did union workers.

The president also signed an order requiring all contractors on federal projects to either use union labor or pay union wages and make contributions to union pension funds that their workers don't benefit from.

The mandate could cut off 80 percent of the nation's private construction workforce from federal contracts. Obama is sending a message to American workers—if you want to join his new government-controlled economy, you'd better sign a union card.

If you don't, you can't expect him to get your back.

Januray 24, 2010

Obama's answer: more populism

Incredibly, the message President Barack Obama is hearing from the revolution in Massachusetts is that fitful Americans want more of the same: more populism, which means a more expansive government that is more intrusive in private markets, which means more spending and more taxes, which means more economic stagnation, which means more unemployment.

In other words, more of everything that's got the electorate already so agitated.

Obama's response to the Democrat's Bay State rebuke was to grab a pitchfork and try to elbow to the head of the mob. It's the greedy bankers you're angry with and not me, he insisted, vowing to renew his war on Wall Street with a vengeful vigor.

It would be easy to assign his denial to tone deafness. It goes beyond that. It's a stubborn resistance to recognize that America doesn't want to go where he's trying to lead it.

Obama is still taking his counsel from the leftist ideologues who are telling him that the trouble isn't that he's too liberal, but not liberal enough.

Two of his most trusted economic advisers, Treasury Secretary Timothy Geithner and National Economic Council chief Larry Summers, urged him not to pitch his punitive tax on large banks, warning it would further bind a credit market already seized up by new regulations that discourage lending.

He ignored them and listened instead to those who advised going on the offensive to deflect heat from himself and Congress' liberal leadership. Wall Street is too easy a target for a president in trouble. So he flogged the banks.

Wall Street responded as Geithner and Summers feared. Stock markets plunged in anticipation of the negative impact of Obama's bank-busting plot.

If that becomes a trend, investors will know who to blame for the reversal of their recent 401(k) gains. Obama is repeating the mistakes of Franklin Roosevelt, who worsened the Great Depression by demonizing private industry and overexpanding the reach of government.

Instead of putting an end to the spending orgy in Washington, the president was back on the campaign stump in Ohio promising a second stimulus package that doubles down on the failed first one. He'll keep trying to create jobs and spark an economic revival with massive spending on welfare and public works projects.

Expect him to attack the deficit not with fiscal restraint, but by raising taxes on investors and job creators.

This may not be a president capable of changing course, as Bill Clinton did when voters spanked him in 1994. He's not likely to waver from the conviction that government should be the dominant force in American society. What he can't do through legislation now that he's lost his Senate supermajority, he can do through regulation.

It will take more than the loss of a Massachusetts Senate seat to make Barack Obama abandon his mission of remaking America into something Americans won't recognize.

May 5, 2011
Obama policies choking growth

Republicans hoping to unseat President Barack Obama and his Democratic enablers in Congress should recraft the campaign slogan Bill Clinton used to topple George H.W. Bush: It's the policies, stupid.

Obama, with no shortage of audacity, is betting he can blur the connection between the decisions of his administration and the still wheezy performance of the economy and convince voters that soaring prices for essential goods and anemic job creation are not his fault.

That was the message pitched by Treasury Secretary Timothy Geithner last week when he told the Detroit Economic Club that the recovery is on solid ground and any lingering economic pain is the fault of the previous administration.

Given the money Obama has spent and the depth of his reach into the private sector, he now owns this economy. And it isn't anywhere near where he said it would be by now when he bullied through an $823 billion stimulus package and seized control of the free market.

Obama hopes to blame big, greedy oil companies for gasoline prices that are more than $4 a gallon today, and could be up to $6 by Election Day if trends hold.

But Obama has used his regulatory power to choke off domestic oil exploration, fueling speculators who are betting on tighter future supplies. The Fed's stubborn commitment to a weak dollar also is impacting oil prices and other commodities, including food.

This is the slowest economic recovery since World War II, and while Geithner tried to shrug that off as typical of a recession triggered by a financial markets crisis, the real blame falls on Obama's policies that are blocking development and spooking investors.

The biggest culprit after huge deficit spending is the Environmental Protection Agency, which has side-stepped Congress to put in place carbon caps that assure America won't have enough energy to power robust economic growth.

Despite spending hundreds of billions of dollars to shore up the housing market, mortgage foreclosures continue to surge. Delaying foreclosures drags out the inevitable and keeps the market from resetting. Home values keep declining along with consumer confidence.

Small businesses complain they can't get loans to expand, and banks say Obama's rushed through financial regulations make it almost impossible to lend money to entrepreneurs.

The uncertainties of Obamacare, growing debt and the president's determination to raise taxes on the investor class make job creators nervous and less eager to risk their money.

Businesses see that Obama has tilted the labor field sharply in favor of unions, impacting decisions on whether to locate new operations here or overseas. Same goes for his corporate tax policies.

From the viewpoint of Main Street, the economy still stinks. Obama will work hard over the next 18 months to shirk the blame. But as the dots are connected, the line of responsibility leads to the Oval Office.

February 19, 2012

Obamacare is liberty's enemy

Obamacare is the third major assault on civil liberties in the past half-century, and may be the one that erases the space carved out by the Constitution where an individual can stand beyond the reach of an intrusive government.

The well-meaning efforts of both parties and all persuasions, acting in the name of the public good, have done more damage to the American promise than those of evil intent ever could.

In reaching for a drug free society, we've made hash of due process and search and seizure protections. The government can confiscate our property on the mere suspicion of a crime.

The war on terror made privacy such an obsolete expectation that there's no point drawing our window curtains. The government is on the verge of deploying drone spycraft in domestic airspace to constantly surveil its citizens.

And here comes Obamacare, which will make criminals out of anyone who refuses to buy health insurance.

Even before the Supreme Court could decide the constitutionality of the individual mandate, the Obama administration tested its ability to expand federal power by ordering church-run institutions to include coverage of contraceptives and abortion-inducing drugs in their employee health insurance policies.

Religious leaders decried the mandate as a violation of their freedom of conscience, and a president worried about losing Catholic votes backed down. But the compromise he crafted is even more offensive to those who still believe government should be subservient to the governed, and not the other way around.

Obama arbitrarily commanded insurance companies to provide without charge the contraceptive benefit to employees of religious agencies.

Asked from where the president derives the authority to compel private businesses to give away their products for free, the administration said, "From the health care law."

If that's true, Obamacare is a most powerful weapon of subjugation. A government that can force individuals to buy a service and coerce businesses to give away their goods is a government that can compel its citizens to do anything.

The freedoms stripped by the drug war were supposed to give us a sober society. The liberties lost to the terror war were billed as an exchange for the right to live serenely.

The latest hijacking is cast as being about access to contraceptives, as if the $9 a month Walmart charges for birth control pills is too high a barrier for employees of religious organization.

As usual, power grabbers fall back on the defense that a majority of the public favors the outcome sought by the government. But the Bill of Rights was not designed to be reshaped by opinion polls. It exists precisely to shield the minority from the tyranny of the majority.

None of the benefits promised by the sacrifice of liberty are worth a tinker's damn if they come at the expense of the inalienable rights that Americans are born with.

November 8, 2012
Blame game won't play in second term

After Barack Obama's first presidential win in 2008, my then 4-year-old granddaughter, the child of MEA Democrats, said to me, "Rock Bama is president, Papa. He's everyone's president. Even yours."

Still true. And as much as I wish it wasn't, my head didn't explode then and it won't now.

While I think the Republic will survive, I don't hold out much hope that Obama will be any more adept in a second term than he was in the first. Yet I sincerely hope I'm wrong.

My pessimism has nothing to do with sour grapes. America needs Obama to succeed; four more years of neglect in the face of a continuing crisis could wreck us. My security and livelihood is as much at risk as everyone else's should the economy collapse again.

But I've seen this movie before.

I wrote during the campaign about the striking parallels between Obama's re-election campaign and the 2006 second run by then-Gov. Jennifer Granholm.

Like Granholm, Obama was a failed incumbent who nevertheless enjoyed a personal popularity that defied his job approval rating.

And like Granholm, Obama faced an opponent whose wealth and business career were easy targets. Obama followed the Granholm playbook in this campaign in blaming his predecessor and obstinate Republican lawmakers for blocking a phantom agenda, while demonizing his opponent. It worked again.

My concern now is that Obama will continue to play out the Granholm script. She failed to use the liberating power of being beyond the reach of voters to shove aside her special interest bosses and take bold action to stop Michigan's free-fall.

She went on dawdling, pushing the crisis into the future and raising taxes right to the end. And conditions in the state worsened.

Hopefully, Obama will make a different choice.

He should learn something else from the Granholm experience: The blame game doesn't work in a second term.

Americans ultimately expect him to take charge and responsibility.

When Granholm left office, she left behind a state Democratic Party that was demoralized and defeated. (Recognize the feeling, Republicans?) Granholm fatigue was so strong that her well-thought-of lieutenant governor decided not to even risk a bid to replace her.

Republicans despairing of the future of their party should remember how quickly fate can turn. If Obama governs in his second term as Granholm did in hers, by the time the 2016 vote comes even many Democrats will be voting Republican, just as they did in Michigan in 2010.

Exit polling depicts an angry, frustrated electorate that believes the nation is on the wrong course and disapproves of the job their elected leaders are doing.

So they re-elected the president, kept Republicans in control of the U.S. House and Democrats in majority in the Senate.

In Michigan, they defeated five ballot measures to alter the constitution, retained a conservative Supreme Court and kept the GOP majority in the state House.

Only in Oakland County, where two Republicans were ousted from countywide offices, did the cry for change play out.

Here's a clue, voters: You don't get change by voting for the status quo.

August 25, 2013
First, defund Obamaphones

Nothing better illustrates the impossibility of killing a federal entitlement than the fraud-riddled Obamaphone program.

The $2.1 billion giveaway, funded by a tax on every cellphone service contract, is a well-documented boondoggle—an estimated 41 percent of the phones go to ineligible recipients.

Earlier this month, my former intern, Jillian Melchior, was able to obtain three of the free phones on the streets of New York City without telling a single fib. Melchior, now a reporter for *National Review*, says the service reps who signed her up seemed completely uninterested in whether she was eligible for the program. She isn't.

While signing up for one of the phones, she was taking calls on her personal iPhone.

Hers was not the first report on Obamaphone abuse. Other investigations have found Obamaphones in the pockets of drug dealers, and families that get phones for every member, including children.

So why hasn't it been axed? Because federal spending programs rarely die, and are even more rarely reformed.

Every dollar the government spends has a constituency. In this case, the private companies providing the phones are perversely motivated to ignore eligibility requirements—the more phones they pass out, the more money they make. The recipients of the phones are voters, and the administration has no incentive to alienate its own voters to save such a piddling amount as $2.1 billion.

Federal programs are judged on their intent, not their performance. For example, the General Accounting Office two years ago identified $18 billion of waste in federal job training initiatives, and yet there's been no move to cut off those funds, because no politician wants to vote against job training.

Although called Obamaphones, the program actually started under President Ronald Reagan and originally paid only for land lines. The hope was that phones would help poor people find jobs, although Melchior was never asked about her employment status. The program exploded in 2008 after it was changed to cover cellphones, and eligibility requirements loosened thanks to Obama's massive expansion of welfare.

Another obstacle to fiscal responsibility is that well over half of all government spending is now done at the federal level. The further spending is removed from the taxpayer, the less accountability. If this were a state or local program so rotten with abuse, voters would know exactly who to punish. But at the federal level, it's easy for politicians to pass the buck.

Congress and the White House are about to engage in another epic battle over whether to raise taxes yet again to reduce the deficit and expand spending. You'll hear a lot about defunding Obamacare, shutting down the government, the unfairness of the tax code.

Before you pick sides, think about the $2.1 billion of your money that is being so casually frittered away to give cellphones to people who don't need them.

No one should pay another dime in taxes until the Obamaphone program and all others like it are junked.

October 24, 2013
Obama is always the victim

Poor Barack Obama. He's been wronged again. This time, the Obamacare health insurance program is hung up on major computer malfunctions, adding fuel to the blazing criticism that this first giant step toward universal care is a flop.

"Nobody's madder than me," Obama declared while trying to explain why three weeks into the enrollment period, most consumers still can't enroll. "I think it is fair to say that no one is more frustrated by that than I am."

Wait a minute—the president's mad? And he's frustrated? At whom? Himself?

Obamacare is his signature and singular accomplishment, the thing that will define his legacy. His own administration was charged with designing the website and making sure it worked. And it doesn't, despite spending $640 million on the healthcare.gov technology.

Now, in typical government fashion, new contracts costing millions more are being awarded to fix it. So we've got delays, cost overruns and operational failures, and Obamacare is just getting started. And we're supposed to believe the government can run this massively complex entitlement?

In his remarks, the president added, "There's no excuse for the problem." And then he went on to tick off a list of alibis, before finally settling on his well-worn favorite: The Republicans did it.

Obama chided the GOP for rooting for Obamacare's failure and urged them to stop. How that would heal the flawed technology isn't clear.

The White House blames those Republican governors who refused to create state health care exchanges for causing the federal system to be swamped. But Obama has known for months those states weren't buying in and didn't prepare an alternative.

The administration also suggests the GOP-led government shutdown contributed to the program's disastrous start, even though no resources were diverted from the implementation. Still, his defenders claim Obama was distracted by negotiating an end to the stand-off and couldn't give his full attention to making sure Obamacare got off smoothly.

Several problems with that explanation. First, Obama proudly declared he wasn't negotiating with Republicans. Second, he knew Obamacare was under fire, and making sure it was ready to launch should have been his highest priority. Finally, are they really saying that a president with the mental dexterity they assign to Obama can't manage two things at once?

This has become a trademark of this administration: It can't execute. The president has shown no interest in the hard work of governing. Jawboning and campaigning, he loves. Making sure the trains run on time, he doesn't.

Despite his posturing at accountability, Obama never takes responsibility for his own failures. It's always someone else's fault. There's always an external reason he can't get things done. Obama is always the victim.

Responsibility used to be a buck that stopped on the president's desk. Now it's a hot potato that never lands in this president's hands.

November 24, 2013
Obamacare will kill middle class

Obamacare is the biggest assault ever on the middle class.

If not radically altered or repealed, it will diminish lifestyles and increase the financial struggles of average individuals and families. Combined with other costly government meddling in the economy, it will destroy the concept of an American middle.

Incomes that over the past decade have barely kept pace with inflation will not absorb the surging cost of health insurance that will come for many, if not most people, on Jan. 1.

We're painfully familiar with Obamacare's impact on the individual insurance market. Those who buy their own insurance are seeing policies canceled and replaced with ones costing two to three times as much. President Barack Obama's fake fix won't provide much relief.

But Obamacare's pain is spread much broader. Those with employer-provided insurance are also getting stung. Policies that previously asked for manageable contributions from employees will now carry either much higher monthly premiums or outrageous deductibles and co-pays, or both. Out-of-pocket costs are leaping to an average $5,000 to $6,000 annually for individuals, and $10,000 to $12,000 for families.

That means a young, middle class couple that decides to have a baby will come home with both an infant and a $10,000 bill for delivery and related care. Maybe it's a good thing Obamacare mandates contraception coverage. Only the poor and the rich will be able to afford to have babies.

These middle-class workers with employer-provided policies likely won't be eligible for government health insurance subsidies. Many will face the unsavory reality that they may be better off not working.

Obamacare was sold as a path to making America healthier by giving everyone insurance coverage. But what good is insurance you can't afford to use? How many people will put off recommended tests and treatments because they don't have the money to pay the deductible?

This is what it looks like when government tries to create a more perfect society by intervening in the private economy and taking away consumer choice. And it's just the latest example. Government regulations cost the economy $1.75 trillion a year, according to the Competitive Enterprise Institute.

That shows up in higher costs for food because ethanol mandates make corn more expensive, for utility bills because EPA regulations restrict the burning of cheap coal, for automobiles because relentless hikes in emissions and mileage standards require ultra-expensive technology.

What those regulations don't do is increase average earnings. While middle class buying power is dwindling, middle class paychecks are standing still because policies such as Obamacare and the war on coal and oil depress hiring and drive down the demand for workers.

The left blames globalization and greedy CEOs for the plight of the middle class. But nothing has hurt middle America more than the government trying to help it.

Chapter 6

Politics

December 17, 2000

Healing the wounds in Washington and Detroit

Healing and harmony are the watchwords of the week. After they emerged from the ring battered and exhausted, the two presidential combatants rhetorically embraced, expressed their mutual admiration and respect, and urged the nation to unite and move forward.

It was a stirring end to a ferocious fight that split America first into two camps and eventually into three—those who backed George W. Bush, those who backed Al Gore and those who just prayed for some relief.

And even if I'm kidding myself, I do find hope in the gracious expressions of both men Wednesday night. I want to believe they were sincere, and that partisan agendas might be set aside while we seek common ground from which to attack the nation's problems.

The message was "good fight, no hard feelings." That's such an American thing.

Our tradition is that we can live with losing, as long we fight hard, and the field is fair. And we don't gloat in victory.

We are passionate about our politics, but we're not fanatics. Reasonable people can disagree without disagreement becoming hatred.

That's what allows us to live together peacefully after the battle is done. Our culture permits compromise without shame. It also allows for reconciliation. We don't need to destroy the opposition to protect our advantage. Even though we know they may beat us in the next round, we recognize that having opponents keeps us honest.

Bush and Gore will sit across a table in Washington on Tuesday to discuss not what's best for themselves, but what's right for the nation. They still have deep differences. They'll probably never be friends. And they may even find themselves in another fight someday. But for now, they are willing to commit to the greater good.

Much closer to home, another battle is drawing to an end. Hopefully, the last of the unions involved in the five-year Detroit Newspapers dispute will ratify a contract today.

Take it from someone who's been here from the beginning—this has not been fun. I lost a lot of friends when the strike started July 13, 1995. The newspapers lost a lot of customers. A lot of good people lost some very good jobs.

Moving forward together will require a great commitment from both parties. There is enormous resentment to overcome. Each side feels it was needlessly damaged by the greed and stubbornness of the other. Hard words have been said. Hard actions taken.

But it's pointless to keep fighting. The newspapers, their workers and this community have been through enough.

With the contracts settled, we can find common purpose in strengthening the business. Tens of thousands of readers left us in 1995, and many have not yet returned.

Rebuilding circulation will not only mean higher profits, but also more money and more jobs for the unions.

But more important, it will protect the newspapers' ability to fulfill their First Amendment responsibilities.

Daily newspapers remain the best source of local news coverage and the best watchdogs of the political process. The more people who read them, the more effective the newspapers can be in that watchdog role. We may never agree on the villains or the causes of the strike. It's not important that we do. All that matters now is that we accept that we have a common interest in maintaining future harmony. A business can't survive if it's constantly at war with its workers.

It's not much different than the challenge faced by Democrats and Republicans in Washington.

In both cases, there's tremendous potential for getting things done, if each side agrees to move away from hard-line positions and take a step or two in the other's direction.

A good fight can be stimulating. The national brawl we've just endured may serve to increase citizen involvement in the political process. The newspaper dispute certainly made us leaner and more efficient, and that should protect future jobs.

But now it's time to cool off. We don't expect a love fest, either in Washington or in Detroit. Just a sincere commitment to cooperation and a promise not to thump each other again for a while.

January 14, 2001

Bill Clinton stays popular because, like Bubba, he is a lot like us

A reporter landed here a few years ago from a small newspaper in Louisiana. When I asked him about his former home, he said, "We like both kinds of music down there, Hank Sr. and Hank Jr."

I liked him right off. He was a Bubba.

For the same reason, I've always had a soft spot for Bill Clinton, even though his kind of politics and mine aren't exactly the same. Clinton is the king of Bubbas, an irresistible rascal with simple appetites and no hope of controlling them.

Clinton's unwavering popularity in the face of scandal has always vexed his critics. But it's not so hard to understand.

We recognize Bill Clinton—he comes to our family reunions and eats fried chicken. He is both blessed and cursed by his charm. No one really expects him to behave, so we're never as shocked as perhaps we should be by his misbehavior.

I suspect a lot of us are forgiving of Clinton because more so than any other recent president, he's one of us. He's no fortunate son—just a kid from a redneck town who caught a break and rode it to the Oval Office. Still, you get the feeling he would be just as comfortable in a double-wide as he is in the White House.

He has a brother no one likes to talk about, and a mother who had three husbands, including one who shot off guns in the house. We may not have lived on that street, but we sure know the neighborhood.

Clinton also has a woman who stands by her man. Hillary may not entirely fit Waylon Jenning's image of a good-hearted woman in love with a good-timing man, but most women I know believe she truly loves him in spite of, if not because of, his wicked ways.

Now it's goodbye Bubba, hello Frat Boy.

George W. Bush wants to be a Bubba. He's got the right accent, an appropriate nickname and a sad-looking hound that follows him around his Texas ranch. But Dubya is a Bubba pretender. If you doubt that, look up the photo of him in that Andover cheerleader's outfit that ran on the front page of the *New York Times* a few months ago.

His nickname may as well be Biff. He can try to be one of us, but it's not really where he comes from.

Though both Bush and Clinton went to Ivy League schools, Dubya came home to an estate on the coast of Maine, while Clinton returned to an Astroturf-lined pickup truck in Arkansas.

Dubya had his wild days, drinking and carousing. But he quit all that when he got religion. Clinton is proof that a real Bubba can get religion quite regular without letting it spoil his fun.

I recently read an interview in which Pope John Paul II said he could never really connect with Clinton. For one thing, the pope said that while they talked, Clinton was looking off at the frescoes on the Vatican walls. Of course, there are a lot of naked babes in those paintings.

Though he stumbles on big words and can do the good ol' boy shrug, Bush grew up in drawing rooms—his father was president, after all. Speaking of that, Bush called his dad "Poppy"; Clinton called his mother Mama, just like Elvis did.

Bush may end up a better president than Clinton, but he won't be as much fun.

In a way, I wish Clinton hadn't messed up as much. It would have been vindication for Bubbas everywhere. But, if he hadn't messed up, he wouldn't be much of a Bubba, would he?

October 12, 2003

The line between conservative and liberal is getting harder to see

Ronald Reagan revived the conservative movement with a simple, easy-to-recognize philosophy: Take as little of the people's money as possible and spend it wisely; shrink the size of government, and leave business alone to create jobs.

But the principles that define conservatives are blurrier. Today, being conservative has more to do with issues of morality and religion than with a commitment to sound economic policy and common sense government.

Say the right thing about abortion, gay marriage and the Ten Commandments and you're in the club. No one bothers to check your fiscal credentials.

While cutting taxes remains sacred—fortunately—cutting spending is a lost art.

The conservatives who are supposed to stand for small, efficient government have presided over the largest three-year expansion of the federal government in a quarter century. They've porked up the budget far in excess of what was needed to cover the needs of homeland security and the terrorism war.

Conservatives are supposed to believe government decisions are best made closest to the taxpayers. That demands a healthy respect for the authority of local bodies like city councils and school boards.

But the conservatives in Washington have effectively nationalized the public school system through the No Child Left Behind Act, making the local school boards all but irrelevant. To get the new federal money, local communities have to cede to the federal government decisions about curriculum, staffing and the testing of their children.

Conservatives are supposed to be pro-business and free trade, believing that tearing down regulations and eschewing protectionism will create stronger economies and more jobs.

But the conservatives in the Bush administration agreed to tariffs on steel imports that have driven up consumer costs, hamstrung the auto industry and killed manufacturing jobs. They also approved a bloated farm subsidy bill, vastly expanding a program that conservatives had once pledged to kill.

And they imposed higher gas mileage demands on automakers, knowing the standards don't work.

Conservatives are supposed to champion the individual, advocating a strict interpretation of the Constitution and a literal reading of the Bill of Rights.

But conservatives in Washington, through the Patriot Act and other measures, have increasingly infringed on individual rights for the presumed collective benefit.

Conservatives are supposed to believe in limiting the power of the central government, allowing whenever possible the people of the states to set their own rules and regulations, based on their own values. But conservatives in Washington are behind an extraordinary move to reopen the Constitution and dictate to the states to whom they can grant marriage licenses.

Conservatives shrug off these erosions of their principles because the people who control the White House and Congress have R's after their names.

But they should remember the inevitability of political cycles. Someday, the more powerful federal government they've crafted will be run by Democrats. What will they say when the National Education Association is writing local school policy?

How loudly will they whelp when those new powers to poke and pry into private lives are in the hands of President Hillary?

July 11, 2004

Edwards' two Americas theory betrays his own success story

John Edwards brings to the Democratic presidential ticket a peculiar perspective of two Americas, one populated by the poor, the other by the privileged.

The message is similar to the populist "people versus the powerful" theme Al Gore failed to sell to voters in 2000.

It's a blatant class warfare pitch that taps our tendency to blame external forces beyond our control for our failure to rise to the top. Little guys can't succeed because the rich get all the breaks, get into all the best colleges, start with all the advantages.

It's a seductive sermon because it excuses the individual who hasn't quite reached the heights he or she desired from any responsibility for falling short. Their dreams were dashed not because they weren't good enough, but because The Man kept them down.

What's odd about Edwards' theory is that it contradicts his own success story.

On the campaign trail he extols his humble roots. Born in a small, hard-luck town in South Carolina, Edwards is the son of a textile mill worker always worried about losing his job and getting the bills paid.

Edwards attended public schools and did a stint in the mill before working his way through North Carolina State University and the University of North Carolina law school.

He became a hugely successful and wealthy trial lawyer, and then entered politics. Just one generation removed from the heat and lint of the textile mill, Edwards has a real shot at becoming vice president.

The way he tells it, nobody cut him any breaks, handed him anything. He got where he through smarts, hard work and determination.

But that rise from the wrong side of the tracks to a view of the White House couldn't happen in the exclusionary America Edwards paints.

He knows that, as we all should. We can look around our own communities, perhaps even our own families, and see people who started with nothing and built lives ranging from comfortable to cushy. Metro Detroit is filled with immigrants who landed here with empty pockets and now have bulging bank accounts.

That's the story of America, as true today as it's ever been. Look at all those young, dot-com millionaires who invested their beer money in ideas busted in college dorm rooms and ended up cashing in.

Yet John Kerry is incorporating Edwards' destructive "Two Americas" vision into the campaign, promising to create one America, where presumably everyone gets to live as well as the mega-millionaire Kerry and the multi-millionaire Edwards.

But when politicians start talking about making the poor less poor by making the rich less rich, it's usually those in the middle who pay the tab.

There are a lot of poor people in America, too many. And there are a lot of rich people, though we could use more. But there are more people in the middle, living better than in any society in history. They're working hard to work their way up, still dreaming, still believing they can hit the jackpot.

And they can. John Edwards is proof of that.

Instead of discouraging them with horror stories about an America hell-bent on keeping them down, Edwards ought to be sharing the secrets of his success.

November 11, 2007
Like his dad, Mitt Romney's a car guy

For a long stretch during the late 1980s and early '90s, my phone would ring and, when I answered, a distinctive voice would boom, "Hello, this is George Romney, and I'm working on a project I want to tell you about."

Romney was always working on a project, and his projects nearly always involved the hard work of convincing his fellow citizens to use their skills in the service of others.

After leaving public life, the former Michigan governor, American Motors chairman and failed presidential candidate became an evangelist for volunteerism and making his home state better.

Mitt Romney inherited that zeal for public service, as well as his dad's looks—a jaw to make caricaturists swoon, Hollywood hair and a rock-steady gaze.

But I wanted to know if his DNA still reads Michigan.

After all, Mitt Romney left the state at age 19 for Utah and Massachusetts, and the motor oil in his veins might be running thin.

But Michigan should take note—when it comes to cars, Mitt Romney is his father's son.

"I grew up in the automobile industry," the former Massachusetts governor and GOP presidential hopeful says. "The biggest time of the year was the auto show at Cobo Hall. And I want to see the American automobile industry succeed.

"It pains me both as a Michigander by roots and also as an American to see our manufacturing base in the auto sector erode. I want that to change."

He'd change it, he says, by helping automakers develop new technologies and by finding ways to reduce health care costs.

Romney gets the auto industry—in fact, he's offered himself up to run an automaker if this politics thing doesn't work out.

You can't say that about any other candidate in either party. Just last week, Democratic front runner Hillary Clinton breezily declared she'd force fuel economy standards of up to 55 miles per gallon.

Earlier, both Democrat Barack Obama and Republican John McCain, in separate speeches to the Detroit Economic Club, offered poorly informed recipes for fixing Detroit's automobiles.

But Romney doesn't buy into the prevailing notion that the domestic auto industry is to blame for its own troubles.

"I keep hearing this thing about why doesn't Detroit build cars that we want, and it drives me nuts," he says. "Detroit is making great cars. Look at the Mustang (he drives one).

"The U.S. auto manufacturers are burdened in excess of $2,000 per vehicle in health care and retirement costs. They have to make a car that is competitive for $2,000 less, and that's not easy to do. They've done a remarkable job. They're really quite creative and able."

That's not the kind of talk you hear much from Washington.

Romney has a long way to go in this campaign and a lot still to prove. He's focused all of his resources on New Hampshire, Iowa and Michigan, where he's doing quite well in the polls. Nationally, though, he's a distant fourth in the GOP contest.

But after watching politician after politician line up to take a free whack at

Detroit's automakers, Michigan has to be intrigued at the prospect of having a car guy in the White House.

November 8, 2009

Jobs a low priority for Democrats

Americans are angry with Washington as much for what it isn't doing as what it is.

What it isn't doing the most is paying attention to the still-raging economic disaster.

Last week's job numbers show unemployment nationally bumping past 10 percent and surpassing 15 percent in Michigan. Unemployment keeps climbing, even though President Barack Obama and Congress nine months ago committed $787 billion to creating jobs.

Since then, neither the White House nor Congress has spent a minute honestly analyzing whether the stimulus program is accomplishing its goal, and if not, what other approaches might work.

Instead, the administration is spinning dismal economic reports into positive news, allowing both it and Congress to ignore the economy while they pursue their ideological ends.

It ought to infuriate anyone who's lost a job, can't find a job, is worried about his job or lives in a community ravaged by a lack of jobs that Congress devotes nearly all of its energy to arguing about health care.

The promise of health care reform was not what got Democrats elected. Voters tossed Republicans on their fannies for ruining the economy, not because they didn't enact wildly expensive social programs.

But while the economy tops every list of public concerns, job creation is not the hot topic in Washington.

In fact, Democratic leaders, obsessed with reworking America, have proved more than willing to sacrifice precious jobs during the worst economic climate in a half-century.

Sen. Barbara Boxer, D-Calif., rammed an energy-rationing bill through her Senate Environment and Public Works Committee last week without a single Republican member in the room.

The bill would greatly limit America's ability to produce the energy it needs to fuel an economic rebound. In other words, it's a job killer.

Democrats are revealing that putting the country back to work is a lesser priority than passing their social agenda.

If that weren't true, they wouldn't even consider any measure that would raise taxes on job creators. Higher taxes, particularly on business, always result in fewer jobs. Both the health care and climate change bills will trigger huge tax hikes for every taxpayer.

Democrats have learned nothing from history. During the Great Depression, each time the economy showed a spark, President Franklin Roosevelt snuffed it with another tax increase or regulatory burden.

Obama is making the same mistake and justifying it by claiming health care and climate change are so urgent they can't be delayed until the economy recovers, and perhaps we can afford the costs.

But one in 10 American workers are unemployed—one in seven in Michigan. Surely, that's the most urgent priority.

If it doesn't become so soon in Washington, the tea bags being hurled at the Capitol will turn into pitchforks.

December 27, 2009
Dems gorge on absolute power

The wisest quote of 2009 came from President Barack Obama, who cut off belligerent Republicans with the reminder: "Elections have consequences."

They surely do. And Americans are paying the consequences of the 2008 election.

The most tangible fallout of the electorate installing single-party rule in Washington is that policy-making has become an ideological exercise, rather than a pragmatic one.

Republicans still represent the views of roughly half of the America people— on health care, it's more like 60 percent—and yet the minority party has had no moderating effect on the health care reform packages moving swiftly to passage.

It's a bill written by Democrats and passed by Democrats, with all of the give-and-take taking place between Democrats. The horse-trading is between the middle and the left, instead of between the right and the left.

So instead of a bill that falls close to the middle, Congress will produce one that is well left of center.

The old saw, "power tends to corrupt and absolute power corrupts absolutely," applies perfectly to the process we're witnessing in Washington.

Moderate Democrats rose to express concerns about the size and scope of the bill, and held some sway. But because the negotiating was intra-party, it was too easy for the Democratic leadership to win over nettlesome holdouts with payoffs.

In the House, freshmen Democrats elected from conservative districts balked at voting for the most liberal bill to move in more than 40 years. They were bought off with promises of plum committee assignments or bullied into line by House Speaker Nancy Pelosi with threats of burial in committee catacombs.

Sen. Mary Landrieu, a Democrat from conservative Louisiana, held out, citing the enormous costs. Ironically, she delivered her vote after getting a promise of $300 million for her pork-laden state.

Sen. Ben Nelson, D-Neb., took up the torch lit by Michigan's Bart Stupak in the House and insisted that the Senate bill ban abortions from public funding. He didn't get his abortion amendment.

But he did win a promise from Senate Majority Leader Harry Reid to exempt Nebraska from the cost of the mandated Medicaid expansion.

Forty-nine other states will have to eat those costs, along with Nebraska's share. In Michigan, it could total $500 million the state doesn't have.

Send some love to Michigan Attorney General Mike Cox, who has joined a handful of his colleagues from other states to challenge the constitutionality of the curious deal.

Reid says this is how legislating works. It is when there's no check on power. Some of the stuff we've seen over the past couple of months would qualify as criminal coercion, vote buying and bribery if it were the private sector writing the checks.

But as Obama pointed out, elections have consequences. So at least for the next year, this Democratic Congress will be able to do whatever it pleases.

February 11, 2010
'Party of No' might be a good thing

Democrats are going full steam at bashing Republicans as "The Party of No."

But what's the downside to obstructing an agenda a majority of the American people oppose?

The GOP should wear the "Party of No" as a badge of honor. They should market it.

Because what Republicans are saying "no" to are the same things the American people are saying "no" to. They're saying no to a massive expansion of government, no to outrageous deficit spending, no to the inevitable tax increases, no to job-killing mandates and no to policy-making from the extreme left.

Who wouldn't say yes to politicians who say no to all that?

Still, the strategy of blaming the GOP for Washington's paralysis is giving new energy to President Barack Obama's media cohorts, who've been flummoxed by the erosion of support for their man. Liberal commentators are demonizing Republicans as the gangsters of gridlock and predicting an anti-GOP backlash.

Obama this week made the grandstanding gesture of inviting Republicans to a bipartisan, half-day, televised health care summit and warned them to come prepared to compromise. At the same time, both he and congressional leaders reaffirmed their commitment to the legislation Democrats passed without including one Republican priority. The question isn't whether Republicans will stop saying no, but whether Democrats will say yes to moving to the middle.

They continue to push a proposal the public isn't buying. Despite an intensive PR effort by the president and his surrogates, despite an advertising campaign financed by big pharmaceutical and health care companies, despite a barrage of scare stories ginned up by the media to create a demand for government-controlled health care—the fact remains that Democrats haven't been able to move Americans behind their plan.

And while there's an element of truth to the claim that Republicans are eager to benefit from Obama's failures, the charge that they don't have health care ideas is another Obama whopper. They've got ideas, but they also have good reasons for opposing what the administration wants. The people who sent them to Washington don't expect them to rubber stamp the most liberal piece of legislation in 50 years.

Republicans are offering a menu of market-driven reforms. Not one is in the final package because Democrats gambled they could leverage their super majority to force through a one-party bill that fulfills a left-wing wish list. They couldn't, and now they're blaming the GOP.

What the Republicans would do with health care is less sweeping than what Obama envisions and less costly. That places it more in line with the comfort level of a public that is increasingly anxious about the exploding federal government.

The GOP has asked for tight limits on medical malpractice lawsuits, expansion of tax-sheltered health savings accounts to encourage patient involvement in controlling costs, increased competition in the insurance market and measures to help the hard-to-insure get coverage. That's what they're saying yes to, and it could form the basis for reasonable health reforms—if the Democrats stopped saying no.

Obstructing unpopular measures carries little political risk.

Republicans can read the mood of the nation; they aren't going to say "yes" to joining Democrats in their refusal to accept political reality.

February 25, 2010
Tea Partiers hold true to the 10th

The latest marginalization of the Tea Party movement dubs its members "tenthers" and finds in their obsession with the 10th Amendment evidence of quackery, or perhaps even racism.

Tea Partiers do like to wave the 10th Amendment, which gives to the states and the people any powers not specifically delegated by the Constitution to the federal government. They find in it justification for their campaign to derail health care reform and other huge expansions of government's footprint. Since the Constitution doesn't mention health care—or education, or the environment or a host of other things the federal bureaucracy now controls—they say, their tax dollars have no business flowing to these programs.

Washington, of course, blew the doors off the 10th Amendment ages ago and no longer acknowledges any limits on its powers. The federal government raises and spends nearly twice as much than all the states combined.

Critics see the Tea Party's failure to acquiesce to this reality as evidence of its outdated mindset. The kindest jabs find it amusingly quaint that its followers would read the Constitution and actually think it means what it says. The more vicious connect the revulsion to an overpowering central government to arguments in favor of slavery and against civil rights. Once again, the attacks go, racists are hiding behind states' rights.

But the Tea Party is fighting on ground that should never have been surrendered by the American people. If this movement can shine a spotlight on the rough treatment of the 10th Amendment, it will have served a noble purpose.

The Founders knew exactly what they were doing when the limits on federal reach were written into the Constitution. They understood that government works best when it works closest to the people. They also recognized that an all-powerful central government in a nation as large and diverse as the United States was even then would alienate and disenfranchise the citizenry. Free people must have considerable direct control of their affairs.

One of the major reasons for Washington's dysfunction is that it is meddling with issues—such as health care—that could and should be resolved at the state level, where community values and local needs can be factored and a public consensus more easily achieved. Massachusetts managed to do it, and though the result isn't perfect, the people can, if they choose, fix it more swiftly than the federal bureaucracy could.

Advocates of an ever-expanding central government have found good allies in the Commerce Clause of the Constitution, which has been used to justify seizure of just about all economic activity, and in its call for Congress to provide for the "general welfare."

General welfare is a wide avenue. It can easily be twisted to give the government the right to impose any mandate, take over any function, ban any behavior in the name of the common good.

Follow that string to the end and Congress can, under the general welfare guise, collectivize any of the rights guaranteed to individuals.

The Tea Partiers see the red flags in this health care bill. They know it will shove the nation beyond the tipping point in its ability to limit the expansion of the federal government. They are hoping, perhaps naively, that the 10th Amendment will be the barrier it was intended.

If not, Washington will grow so fat on health care that there will be no hope of ever shrinking it.

March 27, 2011

Union's tea party goes unjudged

A year ago, Americans spilled into the streets and swarmed capitols to protest what they saw as an intolerable change in the nation's course.

The awakening of an electorate assumed to be immobilized by apathy stunned political pundits and cultural observers, who got to work sorting out what it meant. They disregarded the movement's message, and instead focused on its methods and motives.

Because most were new to political activism and often awkward in the spotlight, the protesters were dismissed as rubes or extremists, satirized and marginalized on both late night talk shows and Sunday morning gabfests. The initial conclusion was that this was a phony production staged by the party out of power.

When they didn't go away, and when their message caught fire with voters, the punditry delved deeper. What they found was something far more sinister than first thought.

The intensity of the discontent, the commentariat concluded, risked unraveling the national fabric. The mass demonstrations outside government buildings, though usually without incident, were cast as potentially explosive.

When members of the movement crowded town halls to shout at politicians whose attention they couldn't get any other way, it was denounced as a hijacking of democracy by the angry mob.

Some of the signs carried by protesters crossed into bad taste, using Nazi references and questionable caricatures of the president. Proof, the pundits declared, that these were racists in patriot clothing.

A few politicians received veiled death threats, and since the protesters were sometimes given to using gun imagery, the movement was deemed to be not only an assault on civil discourse, but a real and present danger. Politicians reminded us constantly of how frightened they felt.

It's a year later, and another group of Americans is spilling into the streets and swarming capitols. They are even louder and angrier than last year's bunch, whose tactics they've adopted and escalated.

But this time the political pundits and cultural observers are entirely focused on the group's message, with little interest in motive or methods.

Although this group is jamming meetings and shouting down politicians, no one is concerned about the impact on democracy. Although this group carries signs depicting politicians in Hitler fashion, no one is disgusted.

Although this group has a history of violence, no one is threatened when the demonstrations turn to rage. Although some also paint cross hairs on signs, and even though politicians have received death threats, no one is worried they present a physical danger.

The first group, obviously, is the tea party and their Republican allies, and the second group is Big Labor and their Democratic partners.

The real difference between them is that the second group has a firm grip on those who spin the message in this country.

September 9, 2012
Presidential politics leaves out the little guy

I've been on a political walk-about the past two weeks, first to Tampa for the Republican National Convention, and then on to Charlotte for the Democratic version of the same.

I've sat in skyboxes with multi-billionaires who could buy everything I own with the change in their pockets.

I've stood on packed convention floors with delegates in loud vests and crazy hats who will remember these few days as among the best of their lives.

I've been jostled by the young and tattooed who, to borrow from the late state Sen. Joe Mack, came to the conventions with one pair of underwear and a $20 bill and never changed either one.

I've watched those who write the checks to pay for this bacchanalia survey the convention halls with satisfied smiles. I've seen a sweaty Ron Paul protester pitch down his wilted picket sign on a sweltering Tampa sidewalk, declaring, "It's too damn hot for this."

Between the two conventions, I visited my Kentucky hometown, populated by the type of people the convention orators professed to care for so deeply— mothers worried about their children's futures, workers doing more for less, small business owners struggling to survive in a broken economy.

In all of these places, I met people who feel isolated by the rigid ideological circles Republicans and Democrats have drawn around their parties. I also met those who are absolutely convinced they are the only ones who are right, and who are making themselves crazy with hate and suspicion.

I met too many who have dug themselves into all-or-nothing bunkers, unable to see any value in consensus.

I wondered if the politicians who streaked through the convention halls trailed by a comet's tail of lackeys, the ones who spoke of these folks so reverently from the platform, ever sat down next to them in their homes.

If they did, they might be surprised, as I was, to discover that despite the dysfunction in our halls of legislation, despite the stagnation in Washington, despite the polarization, they still believe in America.

They still believe in the ballot box, and that by voting this one in or that one out they can make a difference.

They haven't given up on the political process. And their faith merits something better than billion-dollar presidential campaigns aimed at exploiting their fears and dividing them further.

The two parties are offering a real choice in this election, as the conventions made clear. But that choice shouldn't be based on which campaign does a better job of frightening voters or distorting their opponent's positions.

Voters deserve an honest debate of big ideas for solving the country's big problems. They deserve campaigns that offer the hope of healing the national rift after Election Day.

Nothing I saw in either Tampa or Charlotte suggests the two parties are capable of such a campaign. That's tragic, and dangerous. America can't take much more of this destructive style of politics.

November 4, 2012

It's the direction, stupid

It's the economy, of course. It's always the economy. And yet something about the passions of this presidential election suggest something bigger than economic angst is at work.

Something bigger even than the two men running for the office. Eleven months ago, two-thirds of Republicans wanted someone other than Mitt Romney as their standard bearer.

Likewise, in a couple Democratic primaries, the "no preference" choice got nearly as many votes as President Barack Obama.

But now even the most fervent tea partier is all-in for Romney, and the most frustrated Democratic One Percenter hails Obama as his savior.

The boiling emotions voters are taking into the polling booth weren't generated by five-point plans or glossy brochures dealing with tax rates and spending cuts and foreign trade.

No, the fervor grows from an understanding by voters that this is a direction election unlike any they've seen since the Reagan/Carter contest three decades ago. Voters are choosing between two distinct courses for the nation's future, two sharply different political philosophies.

The path Obama has charted over the past four years will continue to move

America toward a European-style social democracy, with an overwhelming government charged with meeting every need, solving every problem for its citizens.

Romney would more closely follow the route laid out by the Founders, who declared the people enablers of the government, and not its subjects.

Romney got close to the core of the election with his misunderstood 47 percent remarks. He had it right in observing that we now have a country in which half the people are dependent on government, and thus are invested in keeping that government large and free-spending. But instead of starting a substantive debate about the impact of such a high level of dependency on the character of the nation, "47 percent" became just another gotcha sound bite.

What we will be as a mature nation is the key question.

Do we still see ourselves as a country whose prosperity springs from individual initiative, entrepreneurship and unfettered capitalism?

Do we still celebrate the success of others and strive for success ourselves, or no longer believe we can climb the economic ladder?

Are we convinced we have less because someone else has more? Have we really accepted redistribution as the only means to achieve equality?

These questions deserved a greater discussion. Instead, voters facing a monumental decision Tuesday were treated to a small campaign. They were short-changed.

And yet they still know instinctively what's at stake. You can tell that by their intensity. So they can't deny an understanding of the consequences of their vote.

It's the direction. Whatever course they choose, they'll be on it for a long time.

January 22, 2014

In defense of L. Brooks Patterson

I've always said if Brooks Patterson weren't so quotable, he'd be governor, or a U.S. senator, or who knows what.

The Oakland County executive is the greatest political talent of the last half-century in Michigan. But every time he opens his mouth it's an adventure. No political foe has hurt Brooks over the years as much as he's hurt himself with unchecked quips and quotes.

He can't help it. If something funny or clever pops into his head, he has to let it out of his mouth or burst.

So is anyone really surprised that Brooks finds himself in the hot seat again for untoward remarks about the city of Detroit?

The comments were made to a reporter from *New Yorker* magazine who, Brooks says, also dug out eye-popping comments dating back 30 years to oh-so-neatly fit the narrative that Brooks is a Detroit-bashing racist running against the current in denying the city's comeback.

It's pure bullwhacky. I know Brooks well enough not to doubt he fed the reporter a notebook full of juicy quotes, each one begging to be a headline. He's unfiltered, and it never seems to occur to him how his words might look in print.

The words make a better story than the reality of what Brooks Patterson has meant to this region, and to Detroit.

The economic strength and sound management of Patterson's Oakland County kept Metro Detroit breathing during the Great Recession, when everything else here was collapsing.

In those long years before downtown Detroit was a cool place to be, Patterson's Oakland County provided the region with a de facto center, offering the housing, shopping and entertainment essential for attracting jobs and residents.

While other political leaders were going to jail and marching their communities to insolvency, Patterson was running an ethical, competent administration recognized nationally for its innovation. His stable leadership kept this region from being written off as a third-world outpost.

Patterson took heat for demanding a greater suburban voice on the Cobo Hall authority. But the governing model he pushed for has changed Cobo from an ATM for crooked politicians and greedy unions into a beautiful, money-making convention center.

He's making similar demands of the new water authority, and rate payers in Southeast Michigan better hope he gets it.

Does Brooks harbor some deep animosity toward Detroit? I don't believe it. I was there last week at the Detroit Economic Club when he extended his hand to new Mayor Mike Duggan and said, "whatever I can do, call me."

He made a similar pledge to former Mayor Dave Bing, offering to loan the city his crackerjack finance team to straighten out the city's books.

He is resentful of the notion that he should sacrifice the interests of Oakland County for the good of Detroit. That's not what he was elected to do. His ego does get bruised when Detroit overshadows Oakland—he once complained to me the media yawns at a new half-billion dollar office development in his county, but gives the opening of a pancake house in Detroit four days of coverage.

And he sometimes can't help but gloat when comparing the government of Detroit to the one he runs. That can lead him to say insensitive things.

This time, he told the *New Yorker* (the *New Yorker*? What was he thinking?) he warns his children not to stop for gasoline in Detroit.

Well guess what? After education activist Sharlonda Buckman's car was stolen from a station at gunpoint last fall, I heard a lot of people—black, white, Detroiters and suburbanites—say the same thing.

As for his comment about the fulfillment of an old prediction he made that Detroit would become the equivalent of an Indian reservation, with the people waiting for corn and blankets to be tossed in, well, the remark was crude, but not far off the mark. Get off the freeways and drive into the city's neighborhoods. You'll see vast wastelands of blight and abandonment, with a population largely dependent on government handouts.

Brooks is blunt. He talks too much. The things he says can make us cringe. He's also honest, effective and totally committed to his people.

I'll take a leader who sometimes puts his foot in his mouth over one that can't keep his hands out of my pocket any day.

February 23, 2014
When to retire the hardest of calls for Dingell

Even approaching 88 years old, even with a back that won't allow him to stand straight, even with a bad leg that keeps him in constant misery, the decision for John Dingell to let go wasn't easy.

I spent Sunday evening with Dingell as he prepared himself to go before the people of the 12th District to announce his retirement as their representative to Congress. The old big game hunter looked as if the bear had finally gotten a hold of him. He was worn out. His eyes were dull. Everything about him seemed slower, more painful than I'm used to seeing.

And yet even then, with the calls made to family and close friends, with his speech written, with the point of no return all but crossed, Dingell was still wrestling.

"I could do another two years," he says as we sit in the den of his Dearborn home, twin stacks of World War II books rising from the floor next to his easy chair. "I could do it well enough to satisfy my people."

But then, after a moment's reflection, "I couldn't do it well enough to satisfy me."

That's how it's gone for two months. Back and forth, weighing the reality of his infirmities against the instinct that he's still got some fight left in him. Friday, he was certain of what he would announce. Saturday, he was second-guessing.

The struggle has taken its toll, mentally and physically.

The difficulty in leaving, even though Dingell at last accepts the time has come, reflects the passion he still feels for public service.

It's an intensity that has kept him going for nearly 59 years in the House. I remember driving into Washington, D.C., with him a few years ago, after a hunting trip. He stopped talking when the Capitol came into view.

"I always get a thrill when I see that dome," he said.

But he's not so enamored of today's Congress, an institution he describes as "obnoxious" because of its bitter partisan divisions.

As he reminisced Sunday evening, he talked of more collegial times, when Congress lived up to the meaning of its name: coming together.

He says, "When (Republican) Joel Broyhill was the ranking member of Energy and Commerce, he used to say to me, 'Damn it, people are starting to think my first name is Dingell.' That's because we passed so many bills together.

"There was an understanding then that though each side started far apart, the process would ultimately bring us to the middle. That's gone now. There's a 'win at all costs' mentality."

A Democrat, Dingell tags Republicans for most of the blame, particularly "the tea party haters." But he has plenty of venom as well for "those damned environmentalists" who made his life miserable as he fought for the automobile industry.

"Everyone today is convinced that they're the only ones who talk to God," he says.

He's fed up. Instead of energizing him as it once did, he now finds Congress draining.

And yet he'd like nothing better than to see his wife of 33 years, Debbie Dingell, replace him in the House.

"She's awfully smart," he says. "She'd do some good down there."

Still, he worries about her stepping into the campaign fray.

"She's tough, but she'll have to get tougher," he says. "She'll have to get some scar tissue. It's a nasty business today."

As the evening wears on, Dingell tires of politics and turns to his favorite subject. He rebounds considerably in retelling a story about a particularly fruitful duck hunt in Argentina.

"We couldn't keep the guns loaded," he recalls "I shot through $500 of shells. And I told the guy, 'That's outrageous. It should have been a thousand bucks. We're leaving too soon.'"

He's smiling now, sitting up in his chair, reaching for a favorite photo of himself and Bill Clinton in a duck blind. It's as if someone threw a light switch.

"Maybe we'll have time to do some more shooting," he says to me.

Maybe we will. ⚡

Chapter 7

Autos

August 8, 2002

Those sweet songs will play again when Detroit delivers sweet cars

Some automobile executives are lately lamenting that Americans have abandoned their love affair with the car. The romance has faded, the thrill is gone.

"In California, people used to write songs about T-birds and Corvettes; today they write regulations," Ford Motor Co.'s Bill Ford complained at the recent automotive summit in Traverse City.

Turn that around. In Detroit, people used to make cars that inspired music. Today they make transportation.

If they want to see the difference, Ford and his mates in the executive suites of Dearborn, Detroit and Auburn Hills should pay some attention this weekend to the 2 million or so car-obsessed Dream Cruisers on Woodward Avenue.

The lust for chrome, leather and growling engines still boils over. The appreciation for a crisp fit and finish, for magical lines, for the automobile as art, is as strong as it ever was. What's missing today is the product, not the passion.

Back when songwriters were penning odes to Mustang Sally and immortalizing the hot rod Lincoln, youngsters used to dream of the cars they'd drive when they turned 16.

Fierce debates raged about the merits of a Firebird over a GTO. Now middle-agers dream of the cars they used to drive as they climb into forgettable German sedans and bulky American trucks. And mechanically inclined teens who a generation ago would have spent every free moment in the garage turning a junker into a chariot are locked away in their bedrooms hacking into computer systems.

Someone once said that they stopped making great rock and roll in 1972. Looking at the classic cars tooling up and down Woodward, it seems that's about when they stopped making dream cars, too.

Maybe, as Ford says, all the sex appeal has been regulated out of vehicles, making them more about function than fun. Maybe the romance shrunk along with the backs seats. Maybe it was disco.

Whatever, there's something strikingly different about those highly polished, highly tuned cars rolling proudly through Oakland County. They're more than just a means of geting from one place to another. They're part of the family, a piece of the heart.

Which of today's vehicles will stand that test in 30 years? Will anyone store a classic Taurus in the garage to roll out on Sundays and have the neighbors say, "Wow, I remember that one"?

Even before the regulators got intimately involved in designing vehicles, Detroit had stopped creating masterpieces on the assembly line. Look what happened to the Camaro, the Malibu and the original Thunderbird.

But consumers still crave the old tunes. That's why they gobbled up DaimlerChrysler's PT Cruiser and Ford's reincarnated T-Bird. Give them something with style and rhythm, and they go wild.

It recalls the old joke about the farmer and his wife, who, while driving home from town in their truck, came up behind a young couple scrunched tightly together in the front seat of a sports car. "We used to sit close like that," the wife complained. "What happened?" After some consideration, the farmer answered, "Well, I ain't moved none."

Car lovers haven't changed. They still have plenty of pent-up melodies inside them busting to get out. When Detroit delivers the inspiration, you can bet they'll deliver the songs.

❧ ❧ ❧

August 17, 2003

Memories remain Detroit's gift to the world

Memory is a giant parking lot, every space filled with the great cars that roared through our lives.

Like Bill Scott's 1959 Impala convertible, red with a white top and rocket ship tail fins. It made my heart leap when I saw it coming down the road to pick up my older cousins for a Saturday night in town. Sometimes I managed to beg a spot in the back seat, where I'd dodge the June bugs that sailed over the windshield and down the neck of my shirt.

He drove pedal to the floor, and the gravel popping off the undercarriage was so loud it almost drowned out the rock-a-billy on the radio.

It was the first time I connected cars to freedom, to the anticipation of adventure, to the sensuality of horsepower.

Some of the most stirring art produced by American culture has come in the form of the automobile. Woodward Avenue was nothing less than a sculpture garden this weekend, displaying the mobile masterpieces from Detroit's stylists and engineers.

Those puzzled by the allure of the Dream Cruise can't see why the rest of us worship the machine, how we hear divine music in the meshing of gears and are spellbound by a perfect fit and finish.

It's all about memories, the reminders of exotic road trips, of good friends and great tunes, of the ones we loved and lost, of steamed windows and backseat boom-whacky.

We've been blessed all week by the appearance on our streets of classic cars prepping for the cruise. Every flash of chrome triggered another moment of nostalgia.

Parked curbside at a Grosse Pointe restaurant was a pale yellow 1966 Plymouth Belvedere coupe. My dad had one of those, though not the 426 Hemi, and certainly not as flawless as this specimen. His cars were always well used and rusty. Getting them from Point A to Point B required considerable coaxing and several quarts of oil.

Slipping through downtown was a 1955 Bel Air, the classic cruising chariot. My cousins pooled their money and bought a sky blue one. After they went into the service, it sat lonely in the yard, reminding us of what was missing.

A '67 Ford Fairlane passed me on Michigan Avenue, mint condition, not so much different from the one my father and I put an engine and transmission in during my sophomore year of high school. It was the most time we ever spent together and was my introduction to serious tools.

Everywhere, there were Camaros and Firebirds, the growling muscle cars I swore I'd drive when I got my license, before settling for a Valiant with an indestructible 225 Slant Six.

The ability of old cars to touch internal chords is why so many people showed up on Woodward to watch their memories parade by, despite power outages and gas shortages.

And why adolescents still turn their heads and count off the days till their 16th birthday whenever they see a flash of a Mustang or Mini Cooper.

My nephew is restoring a 1967 Camaro, a questionable investment for a college student. But when I saw him behind the wheel, my mind drifted to hot summer days when I'd help his father and uncle endlessly polish similar vehicles on the hope that afterwards they'd let me ride along to the pool hall.

Even more than the technology, jobs and transportation, those memories are Detroit's gift to the world.

August 22, 2004

Dream Cruise helps us forget

Cars may be cars all over the world, but in Detroit, cars are the world.

That's why so much wistfulness runs below the surface of the Dream Cruise, the annual paean to the glory days of the automobile that overstuffed Woodward Avenue this weekend.

We love these magnificent cars from the middle stretch of the last century because we built them here. We know how they came together, what makes them roar, their family lines and the legends who brought them to life.

As we watch them roll across Oakland County, our memories are of more than just the passions and pleasures of youth.

We remember when these cars gave Detroit its muscle and respect. When it meant something powerful to be the Motor City. When if a key was turned in an ignition anywhere in the country, chances were that ignition was installed in Detroit, Pontiac, Flint or Saginaw.

My father talked of first coming to Detroit after World War II, and walking up Woodward, and outside nearly every bar recruiters from the auto plants had set up folding tables to enlist workers.

If you had dreams, this was the place they could come true.

Today, Michigan still makes roughly 30 percent of the cars built in America and about 16 percent of the trucks. That's still more than anywhere else in the country.

But when an automotive factory is built, it's more likely to rise out of a hayfield in Alabama than from a Detroit industrial park.

And it's more likely to carry the badge of an automaker from Japan or Germany than from General Motors, Ford or Chrysler. And even Chrysler isn't Chrysler anymore.

Sen. John Kerry, the Democratic presidential nominee, tries to sugarcoat his career-long hostility to Detroit's automakers by saying he wants the battery-powered cars of the future to be built in Michigan.

Fat chance. The new powertrains will be put together in China and shipped to Mexico for installation. The relentless campaign waged by Kerry and others in Washington against the Big 3 is paying off. The automotive industry is more regulated today than the cigarette makers and nearly as hated.

And there's no let up. Make cars cleaner. Make them safer. Make cars burn less fuel. Make cars that no one wants to buy.

Every new layer of regulation switches off the lights in another Michigan auto plant. This industry accounts for one in seven jobs nationwide—one in three in Michigan—and yet it's treated in Washington and on the coasts as a menace that must be contained.

No one thinks about what will happen if Detroit tires of it all and takes its jobs and goes home. Which of the New Economy darlings could fill that void?

Before Silicon Valley, before the nerds in Redmond, Wash., built an industry out of thin air, good, strong workers in Detroit were hanging bumpers on some of the most beautiful creations produced by modern man.

That beauty is what we celebrate and remember as the Dream Cruise inches along Woodward.

It's better, I suppose, than driving down I-75, topping the Rouge bridge and remembering when the assembly lines down below were running full bore, giving Detroit it's character, its strength and its hope.

⤻ ⤻ ⤻

April 4, 2008

Obama should talk to some engineers

If you're a Washington politician or environmental know-it-all, or both, improving the efficiency of America's automotive fleet is as simple as waving a regulatory wand. Pass a mandate and—poof!—Detroit magically begins rolling gasoline misers off its assembly lines.

During last week's Democratic presidential debate, Sen. Barack Obama continued his naive scolding of automakers, urging them to embrace the challenge of reducing oil consumption and greenhouse gases.

Too bad Michigan isn't on Obama's campaign map. Had the candidate stopped by Cobo Center in Detroit last week, he'd have witnessed an automotive industry furiously at work to meet the biggest engineering challenge in its history: pushing the average fuel economy of its vehicles to 35 miles per gallon in 12 years.

I visited the Society of Automotive Engineers convention to talk to the folks who will have to put wheels beneath the arbitrary fuel economy numbers the regulators pulled from thin air.

I had two questions: Can they get to 35 mpg by the government's deadline? And what will it take?

No one downplayed the extraordinary struggle ahead.

"It's scary right now," says Reginald Modlin, director of environmental affairs at Chrysler.

But they're engineers, and engineers get geeked when asked to do the impossible.

"It will be difficult, but we have no choice," says Thomas Baloga, vice-president of engineering for BMW North America.

Baloga pointed out what was obvious on the exhibition floor: Reaching 35 mpg will require a wide range of technologies and vehicles.

At the Ford Motor Co. display, Brett Hinds, advanced engine design manager, showed off the new Ecoboost system, which uses turbo-chargers to force more power from smaller engines with less fuel—and without sacrificing size, safety or comfort.

Re-engineering the internal combustion engine will get automakers part of the way there, but not nearly close enough.

Gasoline-electric hybrids will be a huge part of the mix. Engineers are also at work on aerodynamics, vehicle weight and hundreds of others tweaks.

Everyone agreed the cars of 2020 will carry a lot more technology. And though the engineers say affordability is an equal part of their challenge, making cars greener will also make them more expensive, perhaps as much as $8,000 more.

Automakers will have to find an extra $120 billion from nonexistent profits to cover the research and development.

But again, there were no doomsayers in Cobo. They're confident they'll get the job done.

Unless Congress moves the goal line. The elephant in Cobo Center was the push by California and its congressional allies to raise mileage demands to 43 mpg on an even tighter timetable to combat emissions.

If they win, "we're in enormous trouble," says Baloga.

And so are motorists, who can look forward to driving in super expensive, glorified golf carts. Obama and his ilk might find it useful to consult with engineers, instead of just environmentalists when setting complex policy. He might find a slide rule is a good deal more practical than a magic wand.

January 11, 2009
Detroit has lost the will to party

If you're still looking for an outfit for Friday's auto prom, you might consider sackcloth and ashes.

Heading into the North American International Auto Show, usually a rocking two-week party that breaks winter's dreary hold on Detroit, this town is acting as if it's hosting a funeral.

"Austere" is the operative adjective for describing this year's auto show. Most of the frills are gone, along with most of the fun.

Instead of celebrating the car, Detroit is apologizing for making it, or at least for making it our way. The attitude of contrition forced on automakers by Congress last month has taken root. Our faces are long, our eyes down.

We might as well be sitting shiva for two weeks.

Last year, Chrysler drove a herd of frisky steers down Washington Boulevard to unveil its new Ram pickup. This year, the 6,400 reporters here for press preview days will be lucky to find a cheeseburger.

Automakers have sharply curtailed the parties and free lunches, toned down the wow factor of new product reveals and even cut back on the number of car babes manning the displays.

Sales for the Charity Preview, usually the hottest ticket in town, are off by one-third.

It's partly economic—there's not a whole lot of extra cash in anyone's entertainment account—but it's also driven by perception paranoia. The flogging taken by Big Three executives for flying in private jets to Washington, D.C., is still fresh.

Initially, the execs even balked at cutting the ribbon for Friday's opening, fearful of being seen in their fancy duds with big smiles on their faces. Detroit isn't allowed to smile. And it certainly isn't allowed to party.

They finally agreed to cut the ribbon, but have been carefully coached by their image consultants not to allow themselves to be photographed with champagne glasses in their hands.

What will be going on inside Cobo Center the next two weeks has little to do with the real world auto market.

It's about the auto market that exists in Washington's imagination.

In the real world, consumers are still in love with pickups and SUVs, and only squeeze into matchboxes when gasoline prices soar. They still get a tingle when they stand in front of 400-horsepower tucked inside a carriage of curvy steel, leather and chrome.

Automobiles still touch their pleasure zone, triggering yearnings for sex, speed and sizzle.

But on the floor of Cobo, Washington's auto industry is on display, not Detroit's.

The muscle cars and trucks have been pushed into the shadows. Up front are the politically correct tiny sedans and hybrids.

Green is this show's determined message, even as visitors stumble in from snowstorms that are stubbornly impervious to global warming.

Green isn't the color of glitz and glamour. Green is about sacrifice and smugness. It's about choking down brussel sprouts to save Mother Earth.

Detroit is now green, and humbled, and so very sorry for all of its past sins. And certainly is in no mood to shake its booty.

I think I'll commiserate by sneaking inside the new Camaro with a flask of the bubbly.

≺ ≺ ≺

January 8, 2012

Product drives Detroit revival

Walking from my office to Cobo Center Thursday—the first of a couple of dozen back and forths to the Detroit auto show I'll make over the next two weeks—I felt the familiar anticipation building, the eagerness to push through the doors and join the excitement.

I've covered maybe 30 of these auto shows during my time here. It never gets old. It never fails to rev my engine.

Maybe it's the Detroit in me, but I love automobiles. I can spend a full hour at the show exploring a single car or truck, circling the exterior, running a hand across the curve of a fender, sinking into plush leather, staring at an engine compartment crammed with parts I can no longer identify.

That doesn't change even in the bad years. And there have been some very bad years for the North American International Auto Show, years when even the brightest spotlights couldn't chase the gloom.

Years like 2009. The American automobile industry was such a pariah then that nobody from outside of Detroit wanted to attend, and the press corps spent far more time speculating on the Big Three's demise than it did reviewing the products on display.

That was the year they couldn't give away Charity Preview tickets because no one close to the industry dared to be photographed laughing or drinking champagne.

Three years later, the auto industry is roaring again. Washington types will be knocking each other over trying to get through the show doors Monday. Charity Preview ticket sales are up 20 percent or more.

Ford, Chrysler and General Motors just posted stunning sales gains, and are edging closer to recapturing half of the North American market. Another year like this, and maybe we can lay to rest that grating Detroit Three label and call them the Big Three again.

A lot of folks, particularly in Washington, want to take credit for Detroit's relatively quick comeback. And some of them did help.

But the reason we're smiling and raising our champagne glasses again here is because of what's sitting on the Cobo Center floor.

These are some of the most exciting and marketable vehicles I've ever seen from the Big Three. All three automakers have winning models in nearly every category, from tiny carts to behemoth trucks. I'll admit to being a homer, but it makes me proud to see three companies that had been so recently written off sticking it to the global competition.

I'm particularly eager to spend time with the new Dart from Chrysler. The Plymouth version of the Dart was my first new car nearly 40 years ago. It'll be good to reflect on what's happened to this industry during the four decades between those two vehicles. And it will be reassuring that through all the turmoil, the near-death experiences, the restructurings and retreating, Detroit and its automakers are still here, and look like they will be for another 40 years. If you don't believe that, come to the show and spend some time with the cars. They've never been better.

January 22, 2012
Feds tame Detroit

It was quite a love fest when the National Highway Traffic Safety Administration came to town last week for a public hearing on the tough new fuel economy mandates. Environmentalists were gleeful, of course. They've won a decades-long fight to make large cars, trucks and sport utility vehicles the dinosaurs of America's roadways. They applauded the new rules as a victory for Mother Earth.

United Auto Workers President Bob King testified that forcing automakers to spend $50 billion to $150 billion on technology to more than double current vehicle performance would actually create more jobs for UAW workers. "This is a testament to good government," he said.

Humbled auto executives put on their best fake smiles and dutifully marched to the podium to say, "Thank you, sir. May I have another?"

And the regulators headed back to Washington, pleased they'd finally tamed Detroit.

This meeting should have come with footnotes.

The first one would detail the cost of the mandates. NHTSA wanted only to talk about the great savings consumers would achieve over the lifetime of their new 54.5 mpg vehicles. Maybe that's $6,600, maybe that's $8,200—and all for an investment of $2,000 on the sticker price.

Wait a second, said auto dealers, the only voices raised against the mandates. Those projections are based on vastly higher future gasoline prices and significantly lower technology costs. The actual addition to the sticker price, they said, could be $3,500 to $5,000, and the fuel savings significantly less than NHTSA projects.

Add the second footnote to King's job boom prediction. If the higher sticker prices depress sales—and they could by 14 percent, says the estimate of the federal Energy Information Administration—the automakers and their suppliers will need fewer UAW workers. Some calculations peg job losses at 220,000.

Place another footnote to the automakers' testimony. Yes, they raised their hands in support of the mandates.

But only after they were bullied into choosing between an irrationally high single federal standard and a multitude of irrationally high standards set by each state.

They understand the risk of this course is that consumers won't want the cars the government is forcing them to make, and that the development costs will eat up a huge chunk of their still scarce profits.

The light vehicle fleet average today is about 22 mpg. Getting that up to 54.5 mpg in 13 years will require technology leaps that no one is certain can be achieved. In fact, the Center for Automotive Research in Ann Arbor calls the new standards unreachable.

But the feds don't have to worry about whether or how the mandates are met, or at what cost. They need only say, "So let it be written, so let it be done."

Slap the final footnote on King's assessment that such an arrogant disregard for the marketplace is a testament to good government. ⚹

Chapter 8

Education

May 6, 2001
Community colleges fill void for many students

I had the chance Saturday to say a long overdue thank you to a place that played a major role in my life.

Schoolcraft College in Livonia invited me to the commencement ceremony, where 1,030 students received hard-earned associate degrees, and I picked up a wholly undeserved alumni award.

For about half, the diplomas will take them on to additional education at a four-year university. The rest, enrolled in two-year technical, industrial and health programs, will head directly into the workforce.

I suspect a good number of them came to Schoolcraft for the same reason I did in 1973—they didn't have much choice.

I left Garden City East High School that year with a grade point average that barely poked its head above 2.0, no discernible study habits and not a clue about what I hoped to accomplish. Oh—and no money. Colleges weren't beating down my door.

Schoolcraft was not just the only college I could afford, it was also about the only college that would have me. It was my life preserver. It was either enroll there or go into the factories or the service.

No sane person would have bet much on my chances for success, given my history. But Schoolcraft had a lot of experience with people like me. It quickly shaped me into a halfway decent student, gave me a chance to work on the college newspaper and in two years prepared me to move on to Wayne State University.

Community colleges mark their 100th anniversary this year. Though they stand in the shadow of the big four-year schools, they fill a vital place in the nation's secondary education system. Forty-four percent of undergraduates—about 10 million students—attend one of the nation's 1,100 community colleges.

Most are public, and have liberal admission policies and low tuition—an average of $1,500 a year.

Community colleges once were the neglected step-child of the college system. But no more. They have become community training centers. They are key to the welfare-to-work movement, providing training to people who need to acquire some job skills in a hurry.

They also do custom employee training for companies hoping to upgrade the quality of their workforce.

Schoolcraft President Dick McDowell says the campus has 17,000 students in continuing education programs—computer classes, cooking classes, tennis classes—dwarfing the 10,000 enrolled in credit programs. The college also has on staff a government procurement specialist who has helped local companies win nearly $1 billion in government contracts since 1987.

McDowell notes that Schoolcraft, the ninth-largest of the state's 28 community colleges, is bigger than many state four-year schools.

My schoolmates derided Schoolcraft as Haggerty High, a semi-college barely more sophisticated than the local high school. But the well-groomed campus I saw Saturday gave the impression of a serious place with serious students. Most work. Many work full-time while taking a full load of classes. They aren't there to kill time, but to get a low-cost, high-quality education. It's exactly what I got 25-odd years ago. It was a bargain then, and at under two grand a year, it's still a bargain today.

May 1, 2005

Attitude may make Michigan the new Mississippi

We're doomed. That's the right headline for today's front page story detailing Michigan's sorry commitment to education.

Doomed to a perpetually shrinking economy, budget deficits and service cuts. Doomed to an ever diminishing quality of life.

Doomed to flipping the hamburgers, shining the shoes and sweeping the floors of the states that will prosper as the national economy shifts from rewarding muscle and sweat to valuing brains and knowledge.

Michigan is doomed to be the new Mississippi. A backward state locked to a last-century industry, awash in ignorance and unprepared to seize the opportunities presented by new technologies and scientific advancements.

That's the only fortune to tell for a state where just 27 percent of parents consider a good education essential for a successful life, and nearly half don't agree that everybody should go to college.

When the *Detroit News* first teamed up with the Your Child outfit, a mixture of education groups and pollster Ed Sarpolus of EPIC-MRA, our goal was to measure whether Michigan families understand the crucial role education will play as the state attempts to compete for new economy jobs.

What we found is heart-breaking: There is no culture of education in Michigan.

"This is still a state that believes in the university of hard knocks," Sarpolus says. "We still believe that sweat, not brains, will get us ahead."

Haven't we noticed the plant closings and high unemployment rates of recent years? Blue-collar jobs are gushing out of the state, and yet parents still believe their kids can make it in life with blue-collar skills. Are they bone stupid?

This is nothing short of child abuse.

For years, we've painted parents as the victims of a failed public school system that is not readying their children for the future. And yes, too many commited parents are being failed by too many schools. But the greater failure is happening in homes, not in classrooms.

Certainly Michigan's schools need a tougher curriculum, more realistic career counseling and an environment that demands excellence.

But no amount of structural change in the schools will succeed without a cultural change. Michigan must drill into the heads of its residents that the glory days of pulling a decent middle-class paycheck out of a factory are gone for good.

Michigan's future will hold far fewer manufacturing jobs, and they will pay much less than they do today.

Nothing the politicians and policy makers do will alter that fact.

The state's only hope lies in producing a highly skilled, highly educated workforce.

And yet the poll indicates parents are not challenging their children, not driving them toward success, not helping direct them into career fields where they might actually find jobs. Sixty percent of parents define success for their children without mentioning education or self-supporting employment.

Asked what they'd like to see their children doing someday, the largest response was the so very Baby Boomerish "whatever makes them happy."

That isn't parental direction; its dereliction of duty.

In a state that hopes to rebuild on the strength of automotive research and development, only 3 percent of parents see engineering or computers as a likely career path for their kids.

Few parents say their children master math and science, the foundation disciplines of the new economy. And by the time kids reach high school, half of their parents have given up hope that they'll go on to college. Fixing this will not be as easy as drafting new education policies or flooding the schools with more dollars. The solution rests in getting parents to do the basic job nature gave them: to prepare their offspring to leave the nest equipped with survival skills.

It may take decades to vanquish the myth that Michigan can prosper with smokestacks and assembly lines.

Sadly, it may also take considerable suffering and disappointment on the part of a generation of children who will ultimately decide they don't want to do to their kids what their parents did to them.

June 26, 2005

Stop the party:
High school graduation means nothing

June is waning, and with it the high school graduation celebrations. The tassels are flipped; the hats tossed in the air. And soon, the last of the champagne corks will pop.

Big stinking deal. High school graduation is an archaic ceremony that carries no significance today. It ought to be scrapped.

Parents are wed to the notion that graduation day marks a rite of passage into the adult world; that their children have secured a foothold on the future.

So they snap a few last school pictures to tape on the refrigerator door, throw parties and shake down about everyone they know for a check.

But if high school graduation is the last education milestone young Johnny and Jill mark, then write them off as failures, or more charitably, as having a high probability of leading a marginal life.

Despite what the local windbag said in that commencement speech, finishing the 12th grade is no more significant than finishing the 10th, or the fourth, or the first. It's just one more year in an education career that has to extend well beyond the senior year of high school.

Abe Stokla, this year's valedictorian at Eagleville High School, had his diploma yanked for saying in his speech: "You have given us the minimum required attention and education to master any station at any McDonald's anywhere."

But the kid was telling the truth. High school isn't preparation for a single career. It's certainly no finish line.

The best a high school graduate can hope for today is to start work in a menial, low-paying position and hope that on-the-job training will help him or her move up the economic ladder.

But the odds are the climb will be limited. Over the course of a lifetime, a college graduate will earn $1 million more on average than a high school graduate.

And don't bother me with a nonsensical recitation of all the people who excelled in life without a college degree. That list inevitably starts with Bill Gates, the Microsoft founder and America's richest dropout.

Take an honest look at that kid of yours who isn't interested in college. Is he or she really Bill Gates material?

Will they even get the opportunity to drop out of Harvard, as Gates did?

If the traditional, four-year college track isn't in their stars, they'd better at least be looking at a two-year community college program, or some other technical or trade school training.

We'd serve our children better if we stopped thinking about education as K-12, and started talking in terms of K-14 or K-16.

High school should be a staging ground to direct all students into the next phase of education, and to begin steering them toward careers.

It might be best if we stopped handing out high school diplomas, stopped even recognizing graduation day. That would deliver the message that nothing's finished yet.

Hold the applause. Save the speeches and the checks. Keep the champagne on ice.

Let the celebration begin when there's truly something to celebrate.

February 19, 2006
Sacred cows derail school reform

It took four years of intense teamwork to turn Detroit's Holcomb Elementary into a high-performing school.

But it took only a clause in a union contract to derail that momentum and threaten to send Holcomb back into the ranks of the mediocre. What's happened to Holcomb is just the latest example of how Michigan's public education system places the comfort and security of its employees ahead of the commitment to do better by its students. Four years ago, Holcomb's teachers and principal, admitting the school was falling short, decided they wanted better results from their pupils and from themselves.

So they applied for a grant, hired an outside consultant and embarked on a rigorous reform process that eventually touched every aspect of school life. "We changed the culture of the school," says Michelle Morden, who until last fall taught lower grades at Holcomb. "By the end, the teachers, students and parents were all transformed and working together."

Holcomb teachers mastered new technologies and adopted a curriculum that stressed learning through the practical application of skills.

Test scores climbed. Absentee rates fell. And the Skillman Foundation noticed. Last June, it named Holcomb one of nine highly performing schools in Detroit, awarding it $100,000 to further its progress.

But before the staff that lifted up Holcomb could enjoy the fruits of their labor, Detroit Public Schools announced school closings and layoffs.

That triggered the usual round of bumping, as high-seniority teachers from closed schools claimed the jobs of lower-seniority teachers in open buildings.

The bumping cost Holcomb a quarter of its teaching staff, including Morden, who was later rehired at a middle school.

"It's very frustrating," she says, "to work that hard on a goal and then see it slip away."

Frustrating for Skillman's Carol Goss, too.

"We invested $100,000 in Holcomb because a team came together, put in place a program and were doing a wonderful job," she says. "We can't continue to make those investments if the responsible teams aren't kept together."

Goss is demanding that high-performing schools be exempted from union seniority rules. At Holcomb, instructional specialist Linda Edmondson says the school is struggling to maintain what it achieved.

"We are losing some momentum," she says. "The new teachers don't have the same ownership of the program. But we are working hard to bring them up to speed."

Two steps forward, one step back. That pace won't take Michigan where it needs to go.

We'll know we're serious about reforming schools when we see the sacred cows of the education establishment being sacrificed for the cause of doing what's best for students.

May 21, 2006
Rotting school symbolizes American dream

The Glidewell School can't possibly stand much longer. Wide holes gape in its roof, and the yellow poplar beams that have held it up for well over 100 years are failing. A few more hard winds and the tiny building will lie in a heap of tin and wood.

The schoolhouse sits in a forgotten corner of Clinton County, Ky., among the poorest places in the nation.

Its doors closed 45 years ago when the bus arrived to take the country kids to the school in town.

Glidewell is where my mother attended school, along with her siblings and cousins—up to 50 children packed into one room under the tutelage of one teacher.

They got eight good years of training there, and after that, it was back to the farms and then on to the service, factories and big cities.

But in those eight years, they learned enough about character, common sense and hard work to get by in the world they lived in.

And they took away from there values that still well serve their children and grandchildren.

I hate to see the Glidewell School fall because for me it's a symbol of how far and how quickly a family can still come in America, if each generation accepts responsibility for making life better for the next.

Neither my parents nor most of their brothers or sisters attended high school—it was too expensive and too far away.

But they worked themselves to death, scratched, scrimped and saved to make sure all of their children earned at least a high school diploma.

And now most of their grandchildren are graduating from college.

That means that few, if any, of that third generation will have to struggle, sweat and bleed in the kind of brutal jobs their grandparents took to survive.

They'll lead more financially secure and comfortable lives. They'll have better choices. They'll enjoy more freedom.

And they'll owe it all to those selfless people two generations back who made tough choices and did tough jobs because they believed it was possible to build a better future for their children and grandchildren.

No one talked to us about college growing up. But they did talk about the importance of working hard, striving for a better life and making something worthwhile of yourself.

For me, those values ultimately equated to college. And having seen all of the wonderful places an education can take you, I've preached to my children since birth that not going to college is not an option.

The last one finished at Michigan State University this spring. Getting all three through wasn't easy. Paying for college is like driving a new car into the river every year.

But it wasn't a gift—it was an investment. The only return I expect is that my children will make the same commitment to their children.

Their grandparents worked too hard, made too many sacrifices, for them to allow the generation they're responsible for to slip back.

July 16, 2006
Pay more to keep brightest teachers

Not to ruffle any family feathers, but I firmly believe my daughter is worth more than my son-in-law. And that's not just a father's bias speaking.

Both he and she are school teachers. Both teach middle school students in a solid suburban district. Both finished near the top of their college classes. Both do what they do very well.

And both are on the same salary track.

Fair? On the surface, yes.

But he teaches English, and she teaches science. And the hard reality is that science teachers are a scarcer commodity than English teachers. In any other profession, the employee more in demand would command the higher salary.

But teachers are insulated from real-world economics by archaic contracts that discourage the striving for excellence and drive the most talented to other fields.

Changing those contracts should be a top priority as Michigan moves to implement a tough, new curriculum for high school students.

The more rigorous course schedule places a greater emphasis on math and science. Many districts will have to scramble to add certified teachers in those subjects.

But the state's education schools are still turning out a predominance of elementary and liberal arts teachers.

And why not? Getting those degrees isn't as taxing as math and science majors. And the pay's the same.

Meanwhile, there's not much incentive for a math or science major to choose teaching.

With basically the same degree, they can get a job in private industry that pays more up front and doesn't cap future earnings.

Michigan has to cover the shortage of math and science teachers in a hurry. The best way to do that is to offer higher pay to teachers certified in those subjects. If it doesn't, other states will—some districts in Colorado already are—and Michigan won't be able to compete in yet one more crucial area.

While teachers unions demand that all of their members be treated as equals on payday, the truth is they are only hurting themselves by insisting on equal pay for unequal skills. Math and science teachers have more career options, and too many are being tempted away from classrooms by the more lucrative salaries offered by the private sector.

That doesn't mean we should devalue English or social studies teachers.

A new pay structure should also reward the best teachers in any subject with fatter paychecks than their less gifted peers. That would make my son-in-law whole—he's an excellent teacher. And it would motivate the mediocre to get on the ball.

As Michigan forges a plan to meet the demands of the new curriculum, teacher pay should be on the table. A multi-tiered merit pay scale tied to both performance and subject specialty will give teachers an incentive to work harder and perform better.

And it will keep the best and brightest teachers where they belong—in front of a classroom.

⪻ ⪻ ⪻

December 28, 2008

Detroit blew chance for school rescue

With Detroit Public Schools near disintegration, it ought to be noted that it's been five years since Plymouth philanthropist Bob Thompson was told to take his $200 million and get back to the suburbs.

Thompson, a retired road builder obsessed with spending his fortune to get urban children a high-quality education, ran into a political buzz saw when he offered to open 15 charter high schools in the city that would guarantee to graduate 90 percent of their students and send 90 percent of those graduates on to college.

Community activists denounced Thompson as a white meddler out to steal their children. They were joined in their absurdity by Gov. Jennifer Granholm and Detroit Mayor Kwame Kilpatrick, who threw their lot in with the teacher union.

The rejection of Thompson's millions became a national story of a city so seized by racial divisions it couldn't set them aside even to save its children.

So instead of a network of alternative schools that would have rescued roughly 5,000 students from the sinking DPS, look what Detroit has today:

A school district that fails to graduate 70 percent of its students; a school board that's fired two superintendents and an interim superintendent in four years; 18 of its 19 high schools on the failure list; and a fiscal meltdown.

Five years after Thompson was given the boot, Detroit is officially the worst big city school district in the nation and still sends more children to welfare and prison than it does to college.

Think about how different things might have been. Had the Thompson schools been built, they would be preparing to graduate their first class in the spring. Two thousand Detroit seniors would be making college plans. And Detroit's fast-fleeing middle class would have a reason to stay.

Yet no one has dialed up Thompson to apologize, to say they were wrong, to beg him for a second chance.

In fact, the governor and Democratic lawmakers are stubbornly blocking other Bob Thompsons from saving Detroit's children.

High-quality national charter school operators are lined up to get into the city. A group of Detroit teachers are pleading for the chance to remake a school under the successful Green Dot model.

But state law still traps students in hopeless public schools. Granholm refuses to lift the cap on charter schools, and the state House just passed a law protecting DPS from competition.

Nothing's changed in Detroit.

To his credit, Thompson didn't sulk back to Plymouth. He already had his University Prep Academy up and running, and thanks to a loophole engineered by Republican lawmakers, he's at work on two more schools, a math and science school at the Detroit Science Center and an art school in the Argonaut building.

The pace is less aggressive than he hoped—he once believed other national foundations would match his funds and make even more schools possible—but it's a lot better than nothing.

If Detroit families are lucky, the public school system will collapse in the coming year, and in the rubble, someone will come across Thompson's phone number.

April 16, 2009
Only parents can save Detroit kids

The minds of black children are valued less in Michigan than those of white children—even by their own parents.

It's inconceivable that a failure rate of 70 percent would be tolerated by parents and taxpayers if it were happening in Oakland County's schools.

Or that if education dollars in Macomb County were being squandered on phantom jobs and fat contracts for politically connected parasites while students lacked toilet paper and textbooks, you wouldn't hear a peep of protest.

Or that western Wayne politicians wouldn't be run out of office on a rail for protecting the franchise of schools that send more kids to prison and welfare than to college.

But in Detroit, where 90 percent of the students are black, the extreme failure of the public schools is taken as a fact of life.

The education gap between white students and black is today's major civil rights issue because it will surely result in a wider economic and opportunity gap.

So why, then, aren't Detroit parents and community activists jammed into the Federal Courthouse demanding justice for their children? Why aren't they marching up Woodward Avenue or sitting down in schools?

The answer is because they are the ones who are cheating Detroit's children of their future.

Apologists for the Detroit Public Schools' miserable performance argue that the root cause is money. If Lansing or Washington would send more cash, education quality would be equal to the suburbs. But two weeks ago, Robert Bobb, the emergency financial manager appointed by Gov. Jennifer Granholm, said he found $100 million in misspent DPS funds.

Money went to pay employees who never showed up to work, keep paying those who were supposed to have been let go and cover contracts for vendors whose only contribution to the district is kissing the bottoms of school board members. That cash would have bought a lot of computers, paid a lot of teachers and kept the supply closets stocked with Charmin.

Still, 10 times more people showed up at a rally to protest the sale of Cobo Center than came out to the school board meeting to demand accountability from the members who are stealing from children. The same week Bobb's findings were made public, the AFL-CIO said its endorsement in the Detroit mayoral race was conditioned on a candidate opposing the spread of charter schools.

More than 30,000 students are enrolled in Detroit charter schools, and thousands more are on waiting lists trying to get in. Charters are a life raft for parents who can't leave for the suburbs.

Yet the city's legislative delegation, in deference to the unions, has done nothing to lift the discriminatory cap on charter schools that is keeping high-quality operators from rescuing Detroit children.

Bobb's appointment was the first move Lansing has made in five years to end the genocide of young Detroit minds. Parents can't let it be the last.

They have to stop upholding a school district that better prepares African-American children for life in the 19th century than it does for the 21st.

June 4, 2009

Graduates should reach for good life

The all-time greatest high school commencement speech was delivered by the actor Bruce Dern in the movie "Middle Age Crazy." Dern, playing an aging and embittered businessman, ends a rambling rant to the graduates of his alma mater with this advice: "Give back the (bleep) diplomas; give back the silly (bleeping) hats and stay 18 for the rest of your lives. ... You don't want to be the future. Forget the future. The future sucks."

What a perfect motto for the Class of 2009.

Tomorrow, I'll congratulate graduates of Garden City High School, 36 years after that school handed me a diploma. If I could channel Dern, I'd be tempted to tell these newly minted adults the same thing.

The world we're sending them into does indeed suck; the future we're bequeathing to them has rarely seemed so gloomy.

My greeting to the grads should include an apology. We've certainly made a mess of things, and now we're asking them to help clean it up.

At the same time, as an incentive, we're telling them to lower their sights, to dream smaller, to expect less of themselves and more from their government.

We're rapidly destroying the individual gumption that we'll desperately need from this generation by teaching them dependency and demonizing success.

We've been here before.

The graduates who followed me out of Garden City High in the mid-1970s faced a similar economic meltdown. Like this one, it hit Metro Detroit and its blue-collar, auto-making suburbs hard.

Graduates then, as now, were told that there was something fundamentally broken in America. That the old values of free markets, free minds and free men were no longer applicable. They were preached the virtues of frugality and austerity.

And a generation raised on the bounty of the post-World War II economic boom was assured they'd never live as well as their parents.

Ultimately, we rejected the self-pitying malaise and started one of the longest periods of sustained prosperity in its history. We exceeded our parents' lifestyles by giant leaps.

I hope today's graduates will do the same. I hope they'll refuse to allow their potential to be limited by a government that would kill their initiative with kindness. That they'll recognize that Americans striving for personal reward have been responsible for most of the innovation, creativity and advancement in the world.

I truly hope they won't buy into the nonsense that there's something sinister about wealth. Or allow pop science to convince them to sacrifice the pleasures of life for the sake of a planet that won't be any fun to live on.

I want them to live large. Dream big. Get rich, if that's what they want.

It's OK. And it's possible, as long as they arm themselves with knowledge, work hard and catch a break or two. And protect their ambition from those who see the drive for individual achievement as a threat to their collectivist vision.

The future does suck, at least for now. So take a few years and go to college so you're ready when things get brighter.

And fight hard against anyone who tells you there are things Americans can't have anymore.

May 9, 2010
Hope shouldn't be a bad thing

Driving into downtown on the Lodge Friday afternoon, I spotted a brand new Wayne State University graduate standing on the walkway above the freeway, dressed proudly in his cap and gown.

He would have been hard to miss, jumping straight up and down and pumping his fists into the air.

The sight of him smiling, pointing to his deep green gown and shouting into the noisy traffic jerked me out of my winter of discontent like nothing else could have.

This young man was the very vision of hope. If there was anything irrational about his unrestrained exuberance, his face sure didn't show it. He looked as if he were bursting with eagerness to get out there and conquer the world.

Perhaps I'm projecting on the graduate a confidence he doesn't hold. Maybe he was just really pleased with himself. I never got the chance to ask. When I looked back in my mirror, he had already blended into the mass of students heading toward the football field.

But my instincts are that his happy dance reflects a more optimistic graduating class than we've seen over the past two years, when we sent more graduates to their parents' basements than into careers. We had nothing for the classes of '08 and '09 but defeatist proclamations that America had so fundamentally changed that their opportunities would be forever limited.

But there's something about the American character that won't allow us to dwell long in despair.

I sense our pent-up hope is breaking loose, that our determination to fix things is overwhelming the misplaced conviction that the things that are wrong with us can't be fixed.

You may not read that in contradictory economic reports. Friday's employment numbers showed more jobs created, but a higher jobless rate. Consumers are starting to spend again, slowly, but you still can't sell a house for anything near a decent price.

And yet we seem to have decided we've had enough of this malaise.

I break with many of my political ilk in hoping that's true, and that it sticks. Those of us who are anxious for November to arrive so we can put an end to the unchecked power of the radical left have a tendency to wish for this black cloud to hang around a bit longer so that the electorate stays angry and committed to change.

That's an unhealthy inclination. People can go back to work and start smiling again and still remember what it is they don't like about Obamacare and the explosive expansion of government. They don't have to be angry, frightened or desperate to show up at the polls to reset America's course.

They'll stay motivated even without the incessant badmouthing of the economy. Who knows? It may be that people are more encouraged because they anticipate the election will bring significant change.

I don't care either way. I'm weary of weariness. If that college grad sees enough hope in the future to leap with joy across a freeway overpass, it's good enough for me.

January 16, 2011
Governor, tear down these schools

This ought to be the end of the line for the Detroit Public Schools. New Gov. Rick Snyder is weighing what to do with the district, which chronically defies reform and continues to send more children to prison and welfare than to college.

The solution is inescapable: Tear down the district and start anew with highly accountable schools that are individually run and serve the sole purpose of delivering a quality education to children for whom that is their only hope.

Emergency Financial Manager Robert Bobb has done everything humanly possible to save the district, and he's failed. Evidence of that failure can be found in the turnaround proposals he offered last week. None are acceptable, none are realistic, and none are politically possible.

Bobb is asking the state for a $300 million bailout to erase the district's debt. I have no doubt that with a clean balance sheet Bobb could put together a sustainable, long-term budget. I also have no doubt that he won't get it from a state with a $1.8 billion budget deficit and a long list of other collapsing school districts that would expect similar rescues.

So Plan B is another round of drastic cost-cutting. This time, Bobb would close half the schools and increase class size to 62 students.

Sixty-two students isn't a classroom, it's a holding pen. Little education is possible in that environment; particularly of children who are posting among the worst test scores in the nation.

If Bobb's cuts are enacted, DPS will be drained of students in short order, as parents turn to charters, private and suburban schools.

Or DPS will be hit with a civil rights lawsuit. Neither Detroit nor Michigan can afford to cede control of the district to a federal judge who would make funding decisions without regard to the impact on local and state budgets.

This is the time for boldness. Snyder has the chance and the excuse to do something new and big in Detroit.

The only way to fix an urban district is to move it away from an operating model and toward a management model. In other words, instead of DPS running schools, the district should oversee a portfolio of schools that are actually run by contractors selected from a list of education providers with a proven record of success.

The schools would be autonomous and held to high standards. If they miss their marks, they lose their contracts. They would be free to hire their own teachers and choose the services they want from the district.

The best Detroit schools would be spun off with their existing staffs; the worst would be closed and replaced. This is not a takeover, but a liberation of students from a district steeped in failure. Snyder has few choices. Bobb is gone soon; a replacement isn't likely to post better results. Voters have said they don't want the mayor to run the schools. Returning them to an elected board will enlarge the debt and dysfunction.

Tear down the school district and start over with a bold idea that gives the children of Detroit a fighting chance.

≺ ≺ ≺

May 11, 2014
Teachers need a shield law

Coming out of my junior high cafeteria, I got into a scrap with another boy. There were shoves, a few punches. And then a sharp thump to my chest left me sprawled on my back, stunned.

When I opened my eyes, the gym teacher was standing over me, rubbing his foot across an imaginary wet spot on the floor. "Geez, Finley," he said. "I must have slipped. Good thing you broke my fall."

I didn't run home whining about my trampled rights. My mother didn't show up at the school demanding justice for her poor, abused baby. It was understood that unacceptable behavior had swift and sometimes painful consequences.

But we had an orderly school. We knew who was in charge, and it wasn't us.

Who's in charge of today's schools is anyone's guess. I suspect it isn't the teachers, through no fault of their own.

We've filled their classrooms with under-parented and over-empowered brats fully versed in their rights, who respect nothing and fear no one. We expect teachers not only to turn them into scholars with little or no help from home, but also to keep them from killing each other.

Last week at Detroit's Pershing High School, a teacher was fired for trying to break up an extremely violent fight between two teens who dwarfed her in terms of size. The boys were banging each other all over the classroom, tipping over desks, endangering themselves and their classmates.

The teacher, threatened, frightened and overwhelmed, tried to break it up by whacking at them with a flimsy broom handle. She faces a criminal investigation; the boys received brief suspensions.

Later, one of the boys' mothers appeared with him on TV, defending her son and praising the teacher's dismissal. This mother is raising a wild child, undisciplined and indulged, and she's inflicting him on society. She should have been ashamed to show her face at the school, unless it was to borrow that broomstick to finish the job the teacher started.

A few weeks ago a similar brawl broke out at Livonia Churchill. The boys involved seemed hell-bent on killing one another. The two male teachers who intervened took the worst of the blows—one suffered a serious back injury while trying to wedge the students apart.

Watching the video of that melee, I wondered why someone didn't just grab a chair and break it over the backs of the fighters. Teachers can't do that, of course. They can't do much of anything to deal with out-of-control students. That should change.

State lawmakers should consider a stand-your-ground law for teachers. They should be shielded from prosecution and firing for actions they take in response to violent classroom outbreaks.

Teachers should be able to protect themselves and their students by any means available, even if that's a broom handle.

The videos reveal the high level of chaos and confusion in the classrooms during the fights. Teachers aren't trained to deal with that, and they shouldn't have to.

If we're going to place them in front of students who'd be better served in jail cells than school desks, then at least we should stand behind them. ⚡

Chapter 9

Our Money

September 2, 2001

This taxpayer could actually use more government

Most people of my political ilk are howling for less government. But I want me more government, and right on my doorstep.

I'd really like some Forest Service guys to drop by the house on weekends to help with the yard work. Or maybe a couple of soldiers for the front porch to impress the neighbors. Perhaps I could take my next vacation at one of those South Pacific military bases, or go for a cruise on a Navy submarine.

Best of all would be if George W. could call me every now and then to say hey. "You doing all right, Mr. Taxpayer? We sure do appreciate your support."

Yeah, all that would make me feel better. Because as things stand, I'm not getting near enough government to suit me. In fact, after paying out half my real income last year in taxes, I find I'm not getting one bit more government than the 40 percent of Americans who paid no federal income taxes.

That just doesn't seem right.

W. asked a lot of folks last week what they'd do with their tax rebates. He seemed put off by their nonchalance. Maybe he hoped they'd say, "Thank you —I'm going to use this $300 check to buy my dream house!" Or, "Wow! Now that we have this $600, Junior can go to Harvard."

I wish he'd ask me. My check is going right back to W.

Since April 15, I've been in a cheery correspondence with the Internal Revenue Service. Every few weeks, the IRS sends me a note saying, "Oops! After scrutinizing your tax return under the Hubble telescope, it seems you owe us some more money. Please send a check in 20 minutes to avoid penalties compounded at 200 percent hourly."

This relationship was triggered by the sale last year of some rental property. The return on investment was modest. The tax penalty was not.

The sale threw me deeply into the capital gains swamp. The down side of having a one-time capital gain of any significance is that it triggers all sorts of complex formulas aimed at cheating you out of your other deductions and exemptions. It's an amazingly efficient means of pushing the capital gains tax well above the stated 20 percent.

So it was no surprise when the latest envelope from the IRS bore not my tax rebate, but a bill for precisely the amount my rebate would have been. Now how am I going to stimulate the economy with that?

All of this has me thinking again about tax reform. This year's half-rumped effort to cut taxes hardly qualifies as reform. It gave back only a piddling amount, made the tax code even more complex, and now there's a good chance our congressmen, appalled that they can't cut taxes and spend the money, too, will take much of it back.

Real reform would be to divide the cost of the federal government by the number of working citizens and send each one a bill for their share. Maybe then we'd pay better attention to how much Washington spends.

Since that probably won't happen, we need someone to take up the flat tax mantle. Steve Forbes tried during his long-shot presidential bids. But he was too rich and too odd to be a credible advocate.

But, hey! How about W.? He got us worked up about tax cuts during the campaign and delivered some two-bit rebate. Maybe he can start a serious conversation about bringing fairness and simplicity to the tax system, perhaps even reviving the notion of post card tax returns.

Either that, or he can send a tank by to take me for a ride now and then, just so I feel like I'm getting my money's worth.

⚔ ⚔ ⚔

August 11, 2002

Families, working and otherwise, need protection from government greed

Republicans have lost interest in preaching to their own congregation. They've left their country club cathedrals to chase a Democratic flock, with a Democratic sermon.

That's why President George W. Bush was down south last week, flogging evil corporate executives and pledging to protect workers from boardroom rip-off artists. In Michigan, Dick Posthumus, the GOP's nominee for governor, has donned a denim shirt and is boasting of his union roots.

His post-primary speech might have been written by Jennifer Granholm, the Democrat's choice and a Harvard lawyer, who was moved nearly to tears while emoting about the nobility of those who go to work in stores and factories.

So I'm wondering: If everyone is standing up for the little guy, who's fighting for the fat cats? And what exactly is a working family anyway?

The phrase plays to the myth of an American caste system, where those at the top feed off the sweat and muscle of those stuck at the bottom. That traditional Democratic drivel rings hollow today, with American families enjoying unprecedented prosperity.

But instead of targeting the broad range of voters who own property, have stock portfolios and are fully invested in the economic system, Republicans are speaking the class war language. They've joined the Democratic choir in promising to fight for working families, an ill-defined but apparently quite vulnerable group.

Voters are excused for wondering whether that means them. I suspect mine wouldn't qualify as a working family, even though everyone gets up in the morning and goes to work, and at the end of the day we all feel like we've hit a pretty fair lick. (Maybe we should vote for the candidate who promises to work for fighting families, but that's another issue.)

This working family nonsense would be harmless if it were nothing more than political pandering. But it has influence on public policy.

The economic merits of last year's tax cut were quickly overwhelmed by outrage that wealthier people—those who pay most of the taxes—got the most tax relief. But few challenged the fairness of a plan to give tax rebates to people who don't pay any taxes.

The national economy withers while Washington refuses to take up vital stimulative measures out of fear the rich might benefit.

This demonizing of wealth is un-American. Much of our national appeal is the opportunity to get rich, either through ambition, talent or just plain luck. It's why inventors keep inventing, investors keep investing and immigrants keep immigrating.

Most families, rich or poor, work. Bill Ford works. So does Bill Gates. They get up to an alarm clock just like Bill down at the corner garage. The interests of all families are more similar than they are different.

Thanks to mutual funds and 401(k) plans, 60 percent of American households are invested in the stock market. Two-thirds own their homes. The same capital gains and inheritance taxes that rob Ford and Gates also cheat Bill the garage guy.

If American families need protection, it's from the government, not corporations. Corporations provide paychecks, stock dividends and pension plans. Government sucks the quality of life out of families with waste and high taxes.

Republicans should tend their own comfortable flock. It may be bigger than they think.

November 17, 2002

Want to make Americans richer? Kill the income tax

Intriguing, idea and Washington aren't words that often appear together in a credible sentence. But an intriguing idea is floating around Washington for reforming the way Americans pay for government.

Treasury Secretary Paul O'Neill is quietly exploring a plan to do away with the income tax, that punitive system of taxation adopted in 1913 that spawned an un-American strain of collectivism. The income tax promotes the notion that the first fruits of hard work and enterprise belong to the government, not the individual.

"Currently, the tax code rewards vice and punishes virtue," says Stephen Moore, president of the Club for Growth in Washington, D.C. "The harder you work, the more you save and invest in the economy, the more taxes you pay."

That's where the income tax rubs against traditional American values. It places a high price on success, hard work and risk-taking, and seeks to force equalization by confiscating a greater share as incomes rise.

Moore, one of the leading proponents of nuking the income tax, says the goal of taxation should be to make the poor richer, not the rich poorer.

A tax code designed to redistribute wealth can't accomplish that. But one that stimulates growth and investment can.

O'Neill's embryonic idea would replace the income tax on individuals and corporations with variations of a consumption tax. Corporations would pay a value-added tax based on how much they increase the worth of a product or material as it moves through their hands.

Individuals would possibly pay a national sales tax.

Both taxes would be pegged at roughly 13 percent to make up for the revenue lost from income taxes.

A 13-cent sales tax may sound steep, but remember, you'd no longer pay income taxes, and the cost of goods and services would likely drop because of the change to the business tax structure.

Those who resent wealth will bristle because the consumption tax is not "progressive," meaning it doesn't demand that higher earners cover a disproportionate share of the cost of government. But why should they? Do they enjoy greater government services? Again, taxes aren't supposed to punish success, they're supposed to pay for government in the most efficient way possible without disrupting the economy.

In reality, switching to a consumption tax would benefit lower and middle income earners because it would encourage capital investment and job creation, and lower the prices of most consumer goods.

Americans would have more incentive to save, which should help ease their reliance on Social Security, whose future is suspect. Dollars saved or otherwise invested would not be taxed. Moore says this would turn the U.S. economy into a vacuum cleaner sucking up international investment capital.

Another benefit is that Americans would have to think about the cost of government each time they buy a soda, a suit or a sport-utility vehicle.

It is a sure road to prosperity. But it won't happen soon.

At best, any such proposal will wait until President George W. Bush's second term, if he wins one, and only if he can build on the congressional gains of the recent election and bring federal spending and budget deficits under control.

Lots of ifs, but it does give those of us who long for a fair, sane tax code something to dream about.

⟵ ⟵ ⟵

May 8, 2005

Who cares about the kids?
Save my Social Security check

Having never expected to get this old, Social Security was always an abstract concept, just an annoyingly large deduction on my pay stub.

But now that I've turned 50, I'm thinking I may make 65 after all. I can almost see myself standing by the mailbox to greet the monthly check.

So the Social Security debate has me doing some math. If the system goes bust in 2041, as GOP doomsayers predict, there's a chance I might still be on this side of the sod. If it lasts another 10 years or more beyond that, as Democratic do-nothing advocates insist, I should be beyond caring.

To figure out how to place my bet, I called Robert Kennedy, executive director of the William Davidson Institute at the University of Michigan, who views Social Security from a practical, rather than political perspective.

Kennedy says the Democrats are right, D-Day for Social Security is still decades off. But he says Republicans are right, too, that the fixes must be made today.

"If nothing happens now, the system won't melt down in the next two or three years," Kennedy says. "On the other hand, if we act now, we can make relatively small changes. If we wait, we'll have to make big changes."

By 2017, the Social Security system will be paying out more than it takes in. The Treasury bonds issued over the years in exchange for robbing the system's surplus will cover the shortfall for another 25 years. But that merely shifts the deficit to the general fund. Somewhere, taxes will have to be raised, or benefits cut.

Small benefit trims for future retirees, combined with slightly higher payroll taxes, will keep the system solvent.

And that takes care of people my age, a priority since the power in Washington is held by people my age.

But it's a lousy deal for our children. Kennedy says workers in their 20s can expect a negative return on their Social Security payments. It's hard to see how any private market investment could do worse.

Kennedy adds that allowing young workers to keep some of their money for private retirement accounts is not such a radical idea.

"There's no net cost," he says. "For every dollar diverted to private accounts, the benefit is reduced. It would require some short-term borrowing, but when people start retiring they'll pull less money out of the system. It's a wash."

A wash, perhaps. But politically hazardous.

Fairness to younger workers is not a priority for a Congress motivated by the votes and dollars of richer, older workers.

Republicans are drifting away from private accounts, and even President Bush is buying into the idea of making payroll taxes "progressive"—meaning most middle- and upper-income workers will pay more and get less.

That will make Social Security an even bigger loser for today's kids.

Maybe they'll put up with it out of altruism or an overriding affection for Mom and Dad.

Or maybe when they get the political power in Washington they'll vote to cut us off from the sweet deal we crafted for ourselves at their expense.

October 23, 2005
'Oops' babies are breaking state budget

Ignorance breeds faster than intelligence. That fact of life is busting Michigan's budget.

More than 40,000 babies are born each year on the state's Medicaid system, or about 40 percent of all births. Of those, 26,000 are "oops" babies, unintended pregnancies paid for by state taxpayers.

The price tag just for those mistakes is $286 million a year, or about $11,000 per baby for prenatal care, delivery and post-natal checkups.

Most will go on the welfare rolls after birth, becoming an escalating expense for taxpayers and explaining why welfare eats up a third of the state's General Fund and growing.

Most are also born to single mothers, vastly increasing the odds that they'll be raised in poverty. And most aren't an only child—they have brothers and sisters, often several, whose upkeep also goes on the public tab.

It's no wonder Michigan can't fully fund its public schools, doesn't have the money to support its universities properly and can't cut taxes to forge a job-creating business climate. State taxpayers are working themselves to death to pay for the reckless behavior of their fellow citizens.

The most tempting answer is to tell people not to have babies they can't afford and, if they do, figure out how to support them themselves.

But we are slaves to our compassion, and that won't allow us to make children suffer the consequences of their parents' irresponsibility.

Demanding contraceptive use as a condition of receiving aid is an idea with appeal, but one that fails the tests of privacy and religious freedom.

So we accept that everyone has the right to have as many babies as they want, and taxpayers have the right to pay for them.

For answers, we're left with education and making sure contraceptives are readily available.

Believe it or not, Marianne Udow, director of the Department of Human Services, says many people don't understand how contraceptives work or don't have access to them.

And many of those who are getting pregnant are little more than children themselves.

Gov. Jennifer Granholm has started a pilot program in 15 school districts to teach parents how to talk to their children about sexual responsibility and has asked for a federal waiver to provide family planning services to low-income residents.

Critics say this pushes state government too deeply into matters best handled in the home. Normally, I'd be on their side.

But Medicaid costs Michigan $2 billion and is adding 100,000 new clients a year. One Michigan resident receives public assistance for every six who pay taxes.

At this pace, the ratio soon will be one-to-one, and every taxpayer will have his or her own welfare recipient to support.

Raising my own kids took a big bite out of my wallet. I'd rather not pay to rear someone else's.

If we can cut the dependency bill by making people smarter about where babies come from, then let's do it.

May 20, 2007
Make politicians play by business rules

What if politicians had to play by the same rules they impose on business executives?

"They'd go to jail," says Peter Henning, a professor at Wayne State University's law school.

The meltdown of Enron, Worldcom and other corporations led Congress to rush through the Sarbanes-Oxley act in 2002, heaping oppressive layers of accountability on corporate officers and making it likely a CEO will end up in an orange jumpsuit if someone in finance gets creative with a calculator.

But while Congress rose to protect stakeholders from executives who fudge numbers, it didn't shield taxpayers from politicians who do the same thing.

For five years, Gov. Jennifer Granholm and state legislative leaders have signed budgets they knew were out of whack, using smoke and mirrors to make them appear balanced.

For example, last year revenue from the anticipated sale of Northville Psychiatric Hospital was included in the budget. But the land never sold.

"A business could never say we are going to get X amount of dollars based on a guess and then factor that into the balance sheet," Henning says.

Manipulating the bottom line is what helped send the Enron swindlers to jail, Henning says. "They said one thing and knew another, and you're not allowed to do that in business."

But you are in politics. Before last fall's election, Granholm painted an optimistic picture of the state's economic future, while hiding the fact that some state departments had grossly overspent their budgets.

Concealing harmful information to influence the vote is akin to a corporate executive burning an unfavorable sales report to drive up the stock price.

"You can't sue a politician for making promises they know they can't keep," Henning says. "But you can sue a businessman for that, if it affects the stock price."

Another perk available to politicians but not to business executives are slush funds filled by special interests who hope to influence their decisions. Think about Detroit Mayor Kwame Kilpatrick's Civic Fund, which paid for his family's recent trip to a California resort, or the "administrative" accounts politicians use to pay for luxuries their salaries won't cover.

"That could be viewed as a breach of fiduciary duties if it causes you to act other than in the best interest of shareholders," Henning says. "It has landed people in jail."

While Sarbanes-Oxley put corporate officers under the microscope, most governments, including the city of Detroit and the state of Michigan, have only minimal ethics rules for elected officials.

"The politicians don't act as if they have a fiduciary obligation to the electorate," Henning says. "An officer of a company has to account for what he or she does and show it's in the best interest of the corporation. But once politicians are elected, they don't feel accountable to anyone."

The fix is simple. Sarbanes-Oxley is already on the books. Extend it to cover elected officials and let the politicians live by the same rules they impose on business.

June 9, 2011

End-of-life care is killing health system

The death of Dr. Death is a reminder that the conversation Jack Kevorkian fueled about who should control the dying process has not been satisfactorily concluded.

Kevorkian was too ghoulish in his persona and technique to serve as an effective advocate for the right-to-die movement. But the question he raised of how much suffering a person must endure, and at what cost to the health care system, is relevant beyond the issue of assisted suicide.

Last year, when the debate over Obamacare was raging, end-of-life care was front-and-center as opponents decried the idea of "death panels" made up of cold-hearted bureaucrats rationing treatment.

The image of physicians playing the Kevorkian role and dispatching elderly patients whose care is deemed too expensive was an effective weapon against the program.

I detest Obamacare. But I do think we should have an honest discussion about how much money is spent on care that does little to enhance quality of life or to meaningfully extend it.

When my mother suffered a major heart attack, the family made an emotionally driven decision to send her into surgery in a desperate stab at undoing what was likely already done. That one day cost Medicare and her insurance company more than was spent on her health care during her entire lifetime. And at the end of it, she died anyway.

Yet there was little conversation about value for the dollar—would the surgery, if successful, give her a life anything like the one she enjoyed before the heart attack? How long would it add to her life? The decision was left entirely to the family, even though others were paying the bill.

"Doctors don't do a good job of asking the right questions," says Dr. Michael Stelline of Wayne State University's medical school. "They need to be honest about the family's goals, but are reluctant because it is a difficult conversation to have."

But it's one that can save money and needless suffering. Current law discourages such assessments.

Medicare cannot legally reject a treatment based on cost. The CBS news program "60 Minutes" last year documented the case of a 93-year-old terminal cancer patient who got a surgically implanted heart defibrillator, and of advanced breast cancer patients who received the drug Avastin at a cost of $55,000, even though the treatment added just 90 days to their lives.

When a patient arrives at a hospital already at death's door, needless procedures are performed to satisfy the family that everything possible is being done to save their loved one, even when nothing can be done. "Does the family have the right to claim the resources of the system in pursuit of a goal that's unreasonable?" Stelline asks. "That's an important ethical question."

The clinging to life beyond hope or reason is expensive. Medicare spends $55 billion a year on end-of-life care, and up to 30 percent makes no difference. Such wasteful treatment is a primary cause of soaring health care costs, and it should not be taboo to weigh cost against benefits.

Certainly we have to invest in those who have a shot at survival and the resumption of a quality life. But at some point, we die. How much it's worth to briefly delay the inevitable is a discussion we must have if we hope to keep health care affordable, and in private hands.

July 19, 2012

You build it, Obama will come get it

President Barack Obama's campaign trail declaration—"You didn't build that!"—reveals as much about his view of the role of government as did his candid 2008 explanation to Joe the Plumber that "when you spread the wealth around, it's good for everybody."

That moment of truth in Ohio four years ago accurately forecast a presidency obsessed with the quest to impose its interpretation of economic justice on the American system. It explains why after four years of failure, Obama is still trying to revive a moribund economy by taking money from the rich and giving it to the poor, after laundering it through an exploding federal bureaucracy.

Likewise, the startling announcement to business owners last week that their success stems not from their own sweat, skill and sacrifice, but rather from the benevolence of Big Daddy government predicts Obama's second-term agenda. And that will be to complete the subjugation of the private marketplace to federal regulators and tax agents.

When I heard the president's quote—"If you've got a business, you didn't build that. Somebody else made that happen"—I thought immediately of my friend Cindy Pasky, one of the hardest working people I know. Pasky, founder of Detroit's Strategic Staffing Solutions, started with nothing, not even a college degree, and built her IT business into an international powerhouse. She still works more hours in a week than most people do in a month.

So I called Cindy and asked, if she didn't build her business, who did?

"When you start a business, nobody gives you anything," she said. "You have got to be all-in yourself. Entrepreneurs rise or fall on their own abilities and hard work."

What about Obama's claim that the infrastructure government puts in place and the support it gives to businesses make successful entrepreneurs possible?

"The government gives you nothing," Pasky said. "The only gift you get is opportunity, and how you use it is up to you."

She attributes Obama's remarks to naivete about how jobs are created and private business works.

I think the roots run deeper, to Obama's fundamental view of the relationship between government and the people.

The Framers crafted a government empowered by and accountable to the governed. The "you didn't build that" comment springs from a president who believes government empowers the people, doling out both riches and rights.

A president who sees the nation in these terms is comfortable spreading the wealth around, even if it means confiscating what you worked so hard to attain. Getting the chicken or egg question correct is vital. If you believe that individual initiative and a successful private sector allow government to provide services, you advocate a much different set of policies than if you believe, as the president does, that the government makes all things possible.

This election is about more than fixing the economy or choosing between a stuffy millionaire and a cool cat who smooches his wife on the Kiss-Cam.

We will decide whether to keep trudging down the road to serfdom that Hayek warned of, or make a U-turn back to an understanding that individuals build things themselves, and have a right to keep what they build.

← ← ←

December 23, 2012

Tax code milking cash cow dry

Progressive tax rates have always puzzled me because they assume that government has different value for citizens based on their incomes.

Break government down to the basics and it is essentially a provider of services—defense, transportation, the legal system, schools, etc.—that customers want or need and are willing to pay a price to obtain. In that way, it's little different than a private sector business.

Except in the private sector, goods and services have a set value; all customers pay the same. You don't have to scan your 1040 at the gasoline pump to set the price per gallon.

Only in government does every customer pay a different price for the same thing.

Reader Jon Taub sent me a note last week putting the difference between government and private sector pricing in perspective.

Taub, a corporate lawyer for a Detroit business, notes that the top 1 percent of earners pay for 38 percent of the general fund services delivered by the federal government.

Forty-seven percent of earners pay nothing for these services. And the bottom 40 percent actually get a reverse payment from the federal government in the form of a refund on taxes they don't pay.

Taub applies that same formula to a purchase of a gallon of milk, which currently sells for $2.49 at Kroger, to see what would happen.

"If every U.S. taxpayer purchased a gallon of milk, each person would pay $2.49, and the total cost would be 140.5 million times $2.49 - or $349 million.

"Now let's assume the government treated milk like government services and determined its price the same way it determines tax rates. The pricing would change as follows:

"When the bottom 40 percent of earners buy their milk, they won't pay a dime for it. In fact, the government would give them $1 in reverse payments for every gallon of milk they purchase. The total cost of providing one gallon of milk to each person in this group would be $196.1 million.

"The cost of providing milk to the remaining 60 percent of the taxpayers would be $209.9 million, bringing the total cost burden of all taxpayers' milk to $406 million.

"Under our existing tax rates, instead of paying $2.49 a gallon, the top 1 percent of earners would pay 38 percent of the total milk burden or $109.81 for a gallon of milk."

And despite that absurd price, the milk jug wouldn't be full. Since top earners require less government services than lower earners, they'd get a lot less milk.

Taub urges everyone to think about that example whenever they hear President Barack Obama talk about tax fairness, as they will incessantly over the next few weeks.

The current tax system is unfair, but not because the wealthy don't pay enough.

It's out of whack because it doesn't acknowledge that the rich are paying more for their government milk than it's worth so most others can pay less. And instead of saying thank you, we're milking those cash cows dry.

December 15, 2013
Robin Hood policies hurt poor

President Barack Obama has some bad news for poor and working class Americans: He's going to spend the final three years of his presidency attacking the income gap.

"The combined trends of increased inequality and decreasing mobility pose a fundamental threat to the American dream, our way of life, and what we stand for around the globe," the president said in a recent speech.

No coincidence the pledge to stamp out inequality comes at the same time Obama's popularity and performance ratings are plunging due to the Obamacare fiasco. He always pivots to populism when he gets in trouble.

But this is no grand shift. Obama has been playing Robin Hood since Day One. All his major initiatives have been built on soaking the rich.

And what's happened? Those on the bottom rungs of the economic ladder have less disposable income than they did when he took office, and the fat cats are fatter than ever.

According to Bloomberg, the richest Americans earned a larger percentage of the total national income last year than they have since 1917. The top 10 percent earned twice as much as the bottom 10 percent. January's big tax hikes on investors and new Obamacare taxes targeted at the wealthy haven't slowed the 1 percent's rise.

Workers, meanwhile, captured a smaller share of total economic output than in any year since 1952. Factcheck.org reports real household income is down 5 percent during the Obama years, while the number of food stamp recipients is up 49 percent.

The more Obama has tried to help the poor and middle, the worse off they've become. That's a factor of policies that have throttled economic growth and dampened job creation. Obamacare is hurting the middle class in a number of ways, but mostly because employers are wary of adding new workers due to the costly insurance mandates.

Higher taxes have also discouraged job creation. There are still more workers than jobs in the post-recession economy, and that depresses wages.

The wealthy, meanwhile, are stacking up dollars. Obama's monetary policies have kept interest rates artificially low to offset the damage done by Obamacare and higher taxes, and the low rates are fueling a housing and stock market boom.

It would be better for everyone if the wealthy were gaining by planting their money in job creating enterprises, but unfavorable capital gains rates work against investment.

Try as he might, Obama can't spread the wealth. History is gorged with populist politicians convinced they can work the levers of government to make the poor richer by making the rich poorer. The poor just always end up getting poorer.

Obama should loosen his grip on the private economy and let businesses start creating jobs again. A tighter job market will increase wages for everyone.

If the president stops obsessing about transferring wealth, he'll have a chance of actually narrowing the income gap. ⚞

Chapter 10

Family

June 18, 2000
A father's example to do any job well

Dad's toolbox rests on a shelf in the back of my garage, where it's been for the 22 years since he died.

Well-worn and rusting, the few tools remaining in the battleship gray, Montgomery Ward's box are not much of an inheritance, except for the glimpses they offer of the man who used them.

My father was part of one of the most remarkable generations this country ever produced. Reared during the Depression in a region dirt poor even in good times, he left his Kentucky home at age 17 for the factories up north. At 18, he was a Marine headed for Okinawa and the fiery horrors of that World War II battleground. A photo in his scrapbook shows him and his buddies bivouacked on "Atomic Field" in Nagasaki during the postwar occupation of Japan.

Back home, Dad and his peers went to work building modern America.

And that's what I remember most about him. He worked.

I suspect the highest compliment you could have paid him was not that he was a good husband or a good father, but that he was a good worker.

In his world, a man was measured by his ability to get a job done. Most of the time, the job involved muscle-straining labor with the tools in this box. He was suspicious of hands without calluses and work without sweat. His highest ambition for me was that I become a plumber. When I told him I thought I'd try journalism instead, he asked, "Can you really make a living at that?"

Dads were judged differently then. We did not expect him to nurture us, just to support us. I'd have been stunned had he left work early to attend one of my ballgames, or turned down overtime to take us to the zoo.

Work was not his passion, as it is mine. Nor did he take particular satisfaction in what he produced. His reward came on payday and the certainty that he'd earned his money.

Even at home, he worked—snaking drains, tearing apart washing machines, fixing cars. He would have rather descended into Hell than call a repairman.

There's a worn wrench still in that box. In high school, I bought an old Ford Fairlane, in great condition except for the rusty side panels, a knocking engine and a transmission that wouldn't shift.

He crawled underneath the car to tinker with something, and I stayed up top to fetch tools. He called for his big monkey wrench; I decided to pass it down through the engine compartment.

I can still see the terror in his eyes as the wrench slipped from my oily fingers and came hurtling toward his forehead. Too stunned to be angry, he lay still for a while and then rolled from under the car and crawled into the house, muttering, "You'll never amount to anything."

One tray in the toolbox is filled with odd-looking gizmos designed to service the coin boxes on washing machines. For a while, Dad owned a shabby Laundromat on Forest near Wayne State University. It was a great place to park while I was going to school. After class, I'd nearly always find him in the back, trying to mend a hopelessly blown motor or pump.

As best I can tell, the Laundromat never made a dime. Dad kept it open long after a sane person would have locked the doors, explaining simply, "If I shut down, the people in this neighborhood won't have any place to wash their clothes."

It was a rare moment of softness from a man who was truly Marine tough. The only time I saw him cry was when his mother died. Throughout his 18-month dance with cancer, I barely saw him grimace.

Picking through his toolbox, I'm struck by the economy. The tools are of top quality but there's little duplication and not near the assortment you'd expect for a man whose living depended on this box. Dad made do with what he had and wasn't about to spend hard-earned dollars on some fancy gadget if he could coax a screwdriver into doing the job. I compare that with the heaving shelves of tools in my own collection; too many, too seldom used.

On Father's Day, it's appropriate to think of your dad and what you learned from him. My dad taught me to work, perhaps too well.

Work is not the virtue it once was. I doubt my children will ever look back at the long hours I spend at the office with the same admiration I have for my father's efforts.

But I do hope some of what he taught me about the importance of doing well whatever job is set before you will trickle down to another generation or two.

October 29, 2000
My daughter's political defection

Sometimes despite a parent's best efforts, a child goes bad.

I consider myself a halfway decent father. I think my children respect me. But it seems I've had no positive influence on their political development.

This painful realization came to me the other evening while helping my eldest daughter with a crossword puzzle. The television was on in the background, blaring a report from ABC News on political advertising.

In Michigan, the reporter said, presidential candidates will air a combined average of eight commercials an hour between now and Election Day. That's in addition to a brain-bashing barrage of other ads for congressional candidates, state House hopefuls, judicial wannabes and proposal proponents.

"Yuck," said my daughter, taking a break from Eight Down, a five-letter word for attitudes of a people (ethos). "I wish this election was over."

Welcoming a break from my own struggles with 60 Across, five letters for Annie's Dog (no idea still), I asked what I thought would be a softball question.

"Who you voting for?"

"Al Gore," she replied.

"Surely not," I said, reminding her that my newspaper—the one that has fed, clothed and schooled her all her 22 years—endorsed George W. Bush.

"Too bad," she said, skipping on to 50 Across, pitchfork part, four letters (tine), and sticking one in me. "I'm a Democrat."

"Huh?"

"Democrat. You guys also endorsed the voucher proposal, and I'm voting against that. And Spence Abraham's your guy, and I'm voting for..."

"Stop!"

There are some things a father just shouldn't know. Put the politics of a prodigal daughter in that category.

Further prodding revealed that my offspring, graduating this fall with an education degree from Wayne State University, sincerely believes Gore and the Democratic Party offer a sounder agenda for education, at least from the viewpoint of a public school teacher.

Another young acquaintance told me last week that she liked Bush, but will probably pull the lever for Gore because "he's pro-choice and so am I."

I may quibble with their reasoning, but I was impressed that both these young voters had based their selection on issues important to them. Neither talked about personality or appearance. Their decision came down to which candidate they felt would best represent their interests.

Personally, I'd rather my daughter—and everyone else I know—just hand me their absentee ballots and let me fill them out. Since that's not about to happen, I'm glad she's at least attempting to be an informed and responsible voter. She recognizes that this election presents not just varying degrees of the same candidate, but a distinct choice for the direction of the nation, and for her future.

I prefer one direction, she prefers the other. That happens even in the best of families.

Each morning, I sign on to various political Web sites to check the latest campaign developments. Lately, I've been fascinated by the webwhiteblue. org site. The site is sponsored by a network of the 17 largest Internet traffic centers and attempts to encourage citizen participation in the democratic process. Its primary feature is the Rolling Cyber Debate among the presidential campaigns.

Every day a different question is submitted by readers for the campaigns to answer. It's an excellent way for voters to get a detailed look at the candidates' unfiltered positions on a wide range of issues and a better choice than making up your mind from political advertising.

"Political ad makers are dealing with a couch potato mind-set," says Doug Bailey, a veteran Republican consultant who, with former Clinton press secretary Mike McCurry, co-directs the Cyber Debate. "They have to grab the attention of someone who tuned into the television set to watch a ballgame or soap opera, not to get political information. As such, the ads tend to be more general and perhaps more negative."

With the election so close and so many people still undecided, Bailey says it is essential for voters to have access to information that allows them to make side-by-side comparisons of the candidates. Bailey is also involved with youthevote.net, the largest student voting project ever attempted.

I plan to direct my daughter to his sites, in hope that there's still a chance of bringing her back into the fold. In the meantime, I'm penciling in 45 Down, a three-letter word for hopeless dreamer (Dad).

June 10, 2001
Keep your head while all about you a daughter plans a wedding

The benefit of enduring an arduous experience is the wisdom gained.

For the past year, I've been watching from as safe a distance as possible as my oldest daughter prepares for her July wedding. I am much poorer for the experience, but I've learned some things. For instance:

If asked any question that starts with, "What do you think…?," just answer "Well." This is an old trick passed down through generations of my family that always seems to satisfy the inquisitor, without conveying commitment. Later, when someone asks "What did your father say?," you can't be held to anything except, "He said 'Well.' "

Remember, no one really wants your opinion. Think of yourself as the treasurer of this enterprise, not the auditor. Keep writing checks and don't get too deeply involved in the details of where the money is going and you'll be fine.

Don't take the prospective groom golfing on the day of the prospective bride's wedding shower. You may think you're doing a good deed, but trust me, there is tremendous potential for disaster. Get him back an hour or two late and no one with even a remote stake in the shower cares that the foursome in front of you played too slow. They won't blame him—they still need him to ooh and ahh over gifts. They'll turn both barrels on you.

Don't ask if you can skip the rehearsal dinner just because you missed your own rehearsal dinner when an unsentimental editor called you into work. Certain people don't need to be reminded of certain things. Sometimes, "you'll laugh at this later" just doesn't apply.

Your daughter may look like the same person as before, but she now poses the greatest threat to your hopes of a secure retirement. She has heightened memory. She can recollect every childhood slight, every paternal failure. You are vulnerable here, and she knows it. After all, it is true you didn't buy her a pony for her fifth birthday, so if she wants a $500 ice swan on the gift table, suck it up and write the check.

It doesn't matter that you have a perfectly fine tuxedo hanging in your closet. You still have to drag your fanny down to the formal shop and get measured for a tux. Why? So you look like everyone else at the front of the church. It also doesn't matter that you have 20 years on everyone else you're supposed to be looking like.

Cut the groom some slack. He's suffering more than you. But don't be too enthusiastic in his defense. If the attention is focused on his shortcomings, some of your own may be overlooked. This whole thing is mostly his fault anyway.

If you have another daughter and she starts looking all like this might be a good idea for her, too, act fast and be creative. Tell her that in your culture, if a second daughter marries in the same decade as the first, custom calls for the ceremony to be held in the garage, with Faygo and finger sandwiches. If that doesn't work, make sure her boyfriend gets quality time with the increasingly pitiful groom-to-be. That should buy you a few years.

Finally, steal as many hours as you can to spend with your daughter. In a few weeks, the world changes for both of you. Take her to dinner. Tell her she's beautiful. Tell her how proud she's made you, and what fun it's been watching her grow up.

And make sure she knows that whenever she needs a dad, you'll always be there.

July 29, 2001
Knowing when to let go is toughest task

If you're going to raise children, you have to get used to watching them walk away.

A parent's main job is to ready your offspring to strike out on their own. The challenge is maintaining the delicate balance between encouraging independence and smothering them in an overprotective blanket.

The truth is, you're never as ready for them to take the next step as they are.

I learned that lesson first from my oldest daughter's kindergarten teacher, a grandly plump and glamorous woman whose name I've forgotten, but who was perfectly designed for her profession. When the yellow bus arrived for that first day of school, my daughter climbed confidently up the steps and disappeared.

Panicked, I jumped in the car and beat the bus to the school, where I peered through the classroom window to make sure she was OK. She was doing much better than I was. Particularly after the teacher spotted me and politely but firmly ordered me home.

"She's a big girl now, Mr. Finley. It's time to let go."

Good advice. Tough to follow.

Letting go meant saying goodbye to Candyland and newspaper sword fights, and instead searching for the answers to guide her through braces, biology and boys. The job got tougher by the year. By the time I figured out how to be the kind of parent she needed at one phase of her life, she'd already moved on to the next.

Most often, I felt like Lucy in the chocolate factory, frantically trying to keep pace as she marched forward. The oldest child of too-young parents, she was raised mostly by trial-and-error. And yet she thrived, which, if nothing else, proves you can make plenty of mistakes and still produce a darn fine kid.

The biggest challenge was resisting the urge to micromanage her life.

Under-parenting gets most of our attention—parents who are too busy with their own lives to pay attention to their children. But I'm not so sure over-parenting doesn't do some harm as well.

I read recently about a computer chip we'll soon be able to install in our children's watchbands. Using satellite technology, we will be able to constantly monitor where they go and what they do.

That may keep them on the straight and narrow. But it won't teach them to stand on their own feet, to make good decisions, to discover their appropriate boundaries.

I've been struggling for more than 23 years to find the formula for keeping a child safe, while giving her enough freedom to blossom into the person she was meant to be. As usual, now that I have it all figured out, she's ready to move on to a new place.

This time, it's the biggest move of all. She walked down the aisle last evening, as confidently as she stepped on to that school bus years ago.

Once again, I find myself wholly unqualified to offer any guidance. I can't come up with those wise words to help her navigate a new world of husband and home and bills and career.

But she's well on the way to finding her own answers.

That doesn't stop the worrying. I fear I'm about to learn that the worry part of the job of child rearing doesn't go away, even after the child is all grown up.

But as she stood in the front of the church, that teacher's words came back: "She's a big girl now. It's time to let go."

March 31, 2002

Spring break tests parental nerves

Spring break is the ultimate test of how well you've raised your child, and how much you trust him.

It is the Olympics of parental performance. Get the kid to the beach and back in relatively the same condition as when he left, with some spots on his body that remain unpierced and tattoo-free, and without your losing the rest of your hair or wearing out your cell phone with hourly check-in calls, and you've won. Or maybe you've just got lucky.

Just don't ask too many questions when he gets back and for sure don't insist on seeing the pictures.

My son climbed into a van with five other teen-age boys last week and headed off for his first totally unsupervised adventure—a marathon drive to Panama City, Fla., where the possibilities for disaster are endless. I know. I watched the MTV Spring Break special. From what I can tell, drunk, naked and stupid are the requisite conditions.

Which meant before he left, I got a chance to dust off my parental sermon book. Lecturing a teenage boy on the dangers of having too much fun is fraught with challenges.

First, you have to penetrate the shield of indifference. Driving him to the airport last summer for a student conference in Washington, I gave my standard speech to the bill of his baseball cap, which he pulls over his eyes whenever I start preaching. "There will be a lot of kids down there, from a lot of different places. Don't go wild. Don't mess with drugs or beer or strange girls."

The last clause jolted him awake. "Now Dad, you don't have to worry about drugs or beer, but when it comes to girls, I'm not promising you anything."

So I knew what I was up against on this road trip. After checking off the list of behavioral don'ts—an exercise that's valuable even if it doesn't actually alter behavior because it might at least bring some post-behavior guilt—we sat down with the maps.

The boys had an impressive stack of maps and Trip Tics, none of which they could actually read. They had a vague idea that Florida was somewhere south of Detroit, but didn't seem to grasp the magnitude of a 20-hour drive. I spent the first day and night waiting for a call from an Alabama sheriff. "We got your boy down here in jail; what do you want me to do with him?" Hang on to him till school starts back.

But the time always comes when we can't hang on to them. We have to watch them go places we'd rather they avoid, face dangers we think are wholly unnecessary to tempt. But that's how they grow up and how we learn to recognize they have.

The spring break experience can't help but worry a parent half to death. It is, however, a good introduction to what's to come. A trial separation, a test of the launching pad that will eventually propel him on much longer journeys to much more distant points.

This time, his independence will be brief and, for him, delicious, and he'll return after just a few days filled with stories that are bound to raise the hair on the back of my neck. Too soon, he'll be gone more than he's home, and then home for him will be somewhere else.

This week's high-level of parental anxiety will gradually diminish to a low-grade uneasiness. But it will never go away.

All a parent can really do is trust that some of the sermon found its way through the baseball cap.

February 8, 2004
Grandchildren will pay for our recklessness

I've never been wild about babies. They squawk too much. On an airplane, I'd rather see one of my fellow passengers leading a goat down the aisle than carrying a baby.

But I do have a weakness for redheads. So Brynn Keberly's gorgeous head of strawberry blond hair eased any resentment that she made me a grandfather before my time when she entered the world last week.

I was glad to see her for another reason, as well. In 20 years or so when she joins the workforce, I should be about ready to retire.

My contemporaries and I will need Brynn and her generation to pick up the check for our total unwillingness to make financial sacrifices.

Our gotta-have-it-all attitude will leave a national debt in excess of $30 trillion by the time Brynn graduates from college, if trends continue. Her share will be about $200,000, according to Stephen Moore of the conservative Club for Growth in Washington, D.C.

Because today's parents and grandparents refuse to deal with the inevitable train wreck that is Social Security, Brynn can expect to pay 25 percent of her paycheck to fund the baby boomer retirement boom.

She will have to downsize her life to keep us on the golf course or hiking through the Pyrenees, and to fill our pockets with Viagra.

Grandma may wear a photograph of her little darling silk-screened on her T-shirt when she goes to the casino, but don't be fooled, kids. The old gal is more than willing to mortgage your future so she can get her prescriptions filled for free.

Our grandparents reached deep into their wallets to build a national infrastructure that carried the nation to prosperity. We've ignored the much-needed repairs to that system, preferring to pay for shiny new things like sports cathedrals.

By the time Brynn grows up, the roads she drives on, the bridges she crosses, the lines that carry water into her home and the sewage out will demand tens of billions of dollars to rebuild.

Fixing the pavement and pipes now would mean sacrifice, and sacrifice is not a concept we accept. President George W. Bush submitted a budget last week that is more than $350 billion short of revenue. That would seem to be a rallying cry for slashing programs, for notching in the belt.

But Bush is a classic boomer. Rather than making hard choices that require doing without some things to pay for others, the president wants to have the tax cuts, finance the war on terror and still buy all the other goodies Americans have come to expect.

We'll get through these tough times relatively pain-free and without considering who gets stuck with the bill. It's those grandchildren we claim to think so much of.

Chew on that as this election season progresses. None of the candidates are talking about fiscal restraint, saving for the future, delaying programs until we can afford to pay for them.

Quite the opposite. They all have visions of a much bigger and more expensive government. More entitlements for seniors. Free day care for children. Free college tuition, too. And we won't worry about paying for it today, Brynn. We'll let you worry about that tomorrow.

So go forth and multiply, children. We'll need a whole lot more of you to pay our bills.

⚔ ⚔ ⚔

May 22, 2005

Tobacco buyout brings an end to a century-old family tradition

Owning a farm can be a great conversation starter at parties, until someone asks the inevitable question: "What do you grow?"

Say corn, carrots or butter beans and you're OK. You get an approving smile and perhaps a pat on the back for helping keep alive the American tradition of small, family-owned farms.

Tell the truth and answer "tobacco" and the conversation is over. If you're lucky.

If you're not, your listener gets all damn the pusher man on you. A woman at a business reception in New York City loudly blamed me for her mother's cancer death after I made the mistake of mentioning my one and only crop was burley tobacco.

But not this year. For the first time in more than a century, no tobacco is being planted this spring on my family's farm in Cumberland County, Ky., a modest tract of land that for better or worse now belongs to me.

I could say I've finally taken the moral high ground and turned my back on the despicable plant, decided to accept no more gain from the pain it causes. But that wouldn't be true.

Though I've never smoked and wish no one else did, I've always loved tobacco, loved the smell and feel of its leaves, loved the way it fills the fields in summer and the drying barns in fall.

And more than a few generations of my family depended on tobacco and a little moonshine whiskey on the side to keep from starving, if barely.

So I've endured a tug-of-war between the seductive beauty of the plant and the destructive products the plants ultimately become; between its economic benefits and its devastating impact on health.

The federal government is saving me from my moral dilemma. It ended the tobacco support program this year and is buying out the farmers' allotment.

That means for the next 10 years I'll get a check in the mail for not growing a burley crop.

Given my political leanings, this check ought to trouble my conscience at least as much as raising a carcinogen.

But it isn't the first time the government has paid me for not growing something. I used to get a check in the mail for not planting corn. I had never raised corn, and never intended to, and hadn't asked for the check. But it came anyway.

After a few years, the Agriculture Department must have figured out I wasn't a true corn-growing threat because it stopped sending the money. I had a notion to plant a few acres of corn just to teach the government not to take me for granted, but I lacked the will.

Now, I'm puzzling what to put in those empty tobacco fields.

The land is not hospitable to grain or vegetable crops, and there's too little of it for that kind of farming to be practical anyway.

Once the tobacco checks stop coming, I could ask the government to pay me for not growing everything from artichokes to zucchini, but I suspect it learned a lesson from the corn episode.

For now, I'm growing weeds, and not the profitable kind.

Social conversation should be pleasanter, though. Because now I'll be a true American farmer—I'll be losing money hand over fist.

July 8, 2005

'A minute away,' is too close

One minute is not enough of a buffer zone.

That's how my son, Marshall, described his proximity to the terrorist bomb blasts that shattered London Thursday.

Marshall is at the University of London this summer with Michigan State University's study abroad program, his first trip overseas.

I woke up Thursday morning to the news of the London bombings, and for the next couple of hours waited for the telephone to ring.

When it finally did, the message was typically condensed: "We're about a minute away from where the bombs went off. I'm OK. I gotta go because other people need to use this phone."

He is nothing if not a frugal communicator. An e-mail later in the day was more worryingly descriptive.

"We were sitting in class at about 10 this morning when we heard a very loud explosion. ...We tried to get back to our dorm but we are at the epicenter of the attacks.

"We are in the middle of all three main tube stations in the area that got hit. ... The city is stopped and people are just walking around trying to find their way out. ...

"Had we been in our dorm we would have seen one of the buses that got hit. That's how close to us this is."

Way too close. My business has taken me to some horrific scenes, made me eyewitness to too many terrible tragedies. You take it in stride. But to have a son in the middle of such carnage is unnerving.

And then it occurs that hundreds of thousands of American parents wake up this way every morning. Those who have loved ones deployed in Iraq, Afghanistan and other hot spots live this routine over and over. Listen to the news of a bombing, a helicopter crash, a sniper attack, and then wait for the phone to ring.

The sacrifices demanded by the war on terror have been unequal. Some parents watch as their children march off towards peril, others wave as their kids sail off for a carefree London adventure, never giving a thought to danger.

It is only when terror nudges too near—a minute away, in this case—that we're reminded that this should be our fight, too.

London's bombs will awaken the British, for sure. But it ought to also reawaken the rest of us.

September 11 is drifting away from America's shores, and maybe that's a testimony to the success of the terror fighters in keeping us safe.

But it's also given us the luxury as a nation to spat and sputter about the war in Iraq, while not fretting about terrorists hitting us here.

We've become so indifferent to the threat that we tie ourselves in knots over whether the terrorists we have captured are getting dessert with their three-squares.

Homeland security is becoming yet another rambling bureaucracy, while the money designated to keep us safe is being spent on refrigerators and silk plants.

We go nuts over All-Star Games and celebrities ballroom dancing on the TV, and rarely remember that many of America's sons and daughters are sleeping in the sand—when the mortar fire lets them sleep.

This is no way to fight a war. We should all be engaged in the battle, share more of the anxiety suffered by the parents of soldiers, be reminded every day of what is at stake.

The terrorists didn't go away after September 11. They didn't go away when Saddam's statue fell. And they won't when London washes the blood from its streets.

They'll keep coming back unless and until we destroy every last one of them, or make being a terrorist such an uncomfortable career choice that they give up.

That will take more resolve, more unity of purpose, more sacrifice from all of us. But it's the only choice we have.

Because if we don't fight harder, we can never be certain that the terrorists aren't just a minute away—or less—from the ones we love.

April 22, 2007
Let's raise more Yankee Doodle Dandies

Roughly 2.7 million babies were born worldwide last week. Born in modern hospitals and in ancient huts. Born to mothers free to make the ultimate choice and to mothers never allowed to decide anything for themselves.

Born in places where the arrival of a baby sets in motion college funds, Little League dreams and showers of presents, and in places where life is so uncertain that a birth is as much cause for grief as it is joy.

My interest is in just one of those babies—Logan Russell Keberly, my first grandson and a bit of an infant Goliath. I have no illusion that I'll play Yoda to his Skywalker. I'm not good at that sort of thing and don't have much wisdom to spare anyway.

But I would like him to know this: He hit the jackpot by being among the 77,000 of those 2.7 million babies lucky enough to find themselves in America when they entered the world. That fate, along with educated, committed parents, gives him the head start that is the national birthright.

I'd like Logan to grow up a Yankee Doodle Dandy, convinced of the special place America occupies in the world and aware of the unique privileges and responsibilities of that standing.

I'd rather he be steeped in the corny, Capraesque idealism of righteous might and boundless opportunity than in the national cynicism and self-loathing that poisons the current generation and threatens to infect the next.

The notion of American superiority has fallen out of fashion. We've lost confidence that a nation conceived in liberty claims a higher moral ground than regimes dedicated to despotism and tyranny. We spend more energy dissecting the misfires of this great nation than we do uplifting its triumphs.

Americans who travel abroad are expected to be embarrassed by our country's wealth and power, and our cultural and political leaders are more than happy to accommodate that expectation, tripping all over the world apologizing on our behalf.

Not only don't we celebrate the advantages of our culture, but the very right to claim a distinct American culture is under challenge. We are so enamored of hyphens that the national motto, "Out of Many, One," may as well be "Every Group for Itself."

That's not the America I want to leave my grandchildren.

I'd like them to see their country the way Ronald Reagan did, as a shining city on a hill.

America's endurance depends on the faith of its people that this noble experiment must succeed to keep hope alive for all those in the world still yearning to be free.

We too readily today allow America to be defined by those with no respect for life, liberty and the pursuit of happiness. Or by those who accept no responsibility for spreading freedom and can't understand why Americans are so obsessed with that mission.

The greatest gift we can leave the generations to follow is to school them in the values and ideals that set America apart, and to instill in them not only a love of country, but also a fierce pride.

They should see the word "America" on their birth certificate and know they're holding the supreme winning lottery ticket.

May 10, 2009
Good mothers are our best hope

The best thing I ever gave my children is a good mother.

It's the same gift my father gave me, and his father gave him. It's a legacy of good mothers who took raw material of suspect quality and made it into something useful.

I've been thinking a lot lately about good mothering. It started with the murder of 9-year-old Shylea Thomas, the Flint girl whose body was found inside a storage locker.

Shylea never had a chance because she never had a mother. She was born to a woman whose neglect left her a quadriplegic as a toddler.

Then she was dumped on an aunt who was overwhelmed by the consequences of her own poor choices. And big surprise, no father in the picture.

Shylea lived with six other children, including a 15-year-old with two babies of her own.

Her aunt is now charged with her murder.

It's part of our national creed that an individual can rise from nothing to reach the greatest heights, even the White House.

But it's hard to imagine a child breaking out of the environment Shylea was trapped in.

Fingers are pointing at "the system" for failing Shylea.

State social workers should have done more to protect her, critics say. But the state is no substitute for responsible parents. Not when there are so many children who lack them.

Three-quarters of the babies in Detroit are born to single mothers, many of them teenagers. Roughly 40,000 babies are born onto this state's welfare rolls each year.

They start life poor, in a community whose safety net is strained by too many women having too many babies by too many no-account men.

But this isn't just about poverty. Poor parents can give their children the values and guidance necessary for a decent life.

The house my mother brought me home to as a newborn had three tiny rooms and no running water. I keep a photograph of it in my office to remind me of her determination, sacrifice and love.

It's not just about love, either. Most mothers love their children.

But they have to love them enough not only to lift them up, but to swat them down when they need it. They've got to love children enough not to have ones they are incapable of raising.

And they have to love them enough to be a good example.

I was at a restaurant the other day when a woman walked in wearing a T-shirt with a cheery Winnie the Pooh image on the front.

When she turned around to leave, I saw the back of the shirt, which bore the inscription, F--- U 2. And she climbed into a car filled with children.

As much as anything, that T-shirt symbolizes for me something seriously broken in our culture, when a mother doesn't have the barest sense of appropriateness or recognition that what children see, they do.

You can make anything of yourself in this country, no matter how you start life.

But having a good mother makes everything a lot easier. ⚔ ⚔ ⚔

May 13, 2012

Welcome, kid. Here's your bill

Someone must have enrolled my extended family in the Baby of the Month Club.

So far this year, we've said hey to Solomon, Seth, Ethan, Derek, Ali, Mason, Parker, Bryce, Micah Cole and, just last week, the lovely Addison Leigh.

What to get all these new arrivals? How about a bill for $50,000?

That's their individual share of the national debt that we've been stoking for decades, just waiting for these newcomers to show up and pay it off.

Well, somebody has to. This is real money owed to real lenders, and most of us won't live long enough to see the mortgage stamped "Paid in Full," even if we were inclined to make a few payments.

When I was born a decade after the end of World War II, my piece of the national debt totaled $1,600, a modest sum considering the lingering war obligations and the massive expenditures required for rebuilding Europe and Asia. When my children were born in the 1980s, their liability was notably larger, but a still manageable $4,000 each.

But then my generation got a hold of the national credit card and wielded it with our special "have now, pay later" mentality. There was nothing we felt the nation couldn't afford as long as someone was willing to loan us the money.

Someday, we promised, we'd quit spending and let our inevitable growth pay for what we'd borrowed. But not yet.

No wonder Addison and her cousins bawl so much. Before the first dollar has been saved for their college education, we've placed them in hock for an amount greater than the cost of four years' tuition at the average Michigan public university.

And these babies don't even get a diploma. They didn't get squat for their bill.

They didn't get the Social Security checks, and probably won't.

They didn't get the cash for clunkers, the attic insulation, the free cellphones, the solar panel subsidies, tickets to the Bureaucrats Ball in Las Vegas or any of the other things their parents and grandparents felt they needed so badly that it was worth borrowing from the Chinese to buy them.

America may have some assets left by the time these kids reach adulthood, but it's just as likely that most of the things that were truly worthy of investment will have been auctioned away to pay off Beijing.

I squint at the photos of the squadron of new babies, looking in their faces for glimpses of grandparents they'll never meet.

There's a good chance I won't see their children and grandchildren.

Each generation makes decisions that have impact far down the chain of life. You may not know which of your forebears made the critical choice that caused you to be born in Iowa instead of Ireland.

But we can't pretend we don't understand the burden that our reckless financial decisions are placing on these fresh Americans whose chins we're chucking, and on all the ones after them.

March 10, 2013

Ugh, Happy Birthday to me

Math was my worst subject in school, but lately my head is filled with arithmetic.

Blame it on another birthday, which today takes me undeniably from mid-50s to late-50s, and has got me counting.

Two more birthdays will lead me in to a new decade, one whose name I can't speak.

Seven more to official retirement age. Another 12 years and I hit the biblically allotted three score and ten. And just 17 more birthdays will take me to the age of my mother when she died, the dissonant chords of dementia already playing in her brain.

It's not just addition that preoccupies me. I subtract, too. As in, "Let's see, he died at 68, that's just 10 years older than me, for goodness sake."

Worse are the negative numbers—last week, everyone in the obituaries of my hometown paper was younger than I am.

So it's another birthday panic attack. No sound sets me on edge more than that of a ticking clock. It's hereditary, I guess. My mother threw herself across her bed when she turned 40 and stayed there sobbing the entire day.

I don't necessarily crave longevity. When my doctor says his goal is to keep me alive till I'm 90, I tell him to back off the medicine a bit because I'm not sure my savings will last that long.

But I'm part of a generation that viewed youth as an entitlement and is just now acknowledging that aging is inevitable. Middle-aged turns into senior citizen turns into elderly. Like it or not.

I made peace with my own mortality long ago, accepting the temporal reality of this life. I know there are things I won't see that I once assumed I'd witness: Man on Mars, a cure for cancer, a balanced federal budget.

So it's not the dying that rattles me, it's the dwindling toward death. The loss of faculties, functions, relevance.

My mother was just 73 when her mind began to slip. It was a heartbreaking thing to witness her go from vibrancy to confusion in what seemed like a matter of months.

To think that I might have just 15 more years of clarity stops me cold. I don't want three more decades, only to spend half of them in a fog.

Tell me I can stay fit and lucid until I'm 80, but I have to check out on that birthday and I'll sign on the dotted line, no questions asked.

Most people would interpret this as a moment of epiphany, and scurry to take inventory and make life changes before it's too late. But that's not me.

I've always suspected the pursuit of a balanced life is just an excuse to get out of work. And I like to work. But there may be room for tweaks. Like doing some things to assure there's a good crowd at my funeral, and that they mostly say nice things.

Or spending more time hunting ducks and less watching "Duck Dynasty." Putting more hours in with a book in my lap and fewer with the remote control tucked under my chin.

And devoting less mental energy to counting days and more to counting blessings.

April 18, 2013
Why press ignored Philly doctor's trial

For the past 18 days, the wizards at the University of Michigan Mott Children's Hospital have been working their magic to give my newest grandson the opportunity to live.

Born five weeks early and with a misshapen heart, Jaxson Wade Short is here thanks to the skills and dedication of surgeons, cardiologists and a team of neo-natal doctors and nurses who won't accept anything less than his survival.

They are fighting just as hard to enable the other babies who share his unit, and who, like him, would have been doomed 25 years ago, to go home in their parents' arms to await death.

This personal drama plays out at the same time the controversy rages over why the national media ignored the murder trial of Philadelphia abortion doctor Kermit Gosnell. Gosnell is charged in the deaths of one woman and seven babies in a filthy clinic where, the prosecution says, unspeakable things happened to babies born more viable than Jaxson and his tiny suitemates.

The reason a media obsessed with sensational trials took a pass on this one is obvious. Gosnell's house of horrors doesn't fit the narrative that allows us to think of abortion as a choice rather than an act.

I'm pro-choice because I believe there is nothing more tragic than an unwanted child. But I'm pro-choice in the same way I'm pro-Second Amendment—just as I believe the right to bear arms is subject to reasonable restrictions, some limits can be imposed on abortion rights without trampling the freedom to choose.

But choice advocates, like their counterparts in the gun lobby, fear—perhaps justifiably—that accepting any regulation opens the door to an outright ban.

So we base policies on the discredited premise that while all parents are suspect, all abortion doctors can be trusted, resulting in the absurdity that a teenager who needs parental permission to buy aspirin can get an abortion without those responsible for her well-being ever knowing.

We turn our eyes from the barbarity of partial-birth and late-term abortions lest we have to deal with the uncomfortable reality that a fetus, left undisturbed, eventually becomes a baby.

Not thinking too hard about that lets us make the intellectually bereft declaration that life begins when a mother decides to carry the baby to term, and until then a baby is not a baby, but rather a "cluster of cells," to use the latest sanitized terminology.

Covering the Gosnell trial would force us to confront qualms that aren't acceptable to have today. Like why a doctor in one place works frantically and at tremendous expense to keep alive an at-risk baby, and in another place a doctor destroys a much hardier, healthier baby with the snip of his scissors.

I didn't consider that contradiction until I watched Jaxson's miracle workers in the U-M neo-natal intensive care unit. While I still support choice, I believe that responsibility demands the choice be made early and carried out humanely.

It ought to be OK to be something less than an absolutist on abortion rights without being considered a religious rube or woman hater. But it isn't. You're either all in or all out.

And that's why the press seats in the Philadelphia courtroom were mostly empty until reporters were shamed into covering the trial by an intense social media lobbying campaign—and why we refuse to adopt safeguards to protect women and babies from monsters like Gosnell.

Chapter 11

Terror & War

September 16, 2001

America must define its war correctly to stamp out terrorist threat

War is a muscular word, particularly when spoken by a nation with the military might of the United States.

Drawn into battle, America's arsenal of weapons and warriors can inflict unspeakable horrors.

Our leaders in the days since Tuesday's terror have described the attacks as an act of war and promised to wage war on all responsible. As horrible as the consequences are to contemplate, war is our only choice.

War means defining enemies and objectives. So far, we've been fuzzy on both. Are our enemies limited to those directly responsible for these attacks and those who gave them support?

In that case, this war will have no lasting consequence, because it won't accomplish the primary objective of any war the United States enters—to protect the American way of life and keep its people safe. Wiping out one band of terrorists won't meet that objective.

Our leaders have also talked of bringing those responsible to justice. That's contradictory language. Is this a battle or a prosecution? You don't bring enemies to justice, you bring them to their knees. Different evidentiary standards apply in war than in the courtroom. You kill first, prove your case later. Combat is not done with arrest warrants, but with commando squads.

Nor do you wage war on individuals. War is made on political entities and the ideology that drives them.

That means this war won't be won by dragging the perpetrators into court—or even into an electric chair—and strafing their sponsors with bombs.

Victory can't be declared unless, when the smoke clears, the Taliban is gone forever from Afghanistan, Saddam Hussein is finally dispatched from Iraq, Muammar Khadafy is dragged from Libya, and the political leaders of any country that fosters terrorism are destroyed and their people liberated.

Comparisons have been made this week to Pearl Harbor. That's a good reference point. After Pearl Harbor, the United States rallied to stamp out fascism. Nothing in this country returned to normal until the goal was met.

This time, the ideological enemy is Islamic extremism and the threat it poses to democracy and the civilized world. Nothing should return to normal until every regime controlled by purveyors of that evil ideology are toppled.

Only then will we be safe from the enemy that struck Tuesday. Only then can we say we have protected our way of life.

America's objective is not vengeance, though there's no shame in craving revenge for the bloodiest day on American soil since the Civil War. Nor is it punishment, though a price must be paid by those who so drastically altered not only the skyline of New York, but the psyche of the American people.

The noble goal of this war is preserving what America means, our ability to move about with unrestricted freedom, secure in our own borders. President George W. Bush spoke of a "quiet anger" gripping the country. Anger is the right emotion.

We will need anger to sustain us in this fight, to shout down those who will insist the job is done once we arrest a handful of terrorists, drop a few bombs, and fortify our airports.

The job won't be done until every nest of terrorism everywhere in the world is smashed.

That's what the word war should mean this time.

≺ ≺ ≺

October 14, 2001

America must not equivocate on how it defines terrorism or it will lose war

What exactly is terrorism? That may seem like an odd question, coming barely a month after Terrorism Live.

Most of the civilized world, as well as most of those parts of the world whose claim on civilization is tenuous, agree that the 9/11 assaults meet the terrorist criteria.

Even Yasser Arafat, whose resume as head of the Palestinian movement is written in blood, called such terrorism "a danger to humanity and to the sacred human right to life," and called for its destruction.

Next question: Is it terrorism when a Palestinian fanatic straps a dynamite pack to his chest and blows up himself and a disco filled with Israeli teens?

Now fewer heads nod in agreement. Some argue that the serial murders of Israeli civilians don't qualify as terrorism because they are a legitimate resistance to a repressive occupation. Distinctions have to be made, they say, between evil terrorism and righteous terrorism.

Ultimately, how that question is answered will determine how far the United States is able to go in achieving its goal of obliterating worldwide terrorism, and how long the delicate coalition between the West and the Muslim world holds together.

Right now, the United States has a green light to destroy Afghanistan's Taliban regime and Osama bin Laden and his al-Qaida network.

But while a wide range of voices, from George W. Bush to Bill Clinton, have hinted the war on terrorism won't stop there, not many will say what began in Afghanistan must finish on the West Bank.

The United Nations certainly hasn't. It continues to struggle to define terrorism and has suggested a conference on the subject. The last time the UN held a conference—the recent gathering on racism—it turned into a festival of anti-Semitism. Don't expect much better from a terrorism symposium.

The United States, for all its fist shaking at terrorists, is also timid when it comes to those who target Israel. When Bush ordered a freeze on assets of terrorist organizations, the Hamas, Hezbollah and Islamic Jihad outfits weren't on the list.

The United States also held its tongue last week when Syria, on the unanimous vote of Arab members, gained a seat on the UN Security Council. That's the same

Syria that has provided aid and comfort to the terrorist groups targeting Israel.

Syria is pressing for a definition of terrorism that excludes assaults on Jews in Israel or classifies Israeli military responses to those murders as terrorism as well.

The U.S., no matter how much it needs its Muslim allies, can never buy such a definition.

This is a war with high moral overtones. If it is immoral to slaughter innocents in the World Trade Center, then it is equally immoral to blow apart families in a Tel Aviv pizza shop.

If the United States equivocates on that basic truth, it loses much of the moral justification for this war.

Indications are the strong show of force against the Taliban is making an impression on the tormentors of Israel. Arafat has at last loosed his police forces to disperse extremist protesters and is attempting to enforce a cease-fire agreement.

That's progress that can be built on, but only if America makes it crystal clear that it accepts only one definition of terrorism.

September 30, 2001
As long as evil exists in world, Americans will have to fight

The morning after George W. Bush delivered his speech for history, I stopped by Livonia Franklin High School to watch my son help emcee a homecoming pep rally.

It was everything you'd expect of such an event—marching bands, cheer-leaders, spirit drums and hundreds of kids screaming indecipherable war cries until their already painted faces turned red. Joyous bedlam.

Standing in that gym, still struggling with the emotions stirred by the president's words, two thoughts nearly wasted me. The first, that if war does come, this is what we'll be fighting for—these kids and a world in which their biggest worry is thumping a homecoming rival in a football game.

And then the second: If war comes, these kids, or others like them, will be doing the fighting.

When you have a child—or grandchild, sister, brother, niece, nephew—of fighting age, the cost-benefit analysis of war becomes very personal.

America does not sacrifice its children lightly. That's why, despite our tremendous military power, we limit our wars to repelling domestic threats or restoring peace and justice to the world's dark reaches.

Knowing war means body bags filled with our own sons and daughters is why, even now that we've been viciously attacked within our borders, voices of pacificism are raised.

Advocates of a nonmilitary response would rather focus on bulking up security than stamping out the terrorist threat. They'd pay tribute to terrorists in the form of increased American aid to barbarous regimes and would abandon our ally Israel. They'd prefer to cower behind barriers that can never be high enough to protect ourselves or our children. Anything to avoid a fight.

I can't criticize them—as I said, I have a soon-to-be 18-year-old son. Like any parent, I'd rather fight a thousand battles myself than commit him to one. I'd far prefer watching him on a soccer field to worrying about him on a battlefield.

We have pledged ourselves to raising nonviolent children. We have preached conflict resolution, peaceful solutions, hugs not tugs. Good messages, but now I worry we've forgotten to teach them something else: Sometimes you simply do have to fight.

America's freedom was won with blood and preserved with blood for 225 years. It should not be like that, but freedom is one of the things that evil can't abide, and as long as there is evil in the world, Americans will have to fight.

So I spend more time now talking to my son about the obligations that come with freedom, about the sacrifices of patriots past, hoping he'll understand that it is better to die free than live enslaved to tyranny.

Ancient American lessons, harder for someone of the Vietnam generation to teach.

During World War II, my grandmother walked each afternoon to her little country church to pray for her four sons fighting in places she'd never heard of before. I can't imagine the burden she carried. Nor do I welcome the possibility that her sleepless nights soon could be mine.

We don't want to send our children to war. We want to send them off to college, careers, and future families. That's the way it works in an ideal world. But if the world was ideal before Sept. 11, it certainly isn't now.

And the only way to make things right again is to once more watch our children march off toward danger and death.

No wonder we're so angry.

December 8, 2002

It's time to talk honestly about who the enemy is in war to end terror

The Bush administration might find more support for broadening the war if it would stop tiptoeing around naming the enemy.

Since 9/11, the administration has stuck stubbornly to defining this as a war on terrorism. But terrorism isn't an enemy, it's a weapon employed by an enemy to accomplish its aims. In World War II, we weren't at war with Panzers and Zeros; we were at war with German fascism and Japanese imperialism.

This time, the enemy is a similar evil ideology—radical Islamism—and it's time for George W. Bush to say so.

If he doesn't, he's likely to continue meeting resistance to taking the war into Iraq, and after that into the other places America will likely have to go to crush the extremists committed to our destruction.

Americans now believe the war begins and ends with the al-Qaida outlaw outfit, and victory depends on lifting the head of Osama bin Laden. But if bin Laden were killed or captured tomorrow, and all his henchmen rounded up, Americans would be only marginally safer from terrorism.

Al-Qaida is not a rogue group of evildoers, loosely inspired. It is one unit of a much larger and fiercely dedicated army. That army is made up of Islamist radicals already in control of Iran and vying for dominance in a host of other countries, including Saudi Arabia, Turkey, Pakistan and Indonesia. The enemy is aided financially and physically by Arab nationalists like Saddam Hussein, who share its goal of cleansing the Middle East of Western influences.

That's the terrorism link to Iraq and why Saddam must be dealt with. Instead of explaining that link to the American people and getting down to business, Bush bases his case for invasion on violations of past United Nations resolutions, leading to the current inspections charade. Who knows how long it will be now before Saddam is gone and our sights can be turned to the next target?

The administration has worked hard at using semantics to cloud the mission. Early on, Bush identified the terrorist targets as those "with global reach." That gave him an escape clause from dealing with Palestinian terrorists, who confine their murders to Jews in Israel.

But that name-gamesmanship is crumbling. Al-Qaida is believed to be responsible for the bombing earlier this month of an Israeli-owned tourist hotel in Kenya, acting in the name of its fellow extremists on the West

Bank. That surely qualifies the Palestinian terrorists for the global reach Bush demands.

But just as Bush has been reluctant to tag the Islamist movement with the responsibility for terror, he has resisted connecting the Palestinians to their spiritual brothers in al-Qaida. The followers of Yasser Arafat are every bit as deadly as those of bin Laden. But while we chase bin Laden, we negotiate with Arafat.

Clearly, the administration doesn't want to offend the Muslim world by speaking forcefully against their extremists. Enough walking on eggshells. In war, feelings get hurt. And in truth, Islamist radicals present the greatest threat to the Muslim majority in the Middle East who want to live, work and raise their families in a modern, peaceful and civilized society.

Cloaking war in political correctness is not a strategy for victory. Bush loses nothing by clearly defining the enemy and then moving swiftly to defeat it.

August 24, 2003

To achieve peace, all-out war on terrorism is only path in Middle East

With the blood of its children running through the streets of Jerusalem, Israel has no choice but to crumple the road map to peace and instead draft a battle plan for combatting terrorism.

Any hope for a political solution to the violence in the Middle East vanished in the bus bombing Tuesday, which killed 20 and maimed scores of others, many of them children.

Television cameras showed the surviving youngsters, screaming and blood-smeared, stumbling away from the horrific carnage.

Terrorist groups Hamas and Islamic Jihad competed for credit. There's only one way to deal with those who find glory in slaughtering children: Kill them. The bomber's wife said her husband died fulfilling his dream of martyrdom. The man had two kids of his own, and yet his life's dream was to die killing other people's children.

You can't negotiate with that level of ignorance, hatred and religious insanity.

Yet Israel, at the insistence of the United States, has come to the bargaining table. It has offered extraordinary concessions in the name of peace and taken good faith steps, including dismantling settlements and pulling back troops.

But the peace process has failed again, for the same reason it always fails. The Palestinians are wed to terrorism, and real peace cannot be bargained with a terrorist state.

So Israel has no choice but to seek a military solution, to roll its tanks again across the West Bank and Gaza Strip.

Palestinians blame their violence on Israel's oppression and brutality. But the truth is that Israel has not been brutal enough in the face of terror. Its answer is surgical strikes, targeted assassinations and a catch-and-release prisoner policy.

Meanwhile, terrorist chieftain Yasser Arafat sits unmolested in Ramallah, and the leaders of the terrorist networks hold press conferences and rally crowds in village streets.

Always, Israel's fist is restrained by the United States.

But to end the violence, Israel must strike with terrible force. To be blunt, the Palestinians must be brought to their knees, made to feel the pain of allowing terrorists to act in their name.

The path taken in President George W. Bush's road map to peace did just the opposite. It started the Palestinians toward statehood without forcing them to unstrap their bombs.

Prime Minister Mahmoud Abbas, Arafat's puppet, says he risks civil war by disarming the terrorists. He must be warned that war is coming for certain if he doesn't.

In past Middle East wars, Israel was reined in before it could achieve its final objectives. The conditions are different today. Egypt is a mess. Iraq is gone. Jordan and Saudi Arabia are not in America's pocket. And there's no Soviet Union to pressure the United States to intervene.

So Israel has a golden opportunity to launch its own version of a shock and awe campaign. It can drive the terrorists out of the territories, eliminate the threat from the Syrian-hosted Hezbollah along the Lebanon border and, if Iran chooses to join the fight, good—another problem checked off the list.

Israeli Prime Minister Ariel Sharon has played Washington's game. He's reached across the table, spoken words of conciliation, and restrained his fury in the face of horrible provocation.

It's time to let Sharon be Sharon. He's a warrior. And bringing peace to the Middle East is now a warrior's job.

↞ ↞ ↞

November 27, 2005

Debating strategy for war is not an insult to our troops

Listen to the Bush administration's renewed defense of the war in Iraq and you hear a terribly offensive message creeping through: If you don't support our war, you don't support our troops.

Keep the troops out of this debate. Soldiers don't make the decision to go to war, politicians do. Nor do the troops on the battlefield have much say in how the war is executed, how resources are deployed or how long the conflict will last.

Speaking out against a bad war is no slight to the troops. In fact, sparing them from being sacrificed to a questionable cause is the best support you could give them.

The Iraq war and where it's headed should be vigorously debated, dissenting voices should be heard, and a better defense of administration policies should be offered than if you criticize us, you're betraying the troops.

I supported the start of the war for reasons that went well beyond the fear that Saddam Hussein had weapons of mass destruction.

Saddam was a chronic menace to his own people, his neighbors and the rest of the world, including America. The fight against radical Islam eventually had to come to his doorstep.

The goals of the mission are still sound, even without the finding of horrific weapons stockpiles. A free Iraq would help stabilize the most volatile and threatening region of the world.

But the Bush administration has made too many mistakes in this war.

It went to battle with a political strategy, rather than a military one. Hoping not to offend the hypersensitive Arab states, it brought too little muscle to get the job done.

The weak deployment opened Iraq to outside troublemakers, who poured through unguarded borders and into Baghdad and Fallujah.

America's strategy was to treat the Iraqis as a liberated people, when it should have considered Iraq a conquered nation and its people enemies until they proved themselves otherwise.

So now the broader war against Islamic extremists is at the mercy of a ragged band of lunatics who are effectively preoccupying a good piece of the United States military machine.

Such shabby military strategy can be criticized without disrespecting those in the field who are carrying out the strategy.

I don't advocate pulling out of Iraq. At this point, we'd leave behind the potential for a more dangerous mess than even Saddam could have created.

But we ought to be talking freely about the strategy for wrapping up the conflict and returning Iraq to the Iraqis.

That conversation can't be shouted down by the bogus reasoning that to question the politicians is to insult the troops.

Following that argument, once America commits soldiers to combat, the justification for war can never be challenged.

This is not Vietnam. Americans no longer blame soldiers for the mistakes of politicians. We can have a good, enlightening debate about why we're in Iraq, and how and when we get out, without doing harm to our troops or their morale.

January 3, 2010
We lack the will to fight terror

There's a whole lot of truth in al-Qaida's taunting of America's ability to safeguard itself.

Even though the bomb on Flight 253 fizzled in the lap of its pathetic Nigerian carrier, the terrorist outfit claimed victory because it fully exposed America's vulnerability.

"He managed to penetrate all devices and modern advanced technology and security checkpoints in international airports …" the group declared, "… and defying the large myth of American and international intelligence, and exposing how fragile they are, bringing their nose to the ground, and making them regret all what they spent on security technology."

That's not just chest-thumping by the insane mullah posse.

It's what it is. We've spent billions since September 11 and all we've done is create another pork-peddling bureaucracy called the Homeland Security Department.

Al-Qaida's description of our intelligence as "fragile" is too kind. It's inept. Information doesn't move well between agencies and barely moves at all from the intelligence gatherers to the security forces.

That's evident in both this attack—the warning from the terrorist's dad never made it into the flight screening system—and in the Ft. Hood massacre, where worrisome e-mails picked up by the snoops weren't shared with the Army.

President Barack Obama's response is a promise of more rigorous screening using more advanced equipment. Who's he kidding? Not al-Qaida. It knows we're more worried about stepping on toes than about rooting out terrorists.

Go to the airport right now and you'll see 80-year-old women being patted down from their knickers to their noggins because their artificial hip joints set off the metal detector. But Ulmar Farouk Abdulmutallab, whose name is on a terror watch list and who began his trip to the United States from a terrorist hotbed, was able to waltz on board unmolested.

We're paranoid of profiling. Remember the six Muslim imams who were yanked off a U.S. Airways flight three years ago after passengers became concerned about their bizarre behavior? Only one of the six had luggage, all were on one-way tickets, and they seemed intentionally provocative.

U.S. Airways responded, and was thanked with a federal discrimination complaint. Other airlines have faced similar discipline. Don't underestimate how that dampens their enthusiasm for dealing with suspicious passengers.

Obama is conflicted on terrorism. He won't call it a war, and even has trouble choking out the word terrorist. He prefers to treat them as any other criminal.

That's why Abdulmutallab is sitting in a cozy federal jail cell today instead of in a cold, dark room with Britney Spears songs blaring at him until he coughs up some information.

We don't have the will to protect ourselves from terrorists. And al-Qaida knows it. Sooner or later, that knowledge will result in another airplane crashing to the ground.

January 14, 2010
Support our troops: Free the Navy SEALs

If President Barack Obama wants to establish his credibility as a terror fighter, he should issue preemptory pardons to Matthew McCabe, Jonathan Keefe and Julio Huertas.

The three Navy SEALs were deployed in Iraq last summer when they were given a very dangerous assignment—a common occurrence for SEALs. They were asked to track down a most despicable and dangerous character, Ahmed

Hashim Abed, who is believed to have kidnapped and killed four American security contractors in Fallujah, mutilated their bodies and hung them from an overpass.

McCabe, Keefe and Huertas accomplished their mission. But when they brought in Abed, who was lucky he didn't arrive carrying his head under his arm, the terrorist whined about being roughed up by the SEALs—a punch in the gut, a bloody lip. On the strength of the terrorist's statement, the Navy brought charges against the three. The trials were supposed to start next week, but may be moved to Iraq so Abed can testify.

In terms of war crimes, what the SEALs did—if they did it—is the equivalent of running a stop sign. The prosecution of the SEALs speaks again to America's wrong-headed approach to combatting terror and the absurdity of treating war as if it were an episode of *Law and Order*.

We are placing young men and women in extraordinarily intense, life-threatening combat situations in the most dangerous places in the world. And we expect them to behave as if they were cops patrolling a suburban neighborhood. Say "yes sir" and "yes ma'am" and don't forget to read 'em their rights.

A reflexive action during an out-of-control situation could land any of these good soldiers in prison. We send them out in pursuit of a madman who slices up Americans and expect them to completely control their emotions and tempers. If they slip, we arrest our own men and allow the butcher to stand witness against them. Is this what we call supporting our troops?

In a documentary I watched last year about World War II's Pacific Theater, soldiers offered first-hand accounts of the battlefield executions of Japanese prisoners. The captured couldn't be transported behind the lines because of the ferocity of the fighting. The killing was accepted as a necessary evil of war. I wonder if the Greatest Generation could have waged its epic battle under today's rules.

War is hell, and hellish things happen in combat. We used to understand that. Now we fret about the tender sensibilities of our enemies and treat our own soldiers as if they were the bad guys.

Similarly, the terror agnostics are calling for the heads of CIA agents, State Department operatives and White House lawyers who carried out Bush administration policies on detained terrorists. Those who participated in the so-called torture of captured terrorists, who arranged their transfers to interrogation camps or advised the Bush White House on the legality of what it was doing face the prospect of life-ruining prosecution.

These were folks who thought they were doing their jobs, operating in unchartered waters, believing they were serving their country. And their reward may be a prison sentence.

Our hyper-vigilance against our own terror warriors will only cause them to be less vigorous in their missions and to second-guess every move they make.

This ain't no way to fight a war.

Obama can show he gets that by calling the dogs off the SEALs.

February 21, 2010

New strategy sacrifices troops

Every American soldier should be pulled out of Afghanistan today. It's immoral to commit our troops—our children—to a war without doing everything possible to protect their lives.

That's not happening in Afghanistan.

The politicians and generals have decided to make the safety of Afghan citizens a higher priority than avoiding American deaths and injuries.

They call it a "hearts and minds" strategy, meaning that if the military objectives can be accomplished without inflicting suffering on the civilian population, the people will be more willing to cooperate in defeating the Taliban.

There's no evidence that Afghan civilians are warming to the approach. But there is concern that it is costing American lives.

Lara M. Dadkhan, an intelligence analyst writing in the *New York Times* last week, detailed the effect of a new policy from commanding Gen. Stanley McChrystal to use air strikes and long-range artillery under "very limited and prescribed conditions."

Air support is used to soften targets and provide cover for advancing troops. But Dadkhan contends under the new policy, troops must wait for help from the air and artillery while the civilian impact is weighed.

In one instance cited by Dadkhan, marines last September in the Kunar Province called for air support when they came under fire while searching for a weapons cache. Their request was rejected out of concern for civilians.

An hour after their call for help, the marines, pinned down and running out of ammunition, were finally backed up by helicopters. Four marines and nine Afghan allies were killed, and 22 others wounded.

The Taliban has been quick to exploit our sensitivity to civilian damage. Both U.S. and Afghan troops told the Associated Press that insurgents are using civilians as human shields, placing them on the rooftops of the buildings they're firing from.

New reports from the military also note the emergence of deadly Taliban snipers, who are inflicting great pain on U.S. troops and are able to more freely operate without the worry of air strikes.

Civilian casualties are an inevitable and regrettable cost of war. They ought to be avoided whenever possible. But it's not always possible when the lives of Americans are at stake. Harry Truman rained down hellfire on Japan's civilian population to spare the lives of a half-million allied troops.

He wasn't worried about Japanese resentment. He was trying to avoid sending any more "We regret to inform you ..." letters.

Maybe our kinder, gentler warfare will soothe the Afghan people.

But if it results in higher U.S. troop deaths and injuries, it will lose the hearts and minds of the American people, who have every reason to expect their government to value the lives of their soldiers—their children—more than a PR campaign to win over the people our troops are dying for.

September 9, 2011

10 years later, Sept. 11 hasn't changed U.S. all that much

Everything was supposed to change after Sept. 11. The terrorist attacks were to be the seismic event that would alter America and Americans in ways good and bad, refocusing our priorities, distorting our attitudes and behaviors and engaging us in a united battle for survival.

It hasn't worked out that way. As a truly transformative experience, Sept. 11 sort of fizzled.

Yes, it's more of a hassle to get on an airplane. But while we may pay more attention to our fellow passengers, we haven't significantly switched our traveling habits.

That's true of nearly every aspect of American life that was supposed to be radically reshaped by Sept. 11.

We were sure the attacks would make us more wary, less trustful of our neighbors, skittish about being in large crowds. And yet this coming weekend, on the 10th anniversary of Sept. 11, football stadiums will be packed. Fans may face a higher level of security, but they'll still take their seats. We aren't cowering in our homes.

Credit that to good work on the part of our government and our allies, who have thwarted terrorist plots and kept the heat on al-Qaida. To truly impact behavior, terrorist attacks must come in waves, as they do in Israel.

Aside from the Fort Hood massacre, our tormentors have failed to land another major blow. So we go about our daily lives much the same as we always have.

The doubters of the American character were certain we would turn on Muslim-Americans.

Islamaphobia didn't materialize

A few nut-balls have exploited Sept. 11. But the vast majority of Americans rejected divisiveness. Proof: Seven years after the attacks, we elected a president with the name Barack Hussein Obama.

There was hope Sept. 11 would put an end to our internal squabbling and bring us together as a people against a common foe. That lasted through a few choruses of "God Bless America," and then we were back at each other's throats.

The war on terror deepened our divides as we debated its merits, and gave rise to a more potent strain of partisanship.

Unity still eludes us, and that may not be all bad. Preserving our right to fight among ourselves, to dissent, to challenge the prevailing opinion is as important to our viability as is patriotism.

Are we more patriotic? Somewhat, perhaps. We support out troops—it says so on our bumper stickers. And certainly for the soldiers and their families, life will never be the same. For the rest of us, evidence that we are a nation at war is scant. How have we sacrificed?

While our soldiers fight and die, we indulge ourselves with frivolous pursuits, preferring the faux drama of reality TV to keeping track of the real life-and-death struggles in Iran and Afghanistan.

The biggest expected threat was to our civil liberties. Have we given up some of our freedoms to the war on terror? Yes. But fewer than we did to the war on drugs.

Privacy has suffered. But privacy in the age of Facebook seems a quaint notion.

In truth, the economic meltdown of 2008 changed us more than Sept. 11 did. The erosion of financial security altered our attitudes and assumptions in ways the threat to national security hasn't.

Job losses, foreclosures, plunging home values and vanishing retirement accounts forced us to change our lifestyles, broke our faith in our institutions and placed our presumption to world leadership in doubt.

The Sept. 11 terrorists could have only hoped to wreak such havoc.

Sept. 11 hasn't changed us, at least not much. And that's a good way to define victory in the war on terror.

January 11, 2015

Coddling Islam fueled Paris attack

Part of the entrance fee into a free society is acceptance that while you have the right to believe as you choose, you have no right to expect others will share or even respect those beliefs.

No one should expect to come to a new place and say, "I'm here now, so you change who you are to accommodate me." Newcomers can and certainly do add beneficial cultural layers to a diverse society. But when they demand that their new home become just like the one they left, it sets up inevitable clashes.

Paris saw the most deadly version of that dynamic last week, when two armed Islamic radicals stormed through the offices of a satirical newspaper and murdered 12 people. The jihadists claimed to be avenging the Prophet Muhammad, a frequent target of the publication's cartoonists and writers.

Much of the content of the *Charlie Hebdo* newspaper is vile and disgusting. It features grotesque drawings and inflammatory, irreverent articles that often appear at the most inappropriate times.

It is an equal opportunity offender with a particular fondness for skewering religion, targeting Muslims, Christians and Jews alike. But it is most relentless in poking Islam, likely because that's where it gets the greatest reaction. Satirists have no fun if their victims don't howl.

As a result, *Charlie Hebdo* staffers have been under a continuous death threat and its offices were firebombed in 2011. And yet it has never backed down. That's a show of journalistic courage rare today.

The newspaper, as crude as it is, understands what too few do: Bowing to bullies and acquiescing to their irrational demands only invites more of the same.

Europe has spent much of the past two decades frantically trying to avoid conflict with its growing Muslim population. It has tried to shield them from insult, bent its rules so they wouldn't have to assimilate to European norms, allowed them to live separate from mainstream society, ignored their anti-Semitism and welcomed their religion into the public square.

And still it constantly harbors the fear that even the slightest offense will invite another terrorist bombing. When courage is demanded, it cowers.

In 2006, when Danish cartoonist Kurt Wetergaard was targeted by Islamic radicals for drawing images of Muhammad in an archaic affront to the religion, most European newspapers refused to reprint the cartoons, afraid they would provoke more violence. (Most American publications, including this one, refused as well, to our shame.)

Every newspaper in the free world should have published those cartoons, which were a legitimate news item and well within our standards of good taste. Instead, we granted Islam a concession we wouldn't consider for any other religion.

I wonder if last week's rampage would have happened if *Charlie Hebdo* weren't so alone in its willingness to goad Islam. If the press took off the kid gloves and treated Islam the way it does Christianity and Judaism, would the target have been too big? That's what should happen coming out of this tragedy. It's the only way to honor the martyred journalists. ⚮

Chapter 12

The
Middle East

February 23, 2003

America can march or fight,
but only fighting will secure freedom

Millions are filling the world's streets to implore the United States to turn away from war with Iraq. Better if they marched and chanted against the terrorists and their masters.

Some of the protesters are even planning to go to Baghdad, where they will place themselves as human shields in front of the likely targets of a military strike. Better if they go to Jerusalem and strap themselves to city buses in hopes of deterring the homicide bombers.

The same New York streets now hosting picket signs denigrating President George W. Bush as a power-crazed cowboy were, 18 months ago, overflowing with teary-eyed residents who cheered "Get the bastards!" as the president's motorcade rolled by.

What did we think getting the bastards meant? Where did we think the war on terrorism would take us when we declared it with such passion after the towers fell? Didn't we understand it would be a long and bloody battle?

America has never won peace or security without fighting, and it won't this time.

Protesters blame terrorism on the victims of terror. But terrorism is not rooted in U.S. policies or practices. It springs from the twisted blend of politics and religion that poisons too much of the Muslim world. Our safety depends on its destruction.

The apostles of appeasement would answer this threat by throwing up their hands and crying, "Take what you want, just leave us alone." But when has that strategy ever kept the French safe?

At home, while 150,000 of our soldiers are already in the Persian Gulf region awaiting combat, we are preoccupied with the adventures of a dewy "Bachelorette" as she frolics with a couple dozen frivolous boys. Water cooler chatter is all about *American Idol*, rather than the American heroes preparing to sacrifice so much for our freedom.

For moral guidance, we look to Hollywood's recovered, recovering or yet-to-recover addicts and alcoholics. (This is the culture Osama bin Laden is so hell-bent to destroy?)

We've come to accept the inevitability of the unthinkable, that the terrorists will strike again and harder. And we are uncertain whether we should use our might to stop it.

Instead of demanding our government do more to root out and smash the terrorists before they can smash us, we are pleading for more protective barriers at home, buying emergency supplies and fretting about the vulnerability of our houses.

But surely we know, as much as we dread war, that the only way to protect ourselves is to make terrorism so painful for the terrorists that they will abandon the tactic.

The marchers could actually help. They could take their protests and picket signs to the countries that have nurtured and encouraged the terrorists in a show of solidarity with the victims of terror, stating loudly that this practice will not be tolerated and will not work.

Instead, they preach we can be safe if only we don't provoke those who have proved they will kill us without provocation.

Here's a clue for those give-peace-a-chance nostalgists: This is not the 1960s, and Iraq is not Vietnam. It represents a direct danger to our families and our children right here at home.

We can fight, or we can march. Fighting gives us at least a chance of preserving a free and open way of life in America. Marching will lead us quivering into our cocoons of duct tape and plastic wrap.

≺ ≺ ≺

April 13, 2003

Democracy alone won't liberate Iraq; it must learn to love freedom

Witnessing freedom's birth, watching it take its first wobbly steps before breaking into a jubilant run, thrills the heart. People who love liberty love to see others liberated.

That's why Americans were enthralled last week at the scenes from Baghdad, as Iraqis crawled out from under Saddam Hussein's boot heel to dance and weep and cheer in the streets.

We saw the same celebrations last year in Afghanistan, where women emerged from their burqas and home prisons. And before that, in East Berlin and Moscow and other cities of the Soviet regime.

Toppling the statues of oppression never gets old.

But the parties end, and the hard work of rearing freedom to maturity begins. The mortality rate is high.

Already in Afghanistan, extremists are tearing at the fragile, post-Taliban government. The former Soviet republics continue to struggle with corruption and intolerance.

Iraq will have similar growing pains. This war will bring it democracy, for sure. But democracy alone won't guarantee enduring freedom.

Democracies can be subverted by a populist who appeals to the prejudices, fears and hatreds of the electorate. Many of the worst tyrants in modern history, including Adolf Hitler, first came to power in democratic elections.

Democracy must come with a commitment to the values that sustain freedom. If the people of Iraq don't embrace those values, they will surely end up under the thumb of another brute.

Key among those values is a legal system designed to protect individual rights and liberties, and a respect for the rule of that law. The faith in the law must run so deep that it prevails even in the face of political upheaval.

In this country, half the voters felt the 2000 presidential election was stolen through devious political maneuvering. Still, George W. Bush was allowed to peacefully assume office. There were no riots, no rebellion. Despite their discontent, the losers upheld the integrity of the institutions that handed them their defeat.

For democracy to lead to freedom, it also must be inclusive. Majority rule can't become minority oppression. This country continues to struggle with that concept. But the willingness to keep struggling is what sets America and other freedom-loving democracies apart.

Free people also demand free minds and free markets. Dissent must be tolerated and encouraged. It's what keeps the process honest. People must be free to express contrary opinions and worship as they please. If Iraq develops the affection of many in the Middle East for strict Islamic laws and codes, liberty is doomed, particularly for women.

Democracy works best when twinned with capitalism. A financial stake in the system is a powerful incentive for maintaining stability.

Average citizens must have an opportunity to achieve, to accumulate wealth, to strive for a better life for their children. That means government can't control the nation's tremendous natural resources, but rather must use them to encourage entrepreneurship. Some people will get richer than others, but that's OK. That's how democracy works.

Unfortunately, Iraq has poor models for this type of society among its neighbors. But for the great enterprise to liberate Iraq to take hold, it needs more than democracy. It needs a universal commitment to freedom.

February 1, 2004
Questions mount on why U.S. went to war

Those of us who a year ago were passionately advocating the invasion of Iraq now have an obligation to ask the difficult questions about whether the war was justified.

David Kay, the former top U.S. weapons inspector in Iraq, says he finds no evidence of weapons of mass destruction and doubts that stockpiles existed before the invasion. Secretary of State Colin Powell seconds Kay's frank assessment.

Even President George W. Bush no longer says he expects the weapons to be found, though he claims Iraq was a "grave and gathering threat to the security of America." Without chemical, biological or nuclear weapons, it isn't clear how the threat was manifested.

So there are hard questions to ask, and the Bush administration owes detailed answers.

Chief among them is whether this was a failure of intelligence or an intentional effort to mislead. In an interview with the *Detroit News'* editorial board during the 2000 campaign, Bush said "the president must have the best intelligence gathering in order to make the right decision." Last week, Bush said he still has confidence in the intelligence community.

But if that community, both here and abroad, produced evidence of weapons of mass destruction where none existed, why does it merit continued confidence?

During the same 2000 interview, Bush returned time and again to Saddam Hussein, saying at one point, "If we catch Saddam Hussein developing weapons of mass destruction ... we'll take him out." And at another, "Saddam is an issue, and he's a problem."

There was a sense that candidate Bush was preoccupied with the nemesis of his father. It's right now to consider whether as president he was overly eager to interpret the intelligence in a way that justified taking out Saddam.

On the other side of the intelligence equation, what information was Saddam getting? If he didn't have banned weapons, why did he act like he did? Why would he allow his regime to be violently toppled and himself chased into a filthy hidey-hole when all he had to do was welcome the inspectors? Is it possible he believed America was bluffing, even while coalition troops were amassing on his borders?

The other legitimate justification offered for invading Iraq was that Saddam sponsored the al-Qaida terrorists who attacked America on September 11. But Powell says there's no evidence to suggest a direct link between Saddam and Osama bin Laden. Iraq's support for terrorism appears no greater than that of many other countries in the region, including some we consider allies.

And the Iraq invasion distracted from the primary mission of destroying al-Qaida and finding bin Laden.

That leaves enforcing the U.N. resolutions that Saddam habitually flaunted, and liberating the horribly abused Iraqi people as the case for launching an unprovoked attack.

It's a weak argument to say the United States and its partners acted on behalf of the United Nations, when that body opposed the invasion.

Liberation in a region of the world so controlled by a violent and intolerant religion is too uncertain a prospect to risk American lives and resources.

An Islamic democracy is, for the most part, an oxymoron. It remains a long bet that freedom and democratic principles will take hold in Iraq. With the influence of the religious sects and their power-crazed clerics, it's just as likely the Iraqi people will end up enslaved to a different sort of tyranny.

If liberation is a legitimate reason for going to war, then why single out Iraq, and not Iran, North Korea, Cuba, the Sudan or other places where ruthless dictators oppress their people? Why not China?

None of this is to say the outcome in Iraq is without merit. If democracy succeeds there, it will be a stable island of hope in a tumultuous region.

While Saddam may not have been the gathering threat Bush portrays, he surely would have again caused America trouble.

His removal has taken the starch out of some other troublemakers, most notably Libya's Moammar Gadhafi, and deprived the Palestinian terrorists of a sugar daddy.

But if there were no weapons of mass destruction and no collaboration with al-Qaida, then we must ask about both the reasons for the war and its timing.

Those of us who a year ago believed in the reasons offered by the administration have the greatest obligation to ask.

July 23, 2006
Let Israel exercise its right to defense

Now that there's nearly unanimous international agreement that Israel has a right to defend itself, the question becomes: How much "defense" will the world tolerate?

Already, the cries that Israel is wreaking a humanitarian disaster in Lebanon, wantonly killing innocents and destroying homes and infrastructure, are reaching a hysterical pitch. Calls for an immediate cease-fire are coming from all of the usual squeamish corners.

But to halt Israel in its pursuit of Hezbollah before it dismantles the terrorist group's military support network in southern Lebanon and breaks its stranglehold on that country would be to leave Israel and the Lebanese people as vulnerable as they were before the fighting began.

A premature peace must be resisted, for Israel's sake, for Lebanon's sake, and for the sake of the broader war against Islamic extremism. In crushing Hezbollah, Israel is carrying the water of the West and of the moderate Arab regimes, which recognize the growing power and influence of Iran, Syria and their Islamist surrogates threatens their existence as well.

That's why Egypt, Jordan, Saudi Arabia and others in the region for the first time affirmed Israel's right and responsibility to respond to acts of terrorism. And why even the European leaders finally dropped their thoroughly discredited moral equivalency stance and put the blame for Middle East violence where it belongs, on the terrorists.

As always, the devil is in the details. Exactly how far will Israel be allowed to go to ensure its safety? When the smoke clears, Israel must have a wide buffer between itself and Hezbollah's Iranian supplied rockets. If Lebanon can't guarantee that safe space, then Israel must be free to do it itself. The current fighting has revealed that Hezbollah is armed with missiles far more powerful than previously thought. That makes pushing it back essential to Israel's defense.

There also must be sign-off on Israel's need to separate itself from the hostiles on its borders. Israel is the most precariously positioned country in the world, nearly surrounded by those openly committed to its destruction.

Compounding the hazard is Israel's tiny size. It's less than one-sixth the area of Michigan, with roughly the same amount of people. The enemy is always within shooting distance. If nothing else, we have relearned during the past two weeks that as long as there are Jews in the Middle East, someone will try to kill them.

Israel should not be denied any tool that will keep out the would-be murderers, including and especially the security fence.

And most vital for defensive purposes, there must be recognition that Israel can't be asked to negotiate with terrorists or make any concessions to the demands of terrorist groups, including Hamas.

Before there can be a peaceful solution to the Middle East conflict, the Palestinian people must rid themselves of the Hamas terrorist curse and truly accept Israel's right to exist.

That's what it means to say that Israel has a right to defend itself. An effective defense will inevitably be bloody, and likely brutal. It won't be pretty to watch.

But anything less will bring closer the Islamists' dream of a map without Israel.

December 10, 2006

Draw clear lines in the sand for Iraqis

Now that we've heard from the Iraq Study Group and are left unsatisfied with its strategies for wrapping up the war, we ought to give the Rick's Barber Shop Study Group a shot.

We, too, are a bipartisan body. And we agree with the conclusion of the official commission that Iraq is now a colossal mess. But we didn't need several months and millions of dollars to forge our plan for cleaning it up. Just an afternoon of getting our ears lowered.

We may be dizzy from the bay rum, but we believe the answer in Iraq is simple: Get our troops out, but before they go, draw three lines in the infernal Iraqi sands.

First, put everyone in Iraq on notice that the Kurds are off-limits. In the view from our barber chairs, the Kurds appear to be the only ones left in Iraq whose brains haven't been eaten away by religious poison.

The Kurds just want to be left alone to collect their share of the country's oil booty and avoid the bullets flying everywhere. Unlike their Sunni and Shiite countrymen, they don't hear God shouting "kill, kill, kill" whenever he speaks to them.

Saddam Hussein made great sport of killing the Kurds after the first President Bush left them hanging, and if anyone deserves our protection in Iraq this time around, it's them.

Next, establish a zero-tolerance policy for international terrorist groups. We didn't spend billions in Iraq and sacrifice thousands of our soldiers to see it become a playground for al-Qaida.

Make it crystal clear to the Iraqis that it's their responsibility to keep their doors shut to terrorists who smell opportunity in the chaos.

Finally, let the Iraqis kill each other 'til their heart's content, but don't allow them to export their violence.

They can't become a threat to our interests or our security, or to that of our friends.

The bloodletting they're so fond of must be contained within their own borders.

Of course, lines in the sand are worthless unless there are consequences for crossing them.

Let the Iraqis know that the price for crossing any of these lines will be terrible and swift.

We were obliged to rebuild Iraq after tearing it down to unseat Saddam. We fancied ourselves liberators, but as it turned out, the Iraqis preferred not to be liberated by infidels.

Fair enough. But our obligation has expired. We gave the Iraqis every chance to build a free, safe and prosperous nation. They'd rather use their freedom to settle old grudges.

That's their choice, just as long as they keep their murder and mayhem to themselves.

But if it touches us or our friends, it's a different story.

Our barbershop policy advisers have no stomach for risking the lives of any more American soldiers to keep the Iraqis from cutting each other to pieces. The weapons at our disposal are too horribly efficient to justify again sacrificing our troops in a messy ground war.

We want the Iraqis to know as we leave that if we have to come back, we'll stay only long enough to flatten them. If need be, we can drill through the glass.

December 17, 2006
Holocaust deniers can't hear the names

Sixty-one years is not long enough for David Kahane to forget what the council of devils who assembled last week in Iran is determined to deny: The names.

Moshe-Chaim Kahane, father. Reizel-Toba Kahane, mother. Chaia-Sara Kahane, sister. Hersch-Leib and Zalman-Joseph Kahane, brothers. David Rozenzweig and Sandor Cohen, cherished friends.

The names belong to nearly every blood relative, nearly every person Kahane knew before they were rounded up in their Hungarian village on June 15, 1944, herded onto cattle cars and taken on the five-day rail journey to the Auschwitz concentration camp. All died at the hands of the Nazis.

In Poland, the 15-year-old Kahane was torn from his family and put to work. The others were marched into the gas chamber.

"The next day, I could see the smoke from the crematorium, and a Polish Jew who was a slave laborer in the camp told me, 'You must stay strong,'" he says. "'They have murdered your family.'"

Kahane stayed strong. He survived. And when he stumbled out of his nightmare at the end of the war, stunned to be alive and totally alone in the world, he carried the names with him.

Kahane came to Detroit, where from nothing he built a new life, a new family and a successful business.

"But I never forgot the ones who were killed," he says.

The names Kahane kept were added to an endless list. Six million names. Six million murders. Each meticulously documented by the eyewitnesses and by the compulsive records maintained by the killers themselves.

The evidence is mountainous and irrefutable. Still, many look at the photographs, hear the oral histories, see the tattooed forearms and say, "It never happened."

These Holocaust deniers have a new hero in Iranian President Mahmoud Ahmadinejad, the man who some would "engage" to settle the current war, as if no hand is too bloody to shake.

Ahmadinejad is heir to Hitler's hate and keeper of his frightful flame. His Holocaust Denial Conference gave a platform to the tiresome theories that say the Jews were not systematically exterminated or that their murders were part of a Zionist plot.

If the denial stemmed from utter disbelief that human beings could commit such atrocities, it might be defensible. But the motive of the deniers is to undermine the justification for the Jewish state and build a case for wiping Israel off the map.

It is painful for Holocaust survivors to recount their stories, to gouge again and again at wounds that never heal. It is wrenching for all Jews to collect and display the evidence of the Holocaust in museums and insist that their children stare the horror in the face. It is shameful for decent people of all races to contemplate man's infinite capacity for inhumanity. Burying it would be so much easier.

But the Holocaust remains a living thing, and will as long as anywhere in the world it's a capital crime to be a Jew.

David Kahane speaks the names in his heart so the world will never forget, but also so the world can never deny.

November 11, 2012
Don't reward Hamas terror this time

In the seven years since Israel withdrew from Gaza, Hamas terrorists have bombarded Israeli territory with more than 9,500 rockets, or an average of roughly four a day.

What other nation would endure such a relentless downpour of murderous missiles without responding with full force against its tormentors? Where else would such a campaign of terror be considered routine?

Yet only when Israel finally decides it can no longer tolerate the daily deadly threat to its citizens does the world finally hear the explosions.

And even then it is only the Israeli bombs that get noticed.

We've been down this road so many times the outcome was easy to predict when the cease fire agreement came Wednesday.

In a week or so of hostilities, some Israelis were killed, as were a lot more Palestinians. The Gaza victims were hauled into the town square to be woefully mourned and dutifully photographed as weapons in the greater public relations battle that always decides these confrontations.

Israel was forced to pull back after signing a worthless cease-fire with Hamas.

In a few months the terrorists' rockets will start flying again, and again will be ignored by a world community that deep down believes Israel has it coming. And the countdown to another face-off will begin.

The script was followed to the letter. Leaders in the United States and elsewhere mouthed the right words "Israel has a right to defend itself"—but as always, with a caveat.

This time, it was the worry that an expansive Israeli operation in Gaza would inflame an already volatile Middle East neighborhood and put Egypt's new leaders at risk.

Israel was expected to act for the greater but elusive good of "stability" in the region.

Yet none of the nations that pushed Israel to stand down would put other interests ahead of their own security.

When the United States is attacked, it answers with a terrible swift sword.

Why shouldn't Israel do the same? Why shouldn't it level Gaza, if necessary, to silence the rockets forever? Hamas feels free to continue to torment Israel because it is confident Israel's so-called allies will throw up the stop sign before its military strike brings the Palestinians to their knees.

The press obsesses over the casualty disparity, as if there is a moral equivalency in war. And with the first dead Palestinian mediators from every corner converge on Cairo to sort out the grievances. The United Nations issues a denunciation or two focusing on the illegality of the Israeli occupation but missing the illegality of trying to massacre your neighbor.

Talk turns from Israel's right to defend itself to the PR hit the Jewish state is taking from its brutal retaliation. And again Israel has to make concessions, accept conditions, to stop Hamas from continuing the morally reprehensible act of randomly firing rockets at civilians.

This time, the Israelis agreed to ease restrictions on Gaza and allow the terrorist leaders to go unmolested as they plot Israel's destruction.

In other words, the Hamas terrorists are again rewarded for their terrorism. And that's why it continues.

March 9, 2014

Obama wobbles again on Israel

When all else fails, blame the Jews.

That tired but true formula surfaced again in Washington last week, as President Barack Obama, his foreign policy in shambles, sought to regain credibility on the world stage by spanking Israel.

The president is determined to restart Middle East peace negotiations and his strategy for doing so is to give the Israelis a good, hard shove in the back while stroking the Palestinians. The approach reveals both a chronic naivete about the dynamics of the conflict and a dangerous underestimation of the impact of an American president's words.

Obama, ahead of a visit to the White House by Benjamin Netanyahu last week, first sent a message to the Israeli Prime Minister through the media. He told a Bloomberg reporter that time is running out for Israel, as is America's ability to protect it from what he called "international fallout." And he suggested Netanyahu might not really want to make peace.

Meanwhile, Obama declared Palestinian President Mahmoud Abbas a willing and responsible negotiating partner, hinting that he recognizes Israel's right to exist (but not necessarily to exist, as Abbas himself clarifies, as a Jewish state.)

The comments, many of them repeated during Obama's sit-down with the prime minister, were not well received. Netanyahu's response: "The Israeli people expect me to be strong and stand against pressure and criticism." Good answer.

It's distressing that the pressure and criticism comes from an American president who should understand that any hint of a rift between our two nations emboldens Israel's enemies and makes the Palestinians even more intractable.

Obama made a similar blunder during his first term in pre-conditioning peace talks on a halt of Israeli settlement activity. The Palestinians immediately adopted that as their position, and negotiations failed yet again.

This time, Obama is asking for Israel's trust, assuring Netanyahu he is "absolutely committed" to his country's security.

But the Israelis can't bet their existence on the promises of a president whose commitments have been so wobbly and judgment so flawed. Netanyahu has good reason not to share Obama's confidence that the Iranians are truly motivated to abandon their nuclear ambitions, and rightfully reminded the president of Iran's messianic mission to wipe Israel off the map.

The prime minister also can't be certain Obama will act if Iran does cross the nuclear threshold. Why should he expect the red line in Iran to be any brighter than the one in Syria?

And Israel can see as well as everyone else how Russia's Vladimir Putin is tossing around Obama as if he were a 100-pound weakling.

Netanyahu made it clear Israel will not defer to the U.S. in defending itself. Be certain that if Israel feels imminently threatened, it will act, with or without U.S. support.

As we now know for certain, a weak American president makes the world a more dangerous place. ⚜

Chapter 13

Holidays

April 15, 2001

Easter rewards us for a long winter by restoring hope through faith

If all goes as planned, I'll slip out of the Rose of Sharon church in Cumberland County, Ky., later this morning and grab several cartons of Easter eggs to hide beneath the leaves and clumps of grass in the field next to the cemetery.

It's been my job for years, stretching back to when my daughters were still young enough to wear those little white bonnets with the elastic straps you could snap to sting their chins. My children long ago outgrew bonnets and egg hunts, and now have even outgrown this annual trip south. But I still hide the eggs, and Easter is still my favorite holiday.

Easter is my reward for enduring winter. Gut it out through March, and I'll soon be back on my farm, where the dogwood and redbud blooms chase away the memories of slush and snow. The woods will be greening, but not yet tangled with undergrowth. The golf courses will be open and so will the fishing docks. It really is the best week of the year.

I also warm to Easter because, of all the messages of Christianity, I resonate best to the Easter story. Resurrection and rebirth emerging from death and despair is the basic hope offered by religion. We can pick up the pieces and go on after failure and loss because of the promise that no matter how deep the heartbreak, how bitter the disappointment, how great the grief, the human spirit will survive and thrive again.

Jews have a similar message of renewal in Yom Kippur; Muslims in Ramadan. Nature, of course, confirms all this with its vivid display of resilience as the snows recede in April to reveal brilliant crocuses and daffodils.

A friend left the Catholic Church as a teenager, thinking she'd never be back. There was nothing there for her, or so she thought. She returned as a young adult after hitting a terribly rough spot in her life, was confirmed and now donates her time to her local parish. She needed comfort, hope, a sense of purpose, and the church was the only place where she could find those things.

Faith manufactures hope. That's why religion remains relevant even in this new millennium, when the tree of knowledge has dropped most of its secrets, when we have answers to more of our questions, when we can do things once considered possible only in the realm of miracles.

Despite our sophistication, our wisdom, we still hunger for the hope that faith brings.

Regular church attendance in this country unquestionably has waned, but not so the profession of faith. Although just under half of Americans attend church regularly, 70 percent go occasionally, and 90 percent have some religious beliefs.

A few years ago, I worked with a man who, when asked his religion, said, "I'm a Posturepedic—I sleep in on Sundays." Yet even he roused his family on Easter morning and hauled them to church, observing a ritual that makes this the most heavily attended Sunday service of the year. Another friend is a lifelong agnostic, but dutifully takes her three young children to services each Sunday because, "There's something there I want them to have."

That something will be the sermon subject this morning in the simple country church where I'll worship, the same as it will be in the world's grandest cathedrals. It's an ancient message of hope: No matter how dark the winter, now comes the season of restoration and renewal.

⇜ ⇜ ⇜

December 15, 2002

Nothing destroys Christmas quite like decorating a tree

My mother's demon was not well hidden. It stood in the corner of the living room for a full month each year, wrapped in brightly blinking red and blue lights and draped in perfectly placed tinsel.

Mom had Christmas tree issues, which unfortunately she passed through the genetic code.

My earliest Christmas memory is of Mom dashing through the house, choking in her hands a fully decorated Christmas tree while screaming, "Open the door!" When I did, she hurled the tree javelin-like deep into the back yard. Standing on the porch, rubbing her hands together like Pontius Pilate, she declared, "I'm done with you! You'll never fall over in my house again."

Children learn lessons the hard way. So it was that a mere flash after asking, "Are we going to open our presents outside this year?" I found myself resting in the snow bank next to the equally startled Christmas tree.

When artificial trees came on the scene, we thought they might be our salvation. They're always straight and don't have the dreaded "holes" that seemed to torment her so.

The idea was disastrous. The tree gave new meaning to the word "artificial." It was a deplorable abuse of aluminum.

Sharp, straight wires stuck out at awkward angles from a center pole, and were wrapped with glittery little silver "leaves." The crowning glory was a scorchingly hot spotlight that shone through a spinning, multi-colored disk to give the illusion that the leaves were changing color from blue to red to yellow to green.

It looked less like a yule bush than it did something space age pagans might use to communicate with their gods. We were the Jetsons.

I should have learned from my father, who I don't recall ever seeing anywhere near a Christmas tree. Or near my mother while she was decorating one. He knew what darkness lurked beneath those festive branches.

Instead, I took up my mother's mantle and began my own personal Christmas tree war.

Remember the scene in *A Christmas Story* where the dad turns into Mr. Hyde while repairing the furnace, unleashing a chilling torrent of obscenities from the basement? That was me, sprawled out beneath the Christmas tree, trying to get the #$@%& bolts into the *&#%#@ trunk so the $%&*#@-ing tree would stand up straight.

This was not suitable for children, and mine hid under the bed whenever I dragged out the Christmas tree stand (of which I have three dozen to donate to a worthy organization, having tried every fool-proof stand on the market without finding one that is fool-proof).

My own meltdown came the year I selected a tree that looked perfect on the lot, but was hiding a fatal crook halfway up the trunk. Every night, the tree came crashing to the floor. Every night, I put it back up, with progressively fewer glass ornaments.

On the fifth night of Christmas, I went to the toolbox, got out a hammer and a spike, and nailed the top of the tree tightly to the wall. It stood there for the rest of the season bent over at a painful angle, as if being pulled hard by its necktie.

These days, I give Christmas trees a wide berth.

O Tannenbaum, you win. Stay in the woods where you belong. I'll not try to drag you into the house and deck your boughs with unnatural fruits. Best we both respect the limitations of our family trees.

May 25, 2003
Graveyard connects to the past and the future

For most of the year, the Shy Graveyard sits undisturbed on its hillside, visited only by cows that push through a lazy fence to pick grass from between the headstones.

But on Memorial Day, the cemetery is mowed slick, freed of weeds and ready to welcome the handful of families who will come to remember long passed relatives. That the tiny graveyard hasn't faded into the woods is the legacy of my grandmother, whose ancestors are buried here and who considered the rough, little acre a part of the family.

She would march us there as children with hoes and rakes to slash away at the tangles of briars and tree-of-heaven saplings and prepare the cemetery for the day she called The Decoration. Most of the graves are marked only with slabs of sandstone, with no inscriptions, and no one left to remember who is buried beneath. We'd straighten those the best we could and then move on to the few graves with formal headstones, including those of her parents.

As we worked, she'd tell us their stories, over and over, so they'd be etched in our memories long after the granite eroded away.

Like most farmers of his generation in this part of Kentucky, my great-grandfather was condemned to a life of working rocky, played-out soil that never yielded quite enough to feed a household made up mostly of daughters.

He had higher hopes for his children, seeing them well off the farm and out of these hills, educated and living in comfort. But one by one, the daughters slipped away to marry local farm boys.

When my grandfather showed up to claim his bride, the old man was in the tobacco field. He threw down his hoe in disgust and cursed, "I'll never make a damn thing out of any of my girls!"

I think about that story whenever I visit the graveyard and wonder what he'd say if he knew that just two generations later, his descendants would be scattered across the country, successful and working in every profession imaginable.

That was my grandmother's point. In cleaning up the cemetery, in decorating graves, we weren't just paying homage to cold remains, but acknowledging the hopes and heartbreaks of those who came before us.

She wanted to remind us that the links in the family chain go forward as well as back, and that we, too, have an obligation to dream on behalf of those in the future whom we'll never know.

After she died, my aunt took responsibility for the graveyard, and now it rests with my cousins and me.

None of us have the time or the will to chop out weeds on a sweltering hilltop. So we've swapped rakes and hoes for a checkbook.

The people we hire to ready the cemetery for The Decoration do a terrific job, much better than we could ourselves.

But they don't tell the stories of the graveyard's occupants as they work, and soon those oral histories are bound to simply drift away.

Though we're doing what we promised to do—making sure the Shy Graveyard always looks proud on Memorial Day—we aren't doing what our grandmother did.

We aren't teaching the next generation that beneath the broken stones are those who once had human flesh and human desires, who loved and laughed, worked and struggled, and added a layer to the foundation they stand on today.

December 19, 2004

Merry Christmas, happy holidays, whatever

Christians are drawing a line in the snow this season against any further secular encroachment on their most significant religious holiday.

Christmas, they fear, has been co-opted by consumerism, political correctness and an obsessively misguided construction of the separation of church and state.

Web sites are offering advice to assist Christians in combating the ridiculous banishment of the word "Christmas" from schools, stores and corporate greeting cards. "Happy Holidays" and "Seasons Greetings" don't cut it with them—they want "Merry Christmas," with the emphasis on the Christ.

They may decorate Christmas trees and delight in the glittering displays of Santa Claus, Rudolph and Frosty, but they demand equal time for the star, the manger and the baby Jesus.

Their pique is understandable. Though Christmas is a religious celebration, it now also must do double duty as the high holy day of capitalism.

The sacred rites of Christmas have been twisted into candy canes and reindeer horns. No other religion has had its cherished rituals commercialized in such an unholy manner.

Imagine Ramadan or Yom Kippur being marked by a 12-foot high, blow-up Sponge Bob rising from the front lawn.

But Christians are missing the point by taking offense.

Certainly, the bright and blinking secular symbols and half-off holiday sales are overwhelming the traditional Christian observances, making them seem quaint and awkwardly old-fashioned.

But the true spirit of Christmas also has been appropriated and incorporated into the nonreligious observances of the holiday. And that spirit is deeply rooted in the principles of Christianity.

Even those who X-out the Christ in Christmas know it is a gentler season; a time for sharing and spiritual reflection, for building traditions that keep friends and family close, for charity and children, for love and loved ones.

Celebrants may cringe at holiday hymns. They may never attend a midnight Mass. They might even find it uncomfortable to murmur a Merry Christmas greeting. They may be nonreligious, or of a different religion, or indifferent to religion.

But maybe they will renew a cherished friendship during this season of magic. Or write a check or volunteer some time to feed the hungry and give comfort to the afflicted. Or open their homes and hearts to the fellowship that gives Christmas its special charm.

They may not share the faith of those who come to Christmas on bended knee.

But for the few weeks of this season, they may share a faith that the angel's declaration of peace on earth and goodwill towards men is more than a wish upon a star.

If so, they will touch the spirit of Christmas, and by extension, the goodness of the Christian faith.

The world is a better place at Christmas, for everyone. Isn't that what religion is supposed to achieve?

Rather than bristling because the world is stealing Christmas, Christians should consider Christmas as their gift to the world.

December 23, 2007
Sadness is also a part of Christmas

A few weeks ago I came across a column in a small town newspaper that started with these words: "Back when everyone we loved was still alive..."

I've rolled that thought over and over in my mind, stretching to remember the brief time the writer describes, a time when there was no one missing.

We notice the missing more at Christmas. And now the holiday is at the door, carrying with it both the relentless expectation of happiness and the constant reminder of loss.

This season is an absolute bully in its demand for good cheer.

But there ought to be room as well for some sadness. Because there's no escaping that for all its shouting to let's be jolly, Christmas can be a very sad holiday.

Look around the church during this week's holiday services. Notice the eyes fighting back tears, the shoulders shaking silently. Maybe the loss is fresh. Or maybe the choir is singing the favorite carol of a loved one long passed.

We know exactly what they're feeling. And yet, open expressions of grief at this time of year make us uncomfortable. Pain isn't supposed to be part of the Christmas script. So those who are suffering feel especially isolated.

That's the conflict of Christmas. We make wonderful memories during the holidays, but those memories are eventually the ones that hurt the most.

Charles Dickens captured it perfectly with his Ghost of Christmas Past, whose blend of sweet nostalgia and bitter regret make him the truest Christmas character.

Every new Christmas season seems to bring another empty chair at the holiday table. And at the same time, new faces.

We lose parents and gain grandchildren; say goodbye to aunts and uncles and pick up nieces and nephews; bury siblings and welcome in-laws.

But it isn't a zero-sum game. The newcomers, as much as they're loved, aren't meant to replace those who have left.

Still, the architects of the modern Christmas celebration insist on designing a holiday that is entirely about happiness. Tears of joy, only.

The memories Christmas stirs can make that impossible for many people.

Comfort and joy was once the motto of the holiday, but the secularization of Christmas has pushed the comfort message into the shadows and elevated obsessive merriment as the primary purpose.

That creates an artificial environment, hard for even the least troubled to sustain. With the season now nearly two months long, it can wear out the mind.

We might find Christmas less of an emotional tug-of-war if we were less resistant to taking some time for reflecting on the memories that make us ache and offering more tolerance to those who just can't muster the joy the season requires.

That wouldn't have to turn Christmas into a maudlin affair. Christmas still should be about the gifts and glitter and good times. It really is the most wonderful time of the year.

But acknowledging that a strong stream of sadness also runs through Christmas would make the holiday more honest.

December 21, 2008
Savoring the tastes of Christmas past

It may be that I'm just at the mercy of my ever-expanding stomach, but lately when I think about dead people, I get hungry.

This is the first holiday season since my mother passed away, and my mind is on banana pudding.

She made the best. It was her specialty. You could count on it being on the table at every family gathering.

Banana pudding in a bowl lined with vanilla wafers and topped with browned meringue—you'd better go for that first, because if you waited until dessert, you'd be out of luck.

When a loved one passes from your life, you don't just lose the warmth of their presence.

You lose cookies, cakes and casseroles as well. You bid farewell to comfort foods made just for you and to secret ingredients that tie together families as surely as does blood.

You can pass down recipes from one generation to another. You can also hang a poster of a Rembrandt on your wall. But it's just not the same without the artist's brush strokes.

My beloved Aunt Imy, who died four years ago, set a table in the old Southern style. It didn't matter if it were a holiday or a plain old Tuesday night, supper was a spectacle.

The table buckled under the weight of platters rushed hot from the kitchen. There was barely room to rest your plate, and the serving dishes seemed not to have a bottom.

What I miss most are her dried apple pies. She picked the apples from the trees in her yard and dried them in the back window of her old Ford. I always suspected they were equal parts fruit and yellow jackets.

Fried in lard, they were nasty to look at and you didn't want to dwell too long on the history of those apples, but I'd make a pact with the devil to have one in my hands—and mouth—again.

It's been 25 years since I've sat at my Aunt Noxie's table, but my stomach growls remembering her rich pinto beans and ham soup, cornbread on the side. She was serving up bowls of heaven long before she went there.

These sisters cooked from memory or with bits of recipes jotted down on paper scraps. There's not much of an archival record with which to recreate their delicacies.

Imy once tried to dictate the recipe for her holiday jam cake, but I put down the pencil when she came to the part where you "add a scoop of butter the size of a walnut and mix it up until it looks like it's supposed to."

Miss Thelma Back, my cousin's mother-in-law, had the good grace not to take the secret of her exquisite hickory nut cake to the grave. Somewhere, I have the recipe written down.

But it reads like the formula for making a nuclear reactor. It's well above my skill level, and I wouldn't have a clue where to buy hickory nuts in Detroit.

New foods come into your life, of course, just as new people do. But they don't erase the memory of the flavors that are lost.

Death means empty chairs around the holiday table and empty bowls atop it.

So as always, cherish your loved ones this Christmas season because you never know what a New Year brings.

And remember to savor the tastes as well.

December 15, 2011

Shopping in boycott era is a holiday pain

Holiday shopping is never easy. But this year it's especially challenging. I've pledged to be a socially responsible shopper by honoring the boycotts against those who pierce the thin skin of our vast Victim Nation.

Not willing to throw my lot in with any particular cause, but instead determined to be a non-judgmental boycotter, I am vainly seeking a checkout counter worthy of my Visa card.

In a typical yuletide (can't say Christmas because the word is boycotted by corporate America so as not to offend secular celebrants), I'd knock off my list at Lowe's, stuffing stockings with screwdrivers, cordless drills and lag bolts. But Lowe's is crossways with the Muslim community because it pulled ads from the *Muslim in America* reality series under threat of a boycott from Florida Christians.

No problem, you say? Go to Home Depot instead. Can't. A family values group placed a cross in front of Home Depot's doors for supporting gay pride parades.

So if you were expecting hardware from me this year, forget about it.

Target would seem safe. But not to the Lesbian, Gay, Bisexual or Transgendered community. Lady Gaga says no-no because Target gave money to a group that backed an anti-gay candidate for governor of Minnesota. Same goes for Best Buy.

Don't even ask about Wal-Mart.

I'd hoped to buy my son-in-law a gift certificate to his favorite restaurant, Chick-fil-A, but they're on the griddle for catering a marriage seminar hosted by an anti-gay group.

Gas cards? Nope. BP is station-non-grata because of its role in the Gulf oil spill, Citgo has ties to Venezuelan strongman Hugo Chavez, and Esso denies global warming.

Guns always look festive under the Holiday Tree. But Smith & Wesson and Colt have been shunned for caving in to past gun control schemes.

I can't keep track of the companies boycotted by environmentalists and animal rights activists. You also can't buy anything that may have been made by an illegal immigrant, or in a place that doesn't pay union wages.

Whole countries are on the boycott list, including Israel, as always, and Singapore, which offended soccer fans by charging too much for World Cup broadcast rights.

Forbidden is anything made of wood from the rain forest, or jewelry with diamonds tainted by blood.

Shop online and you'll offend the Buy Local folks. But you can't shop local, at least not in Troy, because Troy's mayor posts dumb things on Facebook.

I'm trying to avoid eye contact with the bell ringers outside the mall, because the Salvation Army is on the list for not declaring gay is OK.

Stocking up for holiday parties is no picnic, either. Cheetos are targeted by parents and teachers for an ad glorifying vandalism, and chocolate maker Nestle has been nixed for pushing formula over breast milk.

I'd just go ahead and give gift cards from the credit card companies, but I don't want Occupy Wall Street in my office.

A group called Buy Nothing Christmas is protesting the commercialization of the holiday by urging no gift purchases.

What other choice do we have?

December 25, 2014

No place like home for Christmas

Growing up, Bing Crosby's "There's No Place Like Home For the Holidays" was my family's Christmas theme song.

We spent most Christmas Eve's in a patched-up sedan, the trunk loaded with Christmas presents and the back seat stuffed with kids. In this pre-car seat era, positions were passed out by seniority; my older sister got the seat, I got the floorboard and we wedged my little sister onto that rear window shelf cars used to have.

We were headed south, to Kentucky, but my parents always just said we were "going home."

No matter how many years we spent in Detroit, how far removed we became from the hills and hollers, that was always home. And home was where you went for Christmas.

It was not an easy trip back then. Aside from the possibility of snow and ice, automobiles weren't nearly as reliable. Inevitably, we'd have to deal with a flat tire, overheated radiator or some other mechanical calamity.

And yet my normally grumpy father never let it bother him. He was headed home. And once he got on southbound I-75, he was a changed man. He'd sing along with the Christmas carols on the radio, and pretend to spy Santa's sleigh in the distant sky.

Across the industrial cities of the north, my aunts and uncles and their families were doing the same thing, all of us headed by different routes to a place barely on the map.

It was a common experience for baby boom children. The years following World War II shuffled the population from farms to factories, and most of our families had resettled far from the places of our birth.

Because of that, I always resonated to the part of the Nativity story that described Joseph and Mary traveling to Nazareth to be counted among their people. It was the very first Christmas homecoming, the start of a tradition that remains strong today.

Michigan parents of my generation are on the other end of that ritual. A decade of lost opportunity here sent our children packing for jobs in other places. If you were at the airport this past week, you saw grandparents joyfully reaching for toddlers who didn't quite recognize them. They'll spend next week sending them back. The airport tears will be painful.

Once we got to Kentucky, we'd pull into the yard next to cars with license plates from everywhere. The whole tribe would jam into a three-room house and begin the fight for a sleeping space. The floor was covered with kids on quilt pallets.

The kitchen table couldn't hold us all, so we ate in shifts; first the men, then the kids and finally the women. I can still hear the low, murmuring voices of my mother and her sisters readying breakfast, while we lay half asleep, reluctant to exchange our warm covers for our half-frozen clothes.

So many of those who filled that house are gone. I realize now that home is people, not a place. As the people fade away, the place gets harder to find.

Still, I'll make the trip once more today. It'll be a lonelier journey. But it's Christmas, and, to quote my grandmother, a body ought to be home at Christmas. ❧

Chapter 14

Drugs

April 29,2001

Why abandon precious values for anti-drug plan that doesn't work?

Count among the casualties of the obsessive drug war many of the values we're supposed to cherish as Americans.

Sacrificed most recently are the principles of redemption and presumed innocence.

Over spring break, the Bush administration announced it would actively enforce a mostly ignored federal law that denies college financial aid to students with drug convictions. Passed in 1998, the original intent of the law was to cut off federal support to active drug users.

But the final version also denied aid to students with past drug convictions.

Never mind if it was a one-time mistake. Never mind if they've straightened themselves out. Never mind that they've done their time, paid their fine.

The law classifies drug offenders as a special class of criminal, far more heinous than any other.

Aid is not denied to those with a conviction for murder. Or rape. Or child molesting. Or drunk driving. It singles out only those with drug offenses.

That George W. Bush would tell students who have made mistakes with drugs that there's no second chance is curious. By his own account, he was a drunken failure until he was 40. And yet he turned his life around, to say the least. He should be the last person to throw a roadblock in front of young people trying to turn around their lives.

Despite a lack of evidence that harsher penalties make any dent in narcotics use, especially among the young, the drug-obsessed moralists in Bush's administration insist enforcing this punitive policy will keep students away from dope. It won't. But it might keep them away from college.

On another front, Americans got a close-up look last week at just how far our government will go to stem the flow of drugs. A Peruvian Air Force jet, assisted by U.S. operatives, shot down a small plane carrying Michigan missionaries. Veronica Bowers of Muskegon and her seven-month-old daughter, Charity, were killed.

CIA-hired mercenaries routinely help Peru target airplanes suspected of carrying cocaine. Since 1994, 30 have been shot down. Who knows how many of those planes carried innocents like the Bowers?

But even if all the planes were involved in the drug trade, how do we feel about the United States participating in a program that metes out capital punishment on the mere suspicion of a crime? Would we tolerate such a shoot-first, convict-later policy within our own borders?

The Peru project reportedly has decreased the flow of coke from that country. But that is replaced by supplies from Colombia and Ecuador.

We're preparing to expand our military action against drug trafficking to Colombia, at a cost of billions, and may leap frog to other countries.

Maybe we'll succeed in reducing the cocaine supply. But those determined to get high will find other drugs, as witnessed by the explosive popularity of the prescription painkiller Oxycotin, as well as Meth, the bathtub gin of narcotics.

We can stubbornly insist on persecuting drug users. And we can continue to shoot down planes with no regard to due process.

But those tactics don't work. Unless we're just hell bent on wasting time, money and lives, we should find something that will.

June 12, 2005

End marijuana hypocrisy to save nation billions

Faced with two bad choices, I'd druther kids celebrate their 21st birthdays with a bag of pot than by pouring 21 shots of cheap liquor down their gullets.

Again, both are poor choices. But a poor choice made with alcohol is far more lethal than one made with marijuana.

Binge drinking, drunken driving and booze-induced recklessness continue to leave empty seats in college and high school classrooms.

Marijuana has its own set of negatives, but it is rarely directly connected to a teen death.

And yet we treat marijuana as public enemy No. 1 when it comes to children. At the same time, we welcome a stream of beer commercials into our homes and don't blink when liquor companies sponsor spring break blowouts.

Parents who roll their eyes and giggle when young Johnny stumbles home tipsy go into complete despair when they find a baggie in a dresser drawer.

It's a very expensive hypocrisy. State and federal governments spend $8 billion a year on the war on marijuana.

The latest education campaign will spend another $125 million to convince children that pot will rot their brains.

We should save our money. Teen pot use is as cyclical as the auto industry. Some decades it goes up, some it goes down, with no correlation to spending on anti-drug programs.

Nearly 40 percent of teens say they've tried marijuana, the same percentage as the general population. While hopefully teens understand that pot isn't good for them, they know first-hand that it is no more harmful—and perhaps less so—than loading up on vodka.

Trying to convince them otherwise will just make them ignore warnings about the more dangerous drugs.

Before dismissing me as a leftover '60s pothead, let me say I have no interest in marijuana, even if it were legal.

But I am a taxpayer who expects a return on his investment. The drug war is delivering none.

Nobel Prize winner Milton Friedman joined 500 respected economists last week in endorsing a Harvard University study that said federal and state governments could realize a $14 billion gain by regulating and taxing marijuana as a legal product.

There is a growing acceptance that this war is not only unwinnable, it is irrational.

Despite spending $35 billion a year to battle illegal narcotics, drug use here is about the same as in the European countries with more liberal drug laws.

But still we fight on. Last week, the U.S. Supreme Court handed a major victory to drug warriors by declaring federal authorities can prosecute those who grow and use marijuana for medical purposes.

The ruling fits the national ideology that in the name of the drug war, the Constitution can be tossed on the garbage heap.

But nothing will keep desperate people from seeking relief, or teens from experimenting.

The war against pot is lost.

Surrendering isn't a defeat. It simply ends our national hypocrisy and leaves more money for more pressing battles.

April 4, 2009

Wave white flag in the drug war

The shocking spectacle of a respected Wayne County judge, a crackerjack prosecutor and two veteran cops standing as defendants in a courtroom confirms the war on drugs is lost.

Former Assistant Prosecutor Karen Plants is accused of wanting a conviction so badly in a narcotics case that she corrupted two Inkster officers and compromised retired Judge Mary Waterstone. All were career warriors in a hopeless conflict.

The slide of good guys to the wrong side of the law epitomizes the drug war's failure.

We've been fighting drugs for 35 years, and yet we haven't gained an inch of ground.

Mexico's drug-fueled lawlessness is surging over our border. More than half our prison inmates are in for drug crimes, contributing to the shameful fact that Michigan spends more on Corrections than we do on colleges.

Detroit and other big cities have been dismantled by the drug gangs.

And the number of addicts remains constant.

This is a classic military quagmire. We respond to losing by deploying more troops instead of questioning the mission's viability. In 1986, Congress escalated spending, with the goal of ending the narcotics trade in 10 years.

And now we're about to undergo another major escalation to keep the anarchy in Mexico from destabilizing parts of our country.

Why not try something new? Take away the crime, and get rid of the criminals.

The drug cartels wouldn't have a market for their contraband if we legalized drugs. They'd be as obsolete as the Purple Gang.

Replacing illegal producers with licensed, legal distributors doesn't stop the use of drugs, but it would bring them under tighter control.

With the market in the hands of criminals, there's no way to regulate the potency of narcotics or keep them out of the hands of minors.

Teens can buy marijuana easier than they can buy beer because beer stores face stiff penalties for selling to minors. Pushers don't check IDs.

Tax dollars reaped from drug sales could be invested in treating true addicts.

It chafes our instincts to think of marijuana, cocaine and heroin stocked in bright packages on store shelves. But we've lost the war. Fighting harder and longer won't bring victory. Even when we fight dirty we can't win—as evidenced by the Wayne County charges.

Better to bring drugs up from the underground, control their distribution with regulation and attack demand with taxation and education—just like we do tobacco.

If organized criminal outfits are going to run the drug trade, I'd rather they be Congress and Corporate America than an army of Mexican hoodlums.

Chapter 15

The Environment

May 20, 2001

Americans must make tough choices on energy

Dad had a sixth sense when it came to thermostats.

He could be miles away, and if one of us nudged up the dial a half a degree, an alarm went off in his head.

His dedication to conservation was purely motivated—he was cheap. His happiness depended on slicing a few bucks off the monthly heating bill.

Energy conservation has lost steam during the past 20 years. Stable gasoline and heating fuel costs took the urgency out of dialing down thermostats and measuring gas mileage.

But now it's back in vogue, thanks to suddenly soaring fuel prices. Both President Bush and his Democratic opponents rolled out energy plans last week, and both touted conservation as a long-term solution to our energy woes.

And in a major flourish of hypocrisy, both also touted conservation as a way to drive down fuel costs.

Nobody has bothered to peel another layer off that onion. Drive down prices and what happens? Consumption goes up, and conservation is forgotten.

Americans have given lip service to conservation for decades. We love the theory of saving fuel and preserving the environment. We've blocked power plants, said no to nukes and placed off-limits signs on oil and gas fields.

We've just been weak on the follow-through. We remain ravenous for cheap energy. Conservation without inconvenience is what we really want.

To some degree, that's possible. Home heating has benefited from high-efficiency furnaces and improved insulation. Automobiles squeeze many more miles out of a gallon of gasoline than they did 20 years ago. But at the same time, our homes and vehicles have grown bigger, negating much of the benefit.

We consume more energy every year, and the only time the growth slows is when prices rise enough to catch our attention.

President Bush is under pressure to foster conservation through government intervention. But we can dial down the thermostat, drive a smaller car, switch off a light and shower with a friend without federal regulations. We just need the right incentive.

So we have choices to make. Is cheap gasoline worth opening our wildernesses and lakes to drilling rigs? If we refuse to build power plants and use coal and nuclear resources, are we willing to be a little colder in the winter, a little hotter in the summer? If we'd rather not dam our rivers for hydroelectric power, will we accept that the lights won't always come on when we flick the switch? Are we committed enough to conservation to give up our SUVs for tiny cars?

Because we can't have it both ways. We can't rage against energy production without curbing our own appetites. If we're not willing to seriously conserve, we have to find more energy.

If higher gasoline prices make us cranky now, wait until winter, when a 50-percent increase in natural gas costs shocks home heating bills.

Conservation should come more natural then. At least it will at my house, where the kids sit around in shorts and T-shirts while the furnace makes January feel like July. They tinker with the thermostat so much I worry my dad's internal alarm is blaring away, disturbing his eternal rest.

But next winter I'll borrow one of Dad's tricks and duct tape the dial at 65. When we're talking about my dollars, I can get as serious about conservation as he was.

↞ ↞ ↞

December 24, 2006

Keep the Christmas lights burning

My neighbor has one of those gigantic, blow-up Christmas things in the front yard, a two-car railroad train with a merry-go-round in the caboose.

It covers most of the lawn and is a terrifically tacky expression of the excesses of the season. I consider it one of the marvels of Christmas, but can't drive by without wondering how much power it takes to keep the blower blowing, the lights lit and the happy little animals spinning about as fast as the disk in the electric meter.

But who worries about such things at Christmas? Too soon, perhaps, all of us.

There's no danger of this Christmas going dark. But in 25 years, America's consumption of electricity will increase by 50 percent, and yet we keep putting off decisions about how we'll meet that demand.

Energy policy today is driven by the myth that conservation and green power sources will be enough to head off the coming crisis. Conservation is a righteous thing, but not something Americans have proven themselves capable of doing, especially as long as energy is cheap.

And the utility companies could put solar panels on all of our backs and windmill beanies on our heads and still not have enough power to satisfy our appetite for things like this year's hottest gift—big screen LCD TVs that suck seven times as much electricity as traditional sets.

Many of our energy guzzling toys come from California's high-tech labs.

Yet California leads the nation in energy denial. It won't allow new electricity plants that produce significant carbon dioxide, meaning no coal, and it won't allow new nuclear plants until a national waste storage site is set.

California's only practical option is natural gas, a commodity that is increasingly scarce and expensive.

If California's mimics in the Northeast adopt similar policies, natural gas will become even more costly, creating severe hardships in states like Michigan, where it is relied on to heat homes.

Let's be honest. We aren't going to conserve our way to a sound energy policy. We have to produce more electricity, and that means ending our resistance to the most logical and economical sources of electricity.

We must invest more in clean coal technology, and tear down barriers to getting coal out of the ground. We have coal reserves to last 300 years, which should be enough time to come up with other energy sources.

We also have to end Nevada's stonewalling of the Yucca Mountain nuclear waste storage facility. Yucca is the safest and most sensible option for housing the waste. But with Nevada's Sen. Harry Reid now running the U.S. Senate, it has about as much chance as a snowball in Death Valley of getting approval.

We have to do whatever it takes to keep America an electric nation. Cheap, plentiful electricity has fueled the development of most of the gadgets and gizmos that make our lives rich.

Not the least of which is my neighbor's enormous, blow-up Christmas train with the merry-go-round inside.

February 5, 2007

Forget ethanol; save corn for bourbon

As a bourbon drinker and grandson of a moonshiner, I naturally perk up when talk turns to distilling corn.

Great-grandpa Finley cooked corn into sour mash whiskey in a process nearly identical to the one used today to produce ethanol.

But while the feds chased Old Pap up hills and down hollers to stop him from running off a batch or two of home brew, the government this year will provide more than $7 billion in subsidies to encourage a massive expansion of ethanol production.

I think Jim Beam could do more good with that corn and money than the purveyors of E-85.

Ethanol is a fraud of an alternative fuel.

It's too costly to make. It can't be shipped economically. It offers only a minimal impact on the greenhouse gasses linked to global warming, while creating other types of dangerous air and water pollution. And it won't break our addiction to foreign oil.

Even if every available acre of cropland in the United States were converted to growing corn, we'd still be about 20 percent short of what is needed for ethanol to replace gasoline.

Ethanol just ain't going to happen here.

But don't bother trying to explain that to the politicians. They're too busy conning themselves and voters that spending truckloads of tax dollars to create an ethanol industry will free us from the oil sheiks and break the earth's rising fever.

If this were nothing more than a waste of taxpayer money, I'd remain in-

December 16, 2007

Gore's warming plan will blister U.S.

Al Gore has met the global warming enemy, and it is U.S.

The former vice president and recent Nobel Peace Prize winner declared with great disdain at the international climate change talks in Bali that the United States bears the blame and shame for stalling the crusade against greenhouse gases.

"I am not an official, and I am not bound by diplomatic niceties," Gore said to applause. "So I am going to speak an inconvenient truth: My own country, the United States, is principally responsible for obstructing progress here in Bali."

It's hard to imagine an elder statesman from any other nation rising to the global stage to hurl mud balls at his countrymen.

But Gore is now bigger than America. He belongs to the world. As such, he's fluent in the international language that translates every wrong into an indictment of Americans.

Gore's condemnation of his homeys reflects the frustration that the Bush administration isn't keen to agree to rigid caps on carbon emissions. Joined at times by other industrial nations worried about becoming deindustrializing nations, the U.S. prefers to leave Bali with a more flexible commitment to addressing global warming without growth-killing carbon mandates.

Gore could have spoken another inconvenient truth at the talks, if he weren't so hell-bent on casting America as the boorish ogre of the global warming drama.

He could have reminded the delegates that in 2006, total U.S. greenhouse gas emissions fell 1.5 percent—and the intensity of those gases fell 4.2 percent—without an international pact.

By contrast, the European Union, which is loudly proud of signing on to the Kyoto Protocol, increased greenhouse gas emissions 0.4 percent.

The decrease in U.S. emissions is attributed to a greater use of natural gas in electricity production, declines in agricultural and industrial methane output and better land-use and forestry practices, among other things.

That's some good news and might have started the conferees thinking about the effectiveness of voluntary, market-based solutions to global warming.

But that would rub hard against Gore's agenda of forcing America to accept a lesser place on the planet.

If last year's reduction proves to be a trend, the United States will trim its greenhouse gas emissions 15 percent during the next decade, without damaging economic growth.

That seems a reasonable strategy. Throwing the nation into an economic tailspin to address a situation we don't yet fully understand would be irresponsible.

But if Gore and his Bali disciples prevail, growth in the United States and other developed nations will grind to a quick halt, while developing nations such as China and India remain free to pollute at will.

That will trigger the greatest transfer of wealth in modern history, as American jobs rush to places with the least regulatory burdens, and more Americans join the ranks of the world's poor.

A generation from now, Americans may well look back at Al Gore as the Benedict Arnold of his age, someone so determined to save the earth he was willing to ruin his country.

July 30, 2009
Do as green gods say, not as they do

A colleague sent me an Internet photo of *New York Times* columnist Thomas Friedman's home in Bethesda, Md. It's hysterical. The global warming warrior who urged the nation's young people to march on Washington for the right to pay a carbon tax doesn't live in a house. He lives on a campus.

The 11,000-square-foot sprawling complex sits on 7.5 acres and replaced a perfectly fine, smaller home that was torn down to make room for his palace. No need for the kids to march on the Mall. The writer could fit them all into his swimming pool.

And yet Friedman is not the biggest global warming hypocrite. That would be Al Gore. The former vice president began the greenwashing of America, urging its citizens to find harmony with the Earth by living smaller, less ostentatious existences. He meant you, not him. Gore's 9,000-square-foot, $2 million mansion in Nashville is slightly smaller than Friedman's. But he makes up for it with a 100-foot houseboat.

Gore calls the lake-liner "Bio-Solar One," so no one will miss the fact that it's outfitted with the latest energy-saving technology. Even with all its twisty light bulbs, I have to believe Gore's aircraft carrier consumes significantly more fuel than the entire fleet of bass boats it's swamping down there in Tennessee.

I also bet I could keep driving my pick-up truck the rest of my days and 100,000 miles into the hereafter and not leave as large a mark on the planet as Friedman or Gore. Or as Madonna, who, the *Times* of London noted when she showed up in England for a Live Earth concert, has a carbon footprint 100 times larger than the average Brit.

I'm not criticizing these eco-hypocrites for their lavish lifestyles. I celebrate them. If I had their money, I'd see their carbon excess and raise it by a couple hundred tons.

My point is that even for these environmental purists, human nature trumps nature worship. The more money people have, the greater their temptation to buy more and bigger things.

And it's why the green gods know so well that the only way to keep me and you from mimicking their offenses is to make sure we don't accumulate too much money. Money really is the root of all evil from an environmentalist's point of view.

Appeals to downsize for the sake of Mother Earth haven't worked. So now the greens are pushing conservation through confiscation.

If they take our money, we can't spend it in ways that will contribute to global warming. Raise the price of all goods and services, as the Obama administration's climate legislation will do, and we'll be able to purchase and use less. Tax us more, as the bills would also do, and we'll be forced into smaller houses and tinier cars.

The enviro-elites such as Friedman and Gore won't have to worry about it cutting into their lifestyles. They're rich enough to buy their way into heaven with checks that erase their carbon sins.

But the rest of us require forced frugality to keep us on the path of eco righteousness.

If we were all allowed to live like Friedman or vacation like Gore, the earth would be a hell of a place.

⚞ ⚞ ⚞

November 26, 2009

Climategate puts warming in question

President Barack Obama is about to stride off to Copenhagen, where he'll sign away any hope that America can return to sustained prosperity.

The president promises next month's international palaver on climate change will be marked by aggressive action to combat global warming and a firm commitment by the United States to shoulder its share of the responsibility.

Translation: Obama will pledge the United States to curbing its appetite for energy, and thus its economic growth, will make reducing emissions a higher priority than creating new jobs and will agree to transfer $1.6 trillion of our wealth to China, India and the other booming developing economies.

And it may be based on doctored numbers.

The so-called Climategate scandal hasn't hit the front pages of American newspapers yet and may never. But it ought to at least raise the skepticism level of a public that has been panicked into believing the sky is falling, or the polar caps are melting, because of manmade global warming.

Purloined e-mails between some of the leading producers of climate change science reveal what seems to be a deliberate attempt to manipulate and distort data to deliver the desired outcome. The e-mails were hacked from the United Kingdom's University of East Anglia Climate Research Unit, an institution that has led in documenting global warming and whose findings have driven United Nations' environmental policy.

The research unit has been notoriously protective of its data, fighting off those who want a closer look at its methodology. Messages between the unit's scientists and officials suggest a deliberate campaign to answer calls for public disclosure with a smear job against those who question the validity of climate change science.

The scandal provides an opening for the United States, which will pay the highest price if a climate change treaty is signed, to say, "Let's call a time-out and look at the tape."

Research skeptical of climate change is denounced as quackery. But science should never be "settled," as the global warming industry has declared this matter to be. Nor should it be cause driven, massaged to align with popular movements.

It should be cold, impassive and willing to prove itself against dissenting theories. It should welcome new evidence, even if it alters its assumptions.

This isn't how climate change scientists work, according to the stolen e-mails. The British center seems motivated entirely by defending its findings to perpetuate the public policies it worked so hard to influence. It also seems willing to destroy findings that dispute its established position.

This is why we can't get a credible answer to why global temperatures have been flat for a decade. The warming warriors who cited every abnormality in weather patterns—falling lake levels, droughts, hurricanes, milder winters—as proof of climate change's impact, now tell us that the reversal or disappearance of those abnormalities are a cyclical blip within the longer trend.

Maybe, maybe not. We can't be sure because the science is settled, and those who would tackle contrary research do so at their own peril.

This matters because world leaders are about to embark on an environmental crusade that will dramatically alter the international economy and the quality of our lives.

We are obliged to make sure the research can be trusted.

December 9, 2010
Rage against the dying of light (bulbs)

Somewhere in Wayne County there's an ACO Hardware store without a single incandescent light bulb in stock. They're all on a shelf in my basement.

The idea of soon having no illumination choice other than those twisty light bulbs has left me a little bit nuts. So now part of my Saturday routine is making the rounds of various stores and loading my pickup with packages of incandescent bulbs.

It's an obsession I bet I share with others who dread the day a year from now when the old-fashioned bulbs become extinct by federal fiat, and all that's left are the smug compact fluorescent lights.

Congress has decided that everyone should use the new bulbs because they are more energy efficient, though I doubt anyone factored the extra energy used to ship them from China, where they're being made instead of the Midwestern plants that produced the old bulbs to price them anywhere near affordable.

I hate everything about the new bulbs. So I've done my best to calculate how many of the old bulbs I'll need to light the rest of my days. I figure I burn out about 25 bulbs a year. If I'm lucky I've got 30 years left. If I'm really lucky and someone comes up with a major life-extending breakthrough, 40 years.

So I'll need 1,000 bulbs. If I've overestimated my expiration date, any remaining bulbs will make a nice next egg for my heirs. I've got to believe they'll be like glass gold once folks can't get them anymore. There may even be a trading exchange.

I've been buying them in every wattage and shape. Three-ways. Spotlights. Sconce. I'm even thinking about stashing away some colored Christmas twinklers.

Revulsion to the new bulbs is rooted in two of my many character flaws: impatience and stubbornness.

It's as simple as this: When I flip a light switch, I expect light. Immediately. The delay between switch and light with the new bulbs is unsettling. No matter how many times it happens, my reaction is always to keep flipping the switch on and off again.

I suppose I could get used to that, but not to what the new bulbs represent. I don't want to use them mostly because the federal government is telling me I have to.

We've been bullied and brainwashed into accepting the ever-growing intrusion of politicians, regulators and do-gooders into our personal decision making in the name of the greater societal good.

We're told that if we give up some of our individual freedom to buy what we want, drive what we want, smoke and eat what we want, the world will be a better place.

But we can't be trusted to make the right decisions on our own just because we understand the need to conserve and may hope to save a few bucks. We need laws to make sure nothing is left to chance.

Those mandates have already saddled us with toilets that won't flush, washers that won't wash, ethanol-laced gasoline that burns up our lawnmower engines and electric cars that aren't nearly as comfortable, powerful or practical as the models they're supposed to replace.

And next, we get crazy-looking light bulbs shoved into our sockets that may or may not come on before we fall down the stairs in the dark.

Well, not my sockets. If I can hoard enough bulbs to make sure I die by the glow of an incandescent light, I'll consider it a small blow for freedom.

If you feel the same way, you'd better get to ACO before I do.

≪ ≪ ≪

April 7, 2011

Where eagles fly, windmills won't survive

Driving along a rural highway in Hillsdale County the other day, I decided for some odd reason to fight off boredom by taking a road kill census.

On this five-mile stretch of lightly traveled two-lane road, I tallied 13 carcasses: six deer, three raccoons, a possum, a skunk and two unidentified furry blobs.

It was a nightmarish slaughter, and one, I thought to myself, that may eventually doom the automobile. No way will the defenders of the animal kingdom allow this carnage to go unanswered.

My concerns were heightened the next day by two emails. The first announced the suspension of a major wind farm project in North Dakota because of fears it would deplete the local bird population.

Windmills, apparently, are second only to housecats as ravagers of our winged buddies.

The second email confirmed why blocking windmills, the keystone of President Barack Obama's drive to get 25 percent of America's energy from alternative sources by 2025, is urgent environmental policy.

The message linked to a snuff film from the American Bird Conservancy. It tracked the slow and unsuspecting glide of a bald eagle into the deadly path of a windmill blade. You can imagine the outcome.

The video will be part of a future commercial aimed at raising awareness of green energy's bloody secret—the conservancy claims 440,000 birds a year are sliced and diced by turbines.

Across the nation, environmentalists are blocking alternative energy initiatives that are designed to replace the coal, nuclear and oil plants that are being blocked by environmentalists.

The U.S. Chamber of Commerce's Project No Project documents scores of hydroelectric dams, windmills and solar farms that are delayed or dead because of environmental objections, many of them based on the potential harm to wildlife.

In California, a solar panel field in the Mojave Desert funded by a $2 billion federal stimulus grant is in court because it may dismay 40 endangered desert tortoises. A corn-to-ethanol plant in Minnesota is targeted because it may taint trout streams.

Nearly every state has a well-meaning green energy project at risk because of environmental concerns. That includes Michigan, where a Lansing hybrid coal/biomass plant has been deemed not green enough.

Dams are no good because they tame wild rivers; solar panels are ugly; windmills are ugly, too, and noisy to boot; and ethanol steals corn from the mouths of the world's poor.

Coal, oil and gas warm the planet. Nuclear is swell until there's an earthquake.

And all of them in one way or the other are hard on critters.

You may rightly wonder where we'll get our electricity if clean energy is as unacceptable as dirty energy. So back to my carcass count. If the greens are willing to sacrifice their own energy agenda in the name of protecting wildlife, wait until they notice what's going on along the nation's roadsides.

We'll all be out of our cars and onto bicycles, and our best hope for meeting our electricity needs will be harnessing the pedal power.

Unless somebody thinks we can get away with cramming billions of gerbils into exercise wheels. ⤳

Chapter 16

Farewells

September 9, 2001

Farewell to Bobby Laurel, the Last of the Two-Handed Set Shooters

Bobby Laurel had a wicked, two-handed set shot that he launched in classic style—thumbs in, elbows out—in an arc so high you'd worry about the ceiling lights.

That shot was museum quality, pre-Oscar Robinson, perfected on the Catholic school playgrounds of Detroit's Irish neighborhoods and seen today only in grainy game films from the '50s and '60s.

Bobby would take a lay-up if forced to. But in the nearly 20 years we played basketball together, I never saw him shoot from inside the three-point line.

He'd linger far out on the perimeter until the defense forgot about him, then take a pass and sail home the set shot.

At 63, Bobby was the oldest of the guys who play Tuesday nights at St. Roberts of Redford. Occasionally, a kid would show up in the gym for the first time, look at Bobby's gray hair and stocky frame, and figure he could let up on the old guy. Bobby would answer by draining three or four in a row from deep outside. The shots would crash through the net with the power and attitude of a monster slam dunk, leaving the defender weak-kneed and quiet.

You'd better keep track of Bobby when he was on the court.

Bobby took three of his patented set shots Tuesday night, before walking off the floor and dropping dead of a massive heart attack. The best efforts of his friends couldn't revive him.

Bobby Laurel was pure Detroit. A musician, he attended the University of Detroit and made his living for years playing piano at the old London Chop House. He wrote the theme song for the late J.P. McCarthy's radio show.

He caught a break in 1987, when he produced The Rosary Murders, a feature film based on the novel by ex-Detroit priest William X. Kienzle. The screenplay was co-authored by Elmore Leonard, and much of the filming took place at Bobby's alma mater, Holy Redeemer High School.

After that, Bobby worked on the fringes of the entertainment industry, promoting musical acts, brokering screenplays and trying to put together movie deals. He drove rusty old cars and worked 15 hour days, always hustling, always hoping for that next big break.

It came earlier this year, when a federal court jury in Ann Arbor awarded him $19 million in a lawsuit against the giant movie studio 20th Century Fox. Bobby convinced jurors that Fox stole his concept for the 1996 movie Jingle All the Way. A local writer had just started a book on Bobby's David and Goliath battle with the studio.

He died before seeing a dime of the award, part of which he joked would go toward buying a new gym floor.

When we started playing together on Tuesday nights, we were all young men, leaner, faster, stronger. We moved through marriages, divorces, children born, children raised, new jobs and new houses, all exchanged on the sidelines in brief chats between games.

The years pass and we stubbornly keep playing, even though knee braces and ankle supports have become part of the uniform.

As the paramedics carried Bobby out of the gym, many of us were thinking the same thing: When do you give it up? How far do you push the calendar?

I never got a chance to ask Bobby when he intended to hang up his shoes. I suspect he'd have said never. Not as long as he could still throw up a rainbow set shot and let the air out of some hot shot kid.

⤙ ⤙ ⤙

January 18, 2004

Wherever Jim Kerwin is, may Victor the Bear be somewhere else

Lafayette Boulevard was once anchored on the east by a state mental hospital and on the west by the *Detroit News*, and it was often hard to tell the occupants of the two buildings apart.

Corporate journalism had already started to tame the newspaper business by the time I walked in the door of the *News* in 1976, but there were still some cowboy days left, and more than a few characters who could have stepped off the frames of *The Front Page*.

Jim Kerwin wasn't the most eccentric of the pack of older reporters who spent more time rared back at the Anchor Bar than they did covering their beats. But he was pretty close.

His wardrobe made him almost indistinguishable from a street bum. His shirts and pants were so worn they held together only by the material's sheer determination not to surrender.

Before a late-in-life marriage, Jim spent many of his nights on a cot in the back of the Anchor. After the wedding, his appearance improved considerably, but never much above the level of rumpled.

With thick black glasses and a lumbering gait, he looked like an overstuffed teddy bear that had been worried to death by a child.

He drew young reporters like a magnet. And not just because he took time to talk us through stories, or to tweak our leads, or to rewrite a paragraph or two on the sly. But because he still had the fire, the passion for newspapering.

He was a hell of a reporter, the highest compliment you could pay then. Jim was among the nation's pioneering environmental writers, and he championed the ballot drive for a bottle deposit in Michigan, much to the chagrin of the newspaper's pro-business bosses. I was sitting in the newsroom with Jim the morning after the bottle bill passed, when the late Martin Hayden, the fearsome editor of the *News*, stormed in.

"Your damn deposit law passed, Kerwin," he snarled. "I hope you're happy."

I was frozen in terror just being in the vicinity of such rage, but Jim was unfazed. As Hayden whirled to leave, he said, "Well yes, Martin, I am. Can I buy you a beer to celebrate? I'll pay the deposit."

Irreverence was the order of the day. Jim chaired the lunch group at the old

Press Club, where the price of admission was a quick wit and the ability to take insults as well as you dished them out.

Jim's moment of infamy came when he accepted a challenge from Victor the Rasslin' Bear as a publicity stunt for the old Olympia Arena. Victor was supposed to go easy, but something about the reporter aroused the bear's beastly instincts. He flat kicked Jim's butt.

Year's later, Jim would rub his back and say, "I haven't been right since that crazy bear got ahold of me." And then he'd retell the story.

I never tired of hearing it or any of the dozens of tales Jim had about the glory days of the *News*.

And I wish I could hear them again. Jim died last week, at age 74, 14 years after retiring from the paper.

Stay around a place long enough and you start to see ghosts in every corner.

The newsroom was gutted and remodeled a few years back. But I can close my eyes and still see the old room, with its dangling wires, worn linoleum floor and Depression-era gray desks. I can also see the legends who filled the room.

And now Jim Kerwin joins them.

February 18, 2007

Mr. K was a teacher who changed lives

You don't forget the special teachers. The ones who encouraged, challenged, mentored. The ones who listened. The ones who applauded. The ones who wouldn't give up.

You don't forget the teachers who did those things for you. But even more so, you don't forget the teachers who did them for your children.

Jack Kalousek took my children under his broad wing as soon as they arrived at Franklin High School and kept them there long after they graduated.

Mr. K. taught social studies and directed student activities at Franklin. He died last week while attending the funeral visitation for the father of a student.

Those who knew him, on learning where he was when he suffered the fatal heart attack, said, "Of course." It's exactly where you'd expect Mr. K. to be when one of his kids needed him.

I spend a lot of time harping on the failures of the public schools and the contributions of the teacher unions to Michigan's education deficit.

In doing so, it's sometimes easy to overlook the individual teachers who pour their hearts and souls into their profession, who give their students confidence, vision and so much more than the paycheck covers. Life-changing teachers like Jack Kalousek.

Kalousek, 60, started with the Livonia schools as a custodian, felt a calling and went back to college to get his teaching certificate. If measured just on his classroom performance, he was worth every dime the district paid him. He made social studies a carnival ride for his students.

But his teaching skills weren't what those students, past and present, were talking about when they packed the Harry Will funeral home to say goodbye to Mr. K.

I asked my kids, now grown, what made Kalousek special. Here's what I heard: He set high expectations for us, but he also helped us meet them. He always stopped and asked how we were doing and what was going on in our lives.

His door was always open. You could talk to him about anything, and he'd listen. His office was a safe haven. He was so much more than a teacher. He was a mentor, a friend, even a father figure. He was connected to us.

That connection didn't end on graduation day. My son, five years out of school, still received emails from Kalousek, checking up on him, offering career advice and passing along news of former classmates.

My son says that when he thinks of his high school years, he always thinks of Mr. K. And for good reason. Kalousek practically lived at the school, orchestrating volunteer projects, overseeing after-school club meetings and nurturing student leaders.

It's not easy today to raise children to honorable adulthood. For a parent, fighting the temptations and negative influences can seem like an all-out war. It's often more than two people can handle alone.

To have someone like Jack Kalousek standing shoulder-to-shoulder with you in the battle is a precious gift.

Mr. K. brought both passion and compassion to his craft. A lot of students, and a lot of their parents, will never forget him for that.

≼ ≼ ≼

July 13, 2008

Tony Snow was a family man first

Shortly after Tony and Jill Snow left Detroit for Washington, I stopped by the ancient row house they were renting in Alexandria's Old Town and found Tony struggling with a honey-do list.

I offered to help with some of the chores and asked Tony if he had any tools. "Of course," he said, and headed off for the laundry room. He returned with a miniature hammer, a couple of useless screwdrivers and a tape measure, all resting in just the cutest little wicker basket.

It was a running joke among his family and friends that when required to use his hands for anything mechanical, Tony was comically inept.

But when it came to the things you fix with your heart, he was a master craftsman.

The recounting of Tony Snow's professional life will note that he was one of the most significant journalists of his generation, that he brought class and civility to a political world that has too little of both and that his ideas helped shape the concept of compassionate conservatism.

But for me, the enduring image of Tony Snow will be of him relaxing on his couch, an arm draped around his young son, the two girls snuggled close against his legs, listening, talking, laughing, loving.

Above all else, Tony Snow was an enormously successful family man, and that answers the question of why he was always smiling, even in the worst of times.

The Snow household is filled with love and chaos, and I guess the two things just naturally go together. Most often, animals outnumber people.

Tony and I were talking in his family room one evening when Eddie, their incorrigible yellow Lab, trotted by, in his mouth a loaf of bread that he'd fished out of a cupboard. Close behind were two kids, shrieking and tugging and grabbing for the purloined loaf. Tony looked, shrugged and kept talking.

This is why he fought cancer so hard. And why he believed so stubbornly that he could manage the disease, keep it in check and stick around long enough to see his children grown.

As much as he loved his family, he loved his work, and the tug-of-war between the two caused him considerable distress.

Last July 4th, just after the cancer returned, I was with Tony in the White House. As he showed me his office, I was struck that it wasn't the power or the influence that held him there when far more lucrative—and less stressful—jobs beckoned.

He was drawn by the history and his place in it, by what he saw as the deep privilege of serving his country. Even after his illness forced him to step down as President Bush's press secretary, Tony was planning for the next phase of his life, talking about speeches and books and columns. And about his family.

Tony was a man of deep faith. He didn't fear death or dread it.

But he was convinced that his great passion for his work, for his wife, for his children would prevail. He believed that to the last.

Saturday, I heard a newscaster say Tony Snow had lost his battle with cancer.

It's hard for me to think of it that way. Tony was a winner, because he knew how to live and laugh even while dying, and he knew how to love.

March 17, 2011
Of newsroom ghosts and Siamese toads

Doug Ilka was part of the cast of cowboys, cads and carousers who staffed the *Detroit News* when I first walked in the door 35 years ago.

My beginning assignment at the newspaper was to help Doug cover western Wayne County out of a ratty office above a jewelry shop in Garden City.

Doug, who died last week of pneumonia, took me on as a cause. He saw his mission as teaching me the things I didn't learn in journalism school. Like accounting.

"Let me see that expense report," he said, grabbing the form from under my pen. "This won't do. You submit this weak expense report and downtown will think you're out here (blanking) the dog."

"(Blanking) the dog" was one of many quaint vulgarities that comprised the dialect spoken in the newsroom, a language as nearly dead today as Aramaic.

Doug was fluent in profanity, having served in the Navy. He schooled me while we sat on barstools waiting for our stories to breathe. It was considered bad form to turn in a story before deadline, as that invited getting another assignment, so we'd cross the street to Joe D's until it was safe to file.

For better or worse, Doug earned newsroom infamy for the tale of the Siamese toads.

He was working in the Sterling Heights bureau when a guy called to report he'd found a pair of toads in his backyard that were connected chest-to-back.

He said he'd had them in a bucket for two days and was certain he'd stumbled on one of nature's rarities.

Doug interviewed him over the phone, called a local college professor for some quotes on the uniqueness of the find and dispatched a photographer to snap a picture.

He wrote the story so well that it landed on Page One the next day.

The scoop was spoiled by another phone call from the toads' discoverer the morning the story ran. During the night, the toads had come apart.

Turns out it wasn't a case of conjoined toads but conjugal ones. They were doing what toads do when the spring turns tumescent. The only upside is that it produced the most hilarious skinback ever printed by the *News*, which ran under the headline, "About those toads ..."

We teased Doug relentlessly for years afterward, and he was never again keen for animal stories. But he took it well. "I'm no expert on amphibians," he'd shrug.

For sure, that. But he was a fine reporter and gifted writer who gave the *News* 40 years of devotion and quality work.

Doug made his mark on this town with an investigation of high cancer risks in automotive model-making shops. His reporting changed industry practices and saved lives.

He was also a good family man, and as likeable a guy as you'll meet in this business. And, having studied engineering at Michigan Tech, he could do math, a skill much appreciated in our right brain world.

We'll miss him.

A couple of days before Doug's death, Earl Dowdy, a former travel editor at the *News*, also passed away. Earl always had the look of a guy who knew he had the world by the tail, and he did—he got paid to travel it.

He was also a master storyteller and a first-rate wit. In retirement, he drove a hearse part-time, and if anyone could get a chuckle out of a corpse, it would have been Earl.

Two more ghosts for a newsroom that's getting crowded with them. ⚚

Chapter 17

Freedom

September 14, 2003

Protect freedom's safeguards

Fifteen years ago, Americans were asked in a Gallup poll whether they'd trade some of their civil liberties for a victory in the drug war. Sixty-two percent said yes.

This year, Michigan State University posed a similar question, asking Americans if they'd sacrifice individual freedoms to be secure from terrorism. Fifty-five percent said they would.

The trap here is obvious: While there is no end to national crises, security threats and social scourges, civil liberties are finite. The safeguards intended to perfectly balance the rights of the individual against the power of the government are much easier to surrender than to reclaim.

The Bush administration is again shaving the edges of the Bill of Rights as it tries to gain the upper hand in seeking and prosecuting would-be terrorists. And the longer the war on terror goes on, the more likely Americans are to support placing security ahead of rights.

"People have seen that the war on terrorism is, in fact, ongoing and that we're going to have to continue to make some concessions," says Brian Silver, the MSU political scientist who conducted the nationwide survey.

A year ago, we were more wary of coughing up our constitutional rights to the government. Silver's first poll, conducted in the months after the Sept. 11 terrorist attacks, found roughly three-quarters of Americans placed a higher priority on preserving liberties than on fighting terror.

"The change is real," Silver says. "People might have hesitated in 2001. But they've had more time to reflect, and as they reflect, they say, yes, society is different, we have to do this."

Americans said the same thing about the drug war.

That fight has cost us sizeable pieces of our protections against unreasonable search and seizure; it has turned on its head the concept of innocent until proven guilty, and it has excused the police from judicial oversight in targeting suspected drug dealers and users.

President George W. Bush last week cited the special Bill of Rights exemptions granted drug warriors when he proposed extending them to the terror war.

Silver's polling would suggest that a majority of Americans nodded their head in agreement. Most probably believe they'll never need the due process rights that would be restricted.

But the warrantless searches Bush wants for terror investigations cost a 63-year-old California grandfather his life. Mario Paz was killed when 20 narcotics officers shot their way into his home. As it turns out, Paz was not a drug dealer—his neighbor of 15 years earlier was. The police informant got it wrong.

A tragic and unintended mistake, but an innocent citizen was executed. The Bill of Rights exists to shield individuals from this sort of overzealous law enforcement. Paz's killing is all the reason a law-abiding citizen should need to demand a hands-off policy on due process.

If the righteous crusades against drugs, terror and other evils can't be won without trampling liberty and suspending the rules that keep innocent citizens from joining the victims' list, then maybe they aren't worth winning.

February 4, 2001

Don't let advances in technology make a blind-sided hit on privacy rights

It was just a small item in the sports section, but the impact was jarring. During last Sunday's Super Bowl, the face of each fan who walked in the gates at Raymond James Stadium in Tampa Bay was photographed, digitized and run through computers. The computers matched the 100,000 faces against those on file with the FBI and various other law enforcement agencies.

They were searching for terrorists who might have considered the year's premier football game an opportunity to make a grand statement. Presumably, no matches were found, since no one was detained.

Perhaps fans will feel safer knowing such super high-tech security techniques are at work at big sporting events. But it makes me uneasy.

I feel the same way about the new technology that uses satellites to track the movement of cell phones and their owners. If the phone is on, police can pinpoint your whereabouts. The system was designed to help rescue workers respond to 911 calls. But it's sort of creepy to know that your every movement can be tracked.

Earlier, the *News* printed a story about a suburban community that planned to mount cameras at intersections. If you run the red light, the camera takes your picture and later on you get a ticket in the mail.

Too much.

Privacy is precious. It's equally precious as being able to sit in a football stadium with the confidence that the person in the next seat is not a mad bomber.

It's just as precious as equipping police with a tool to help them respond quicker to cell phone emergency calls. And it's more precious than making sure motorists pay better attention to traffic signals.

It is a basic right that we shouldn't relinquish casually in the hope of creating a safer, more secure world.

Adam Thierer, director of telecommunications studies at the libertarian Cato Institute, says we should worry about the increasing ability of technology to monitor constantly what we do and where we go.

"These technologies do pose serious privacy concerns," Thierer says. "When your government is snooping on you, it should make you uncomfortable. You should at least be informed that it's being done."

The danger is that such surveillance efforts treat law-abiding citizens like criminals without cause.

"You should be asking why the government is collecting such information, and if there's a permanent record being compiled of your personal movements," Thierer says.

Terrorism at the Super Bowl is a recurring theme of books and movies. And though it has never occurred, officials may have had good reason to fret about hostage-taking or bombings. If that was the case last Sunday, those walking through the turnstiles should have been informed their photographs were being fed into a computer. That's a big step beyond training security cameras on a crowd.

Fans should also be assured that the files are destroyed after the game. You may have some very good—and non-criminal—reasons for not wanting photographic evidence to remain of your Super Bowl visit.

A balance must be reached between taking advantage of the most advanced and sophisticated technology to protect citizens and protecting the privacy of citizens from undue government snooping.

October 21, 2001

Take a lesson from the drug war before exchanging liberty for security

Americans profess to love liberty above all else, but when threatened, we too often hurl our liberties on the barricades.

Once again, we are allowing an atmosphere of fear to be used as an opportunity to chisel away at our freedoms.

The House and Senate are near agreement on a package of anti-terrorism bills that will greatly expand police powers and greatly diminish privacy and due process protections. Had the House not adjourned at mid-week due to the anthrax scare, a bill would already be on its way to the president.

Hopefully, Congress is using the furlough to take a second look at the long-term impact.

Our generation has already allowed the 25-year drug war to horribly erode the Constitution.

Protections against illegal search and seizure and self-incrimination aren't strong enough to keep you from being yanked off the job without cause and forced to take a drug test—unless you work for the government. The sanctity of property rights is weaker than the forfeiture laws that allow prosecutors to seize and sell your car on mere suspicion of a crime. Search warrant safeguards are now twisted into a pretzel of exceptions and rationalizations that give police broad authority to snoop and trespass.

The result? No less dope, but a lot less civil liberties.

We seem to have learned little from that miserable failure, and are ready again to empty the drawers of the Fourth and Fifth amendments.

Atty. Gen, John Ashcroft is asking Congress for a laundry list of insidious measures like the sneak and peak provision, which would open the doors of a home or business to officers who could sort through personal belongings, take photographs, examine computer hard drives, without ever notifying the owner. The lack of notification makes it awfully tough to mount a constitutional challenge to the search.

The new anti-liberty bills would also greatly expand surveillance powers, particularly on the Internet. The government wants to monitor the Web for suspicious activity and intercept e-mail without warrants.

Also under assault are probable cause provisions limiting when the government can eavesdrop. The current standard of suspicion that a crime has been, or is about to be, committed would evaporate.

Non-citizens would lose most due process rights, and could be detained indefinitely if the attorney general—not a judge—suspects they are involved in or know about terrorism. The burden of proof would be on the accused, not the accuser.

You may think all this is reasonable given the present danger. But even Ashcroft acknowledged that had these laws been in place prior to Sept. 11, they may not have prevented the attacks.

"Anyone who thinks we can surrender some civil liberties and be safer is being misled," said Timothy Lynch of the Libertarian Cato Institute. "Because of the gradual chipping away at the safeguards of the Constitution, the next generation is not going to have the constitutional rights we have, and certainly not the ones our grandparents had."

Many in Congress who might normally rise in defense of civil liberties are silent for fear of seeming unpatriotic.

Lovers of liberty should remind them that preserving our ability to pass to our children the rights and freedoms our parents passed to us is the highest form of patriotism.

July 7, 2002

Oklahoma student stood up for liberty; don't let her stand alone

Lindsay Earls calls herself a goodie two-shoes, a straight arrow who sticks to her books and stays out of the fast lane.

She's also my new hero, a fine, young patriot whose instincts for liberty would make Thomas Jefferson proud.

Lindsay was a 16-year-old at Tecumseh, Okla., High School in 1998 when the local school board demanded that all students engaged in extracurricular activities take a drug test.

Lindsay balked, sensing this unprovoked testing was a huge violation of her privacy. With the support of her parents and the state chapter of the American Civil Liberties Union, she filed a lawsuit that eventually ended up before the United States Supreme Court.

And that's where freedom failed to find a defender. The court last week ruled 5-4 that students who volunteer to participate in after-school programs should not expect privacy.

The majority opinion was written by Justice Clarence Thomas, whose own privacy was so despicably trampled during his confirmation hearings. Presumably, Thomas now also believes a judicial candidate who volunteers to have his or her name placed in consideration likewise should have a lower expectation of privacy.

Lindsay and her family were bucking a frightening movement in this country that is willing to forfeit long-established civil liberties for the greater good of stamping out a momentary menace. First drugs, then terrorism and next, who knows? There will always be an evil whose defeat demands freedom's sacrifice.

"They can't do that," is what Lindsay's father said when she told him about the drug testing. "It's un-American."

The writers of the Constitution provided a solid framework for our laws. The suspicion-less drug testing adopted by Lindsay's school violates protections against privacy intrusions, unreasonable searches and self-incrimination. The court's interpretation that those rights don't apply because the students can avoid the tests by dropping out of after-school programs is a perversion of the document's intent.

We can't allow our freedoms to become so conditional. If you can drag a good kid like Lindsay out of the school choir and demand that she give a urine sample or go home, how soon before we yank everyday Americans off the street and force them to do the same?

How soon before authorities can show up at homes and rummage through drawers and closets looking for drugs?

There aren't enough Americans like Lindsay to stop it from happening. A *Detroit News* cyber-survey after the court's ruling indicated solid support for the drug tests. Many respondents said the same thing: If you have nothing to hide, why not take the test? Isn't that what they say in a police state?

David Earls doesn't want Lindsay, now a freshman at Dartmouth, to surrender her rights so easily. That's why he encouraged her to fight back.

"People think this is just about peeing in a cup," says Earls, whose daughter has been taunted in the town of 7,000. "But I told Lindsay there were people who fought and died for the Constitution of the United States and what it stood for. Don't we as citizens owe them a little debt of gratitude by standing up for those rights?"

We owe Lindsay one as well. Even though she lost, she at least tried to slow the erosion of liberty, to stop pushing back the point at which we say, "They can't do that."

May 9, 2004

Feds destroy lives and property rights

John Rapanos has lived both the American dream and the American nightmare.

Rapanos, 68, is the son of immigrant Greek fruit peddlers who went broke in Chicago during the Depression and fled to Midland, where they prospered. So did their son, as a developer of subdivisions and commercial sites.

It was a fine life until 1988, when Rapanos decided to develop 200 acres of fallow farmland he'd owned since the late 1950s. He cleared off the scrub trees and graded part of the property, hoping to attract a retail strip mall. When that idea washed out, he leased the land to a local grain farmer.

That's when the government climbed on Rapanos' back, and he hasn't been able to peel it off since. Sixteen years later, Rapanos is facing up to 56 months in jail and $10 million in penalties.

"They're out to destroy me," Rapanos says. "They won't stop until I'm behind bars."

His crime: Destroying a wetland that never existed.

John Rapanos' story is a chilling example of what can happen when government loses all respect for property rights and starts looking at private land as a communal asset.

The acreage Rapanos cleared lies along US-10, so it's not surprising that his activity was noticed by an agent of the state Department of Environmental Quality. The agent visited the site and determined that Rapanos had drained the land and brought in more than 300,000 yards of fill dirt.

Later, the DEQ handed off the case to the federal Environmental Protection Agency, which confirmed the finding and began prosecution. Rapanos was convicted by a federal court jury in Flint and lost several appeals.

Here's the kicker: Rapanos' land is surrounded on all sides, and divided down the middle, by drainage ditches dug by the county drain commission in 1904. The land was tiled at the same time to further aid drainage so it could be used for farming.

The combination of drainage ditches and sandy soil means the land couldn't be a wetland if it wanted to be. It won't hold water.

"I don't see any way that could have been a wetland," says Russ Harding, director of the DEQ under former Gov. John Engler and now with the Mackinac Center, a free market think tank in Midland. "There's no evidence that wetlands had been disturbed. It's a typical Michigan corn field surrounded by drainage ditches."

Harding visited the property and dug 18 holes, each four-feet deep, at various spots. He found no trace of water, and no evidence of fill dirt. Rapanos says he didn't dump a single load of fill on the property.

Standing in the cornfield, Rapanos' land appears no different from the surrounding farms. It's no higher, no wetter.

Harding says if Rapanos had brought in as much fill dirt as the government claims, it would have raised the topography by six feet. Experts testified in court that there was no fill and no wetlands.

But prosecutors pressed on, even after learning it was the drain commission, not Rapanos, that dug the ditches.

Harding says he believes the EPA targeted Rapanos because he is a well-known developer in mid-Michigan, and they wanted a high-profile example. He calls this "a very bad case."

It's worse than that. After the jury returned its verdict, U.S. District Judge Lawrence Zatkoff set aside the conviction, ruling prosecutors wrongly accused Rapanos of concealing evidence. The Justice Department appealed to the Sixth Circuit Court of Appeals, which reversed Zatkoff and ordered him to sentence Rapanos.

Zatkoff again tried to inject sanity into the case by sentencing Rapanos to 200 hours of community service, probation and a $185,000 fine, all of which he fulfilled.

Noting a drug dealer was in his court the same day, Zatkoff said from the bench: "Here we have a person—who commits crimes of selling dope and the government asks me to put him in prison for 10 months. And then we have an American citizen, who buys land, pays for it with his own money, and he moves some sand from one end to the other and (the) government wants me to give him 63 months in prison. Now, if that isn't our system gone crazy, I don't know what is. And I am not going to do it. I don't believe he got a fair trial."

Amen. But the government had a hold of Rapanos like a bulldog on a pant leg. It returned to the Sixth Circuit, demanding Rapanos get the jail time, and the court agreed. The sentencing is on hold pending Rapanos' third appeal to the U.S. Supreme Court, which has twice refused to hear his case.

A companion civil suit seeks $10 million from Rapanos to build wetlands on another 81 acres he was forced to buy. A government mitigator visited the original land and came to the same conclusion that Harding did: The land can't be restored to wetlands because of the drainage ditches.

And that brings us back to the beginning. Rapanos couldn't have destroyed wetlands because wetlands couldn't have existed on the property because of the drainage ditches, which were built and are still maintained by the government, which is hell-bent on locking him up for something the government did 100 years ago.

The rapids of injustice may quickly turn into a waterfall. Rapanos faces judgment in the civil suit on June 9 before District Court Judge Bernard Friedman in Detroit, and likely sentencing in the criminal case later this summer.

It's so late in the process that Rapanos is running out of options for avoiding jail time and crushing civil fines.

The Supreme Court is unlikely to intervene, given its past indifference. Zatkoff's ability to continue as a bulkhead of common sense has been sharply limited by the Sixth Circuit.

It's a long shot, but President George W. Bush could issue a presidential pardon and free Rapanos from further harassment. That won't recover the $1.5 million he's already spent on the case, or the $4 million in lost revenue from the property the Justice Department has tied up.

But it's the least that should happen for a man who has received such mean treatment from his own government.

August 29, 2004

Popping johns makes money for cops

A hooker says she was paid $60 to jolly up Butch Hollowell in the front seat of the former state Democratic Party chair's car near Detroit's Palmer Park.

Sheriff Warren Evans collected $900 from the same encounter and didn't have to take off a stitch of his clothes.

Why Hollowell would be shagging hookers in his own neighborhood is still unanswered. Why the Wayne County Sheriff's Department is running prostitution busts in Detroit may be the better question.

The Sheriff's Department has limited law enforcement responsibilities. Its primary duty is to operate the county lock-ups and provide support services to other county police departments. It does the prostitution detail, Evans says, at the request of Detroit police.

He says hookers and their customers are ruining communities, are a nuisance to residents and create the environment for other illegal activity. All true.

But it's also true that every john busted in a car has to pay the county $900 to get his vehicle back. Under the civil forfeiture law, the county keeps the money even if the defendant is never charged or convicted of a crime.

The fines are an important revenue source for the sheriff and the Detroit Police Department, which also works feverishly to sweep the streets of johns and their cars.

Evans estimates forfeiture fines bring in $1 million a year, money he says that covers the cost of the unit. He says it's not a profit center and is having an impact on prostitution.

Defense attorneys say the motive for the cops is the same as for the prostitutes—shaking money out of the johns.

"They can grab as many as 100 cars a night," says Dearborn lawyer Majed A. Moughni, who has unsuccessfully challenged the civil forfeiture law.

It's such a fabulous scheme it's hard to believe the government came up with it. Defendants who feel they were wrongly arrested have a choice: Pay $3,000 for an attorney to challenge the seizure, wait 60 days for a court hearing and risk the sort of public humiliation Hollowell is enduring. Or pay the $900, get the car back right away and hope whoever is waiting at home never finds out.

Moughni says his files are full of cases where defendants claim they were arrested for simply rolling down their car window when a police decoy knocked.

The attorney also contends some prostitutes work in cahoots with the cops, giving up their clients after they've been paid for their services. "It's racketeering," says Moughni. "It's all about the money."

The goal of ridding neighborhoods of illicit activities is a fine one. But ignoring civil liberties as a means of getting there is unacceptable. Grabbing a car and holding it hostage to a $900 fine—plus towing costs—trashes the concept of innocent until proven guilty.

Like nearly every defendant in his predicament, Hollowell claims he is innocent, the victim of a misunderstanding. Maybe so, maybe no.

But with so much money in play, and so few due process safeguards in place, it's easy to see how the system could be gamed.

Moughni's advice: "If you're driving through Detroit and see a pretty woman on the curb, don't stop, don't roll down your window, don't even wink."

March 25, 2010
Nanny state will turn U.S. into Europe

Passage of a national health care bill begins fulfilling the fantasy of the left of making over America into something resembling its refined and compassionate European cousins.

Throughout the health care battle, President Barack Obama asked, if European nations can deliver expansive universal health care to every citizen, why can't the United States do the same? The president, an ardent Europhile, poses that question about everything from high-speed rail to cheap college tuition.

The answer is that we can—if we're willing to live a European lifestyle.

That's a dandy thought for those who look longingly at Europe's rich social welfare programs, efficient public transportation and teeny carbon footprints.

But most Americans will chafe at giving up their personal choices and elbowroom to make Euro-socialism work here. The Nanny State is anathema to our natural individualism. But once government takes over the care and feeding of its citizens, nothing is beyond its reach. France and Denmark, for example, claim veto power over baby names. A people conditioned to view the government as the dominant force in their universe accept any government intrusion.

They also accept less of everything.

The average European has 396 square feet of living space, compared to 721 square feet for the average American. Even the poor in the United States have more personal space than the typical European.

Americans love their single-family homes, with as much green space as they can afford between them and their neighbors. In Europe, much of the population is stacked in bleak Bauhaus boxes surrounding cities glorious for their historic architecture, but where nothing of significance has been built in 50 years.

Being cramped at home helps condition them for the toy-sized automobiles mandated by Europe's high gasoline taxes. Imagine those clown cars squeezed full of Americans, who weigh on average 10 pounds more than Europeans (something we aren't so proud of, but will be remedied when government health czars start planning our menus, a la New York's salt ban).

Three-quarters of Americans own an automobile, compared to 50-60 percent in western European nations, and nearly half of us drive trucks or SUVs, a sight as rare on the streets of Europe as an honest taxpayer.

While 85 percent of Americans obey tax laws, the rate in Western Europe ranges from 60-75 percent. In Belgium, which has one of the world's biggest tax burdens, 22 percent of the economy is black market.

Who can blame them for cheating the taxman? In Europe, government spending is equal to 40-50 percent of gross domestic product, compared to 28 percent in the United States, and top tax rates reach 60 percent.

That's why Europeans don't knock themselves out earning money. Productivity gains in Western Europe are half the U.S. average, while unemployment averages twice our rate.

One thing Europe doesn't spend money on is defense. Military spending as a percentage of GDP averages less than 2 percent in Europe, compared to 4.5 percent in the United States, which accounts for 41.5 percent of worldwide defense spending.

As long as America is the world's Great Protector, European countries can afford to skimp on guns to buy butter. But if we are now to become the Great Nanny of our own people, that equation will have to change.

Yes, we can have what Europe has. But we can't have that and what America has as well.

≺ ≺ ≺

January 20, 2011

Missing the real lessons from Arizona

How convenient for the politicians that they were so quickly and earnestly made the victims of the Arizona shootings. Pinning the blame on the nation's overheated and sometimes uncivil political discourse fit neatly into the left's theory that a conservative mob has hijacked the nation and is willing to resort to anything—even violence—to derail the good liberals are trying to do.

And it also neatly excuses Congress from addressing the real roots of this attack and too many like it that happen on an almost weekly basis across the country. Damning conservative talk show hosts and the far right's shrill shrews is easier than fixing a busted mental health system or holding the entertainment industry accountable for saturating our culture in blood.

Instead of tackling these prickly issues, Congress is weighing a law that will shield its members from criticism and another that would ban anyone from carrying a gun within 1,000 feet of a federal official.

What about the rest of us? No law is likely to emerge from the shootings that will do the public any good, even though 18 others were shot along with Rep. Gabrielle Giffords, and six were killed, including a 9-year-old girl— what was her name?

Even though it's overwhelmingly apparent that Jared Loughner is a deranged man with a history of bizarre behavior and no hint of political involvement, the talk remains about the dangers of name-calling.

No one seems eager to tackle the reality that our mental health codes give families too few options for intervening on behalf of a disturbed loved one, and law enforcement officials too little authority to act before the mentally troubled hurt themselves or others.

Nor is there much interest in addressing the fact that in Michigan and other places, the violence-prone mentally ill are as likely to end up in prison as in a treatment facility.

And does anyone see the irony in liberal commentators so quickly drawing a link between the shootings and the veiled violent references in political give-and-take, but resisting the possibility that the incessant images of bloodshed and mayhem pumped into young people from movie screens, television sets, video game consoles and iPods could trigger anti-social impulses?

Hollywood gets a free pass again. Its princes and princesses can show up at televised awards ceremonies and wax sanctimoniously about the need for a more civil society, and then go back to work creating chaos.

Turn on the television set tonight and count the number of programs that carry a "V" for violence warning. These programs are increasingly gruesome and realistic. And they're mixed in seamlessly with shots of real life violence on news shows.

Yet we convince ourselves that our children can distinguish between what's real and what's fiction, and that parents are there to teach them the difference.

Looking at Loughner's photo, it's easier to imagine him spending hours spraying virtual bullets in a game of *Call of Duty* than sitting rapt before a Fox News program.

But taking the debate in that direction serves no political agenda.

So we walk away from what should have been a wake-up call for our society thinking that the only lesson from Tucson is that politicians ought to be a protected species, shielded from rudeness and loud voices, lest the safety of the nation be placed at risk.

July 26, 2012

In defense of the maligned assault weapon

Hysteria and facts don't mix well, so it's not surprising that missing from the righteous outrage about free-flowing assault weapons and America's gun-crazy culture is this inconvenient truth: Gun-related homicides in the United States have fallen in half over the past two decades, according to FBI statistics, to 8,775 in 2010 from 17,075 in 1993.

Note that the gun homicide total continued to drop even after 2004, when the federal ban on assault weapons expired. Per-capita gun deaths today are about where they were in the early 1960s.

Note also that the downward trend in gun deaths has corresponded with an increase in gun ownership.

That doesn't fit the narrative favored by the anti-gun fanatics, but not much about their obsession with banning firearms is rooted in reality.

Start with the "assault weapons" moniker—a term made up by the media and the anti-gun lobby to make those firearms seem more sinister than grandpa's trusty squirrel rifle.

One of the firearms used last week by the Colorado movie theater shooter was an AR-15 rifle, which was described in coverage as a "military-style" weapon.

Military style doesn't mean military issue. While the AR-15 is a cousin to the M-16 used by the armed forces, there's a big difference between them.

The AR-15 is not a machine gun. It won't spray bullets with a single pull of the trigger. It's a semi-automatic, meaning that the trigger must be pulled for each round fired. And while it looks more fearsome, in practical application it's no different and certainly no more deadly or powerful than many of the deer rifles favored by Michigan hunters.

What can set it apart from hunting firearms is the size of the magazine. Most hunting rifles have a five-round magazine to comply with state hunting regulations. The magazine in the gun the Colorado shooter used reportedly held 100 rounds.

In theory, that would allow the shooter to discharge more bullets in a shorter time. But in reality, a moderately experienced shooter can change a magazine in a couple of seconds, making the difference in lethality minimal. And the larger magazines have a tendency to jam, which is apparently what happened in Colorado.

The failure of the gun didn't stop the killing. The shooter also had in his arsenal a .40-caliber Glock, a popular handgun, and a Remington 870 shotgun, which can be found in nearly every duck blind in America. It turns out those common weapons killed as efficiently as the assault rifle.

Most gun owners don't use their weapons for hunting. They have them for either personal protection or because they like to target shoot.

So you can't dismiss firearms that aren't suitable for the field as illegitimate.

Many recreational gun users enjoy shooting rifles that resemble the ones used by the military, and the larger magazines enhance the experience. Mass shootings are an anachronistic crime. They spike and they fall regardless of whether assault weapons bans are on the books or off, or whether the homicide rate is rising or falling.

We can rush to ban certain firearms types based solely on cosmetics. We can reduce their ammo capacity. But those are feel-good measures that won't prevent the next nut-ball from going on a killing rampage.

⚔ ⚔ ⚔

December 19, 2012

Gun laws didn't stop Newtown

There are few physical things I love more than guns. But I would've melted down every rifle, shotgun and pistol I own had I thought it would spare the life of even one of those precious children massacred in Connecticut last week.

It wouldn't have. And the post-shooting solutions being demanded in response to the slaying of 20 pupils and six adults at Sandy Hook Elementary in Newtown won't prevent another outrage.

But here we are waging a culture war instead of coming together to figure out if there's actually something we can do that might work.

More gun control, at least not the proposals on the table, won't do it. Connecticut has some of the nation's toughest gun laws—including restrictions on assault weapons, a waiting period for firearm purchases and no-carry zones covering schools.

And yet none of those measures stopped a disturbed Adam Lanza from loading his mother's guns into his car and carrying out his slaughter of innocents. Similarly, the gun control measures offered by Sen. Dianne Feinstein, D-Calif., mostly restore the assault weapons ban in place between 1994 and 2004, laws that didn't prevent Columbine and other mass shootings during the period.

Her proposal grandfathers the nearly 300 million firearms currently in private hands, including the semi-automatics that are the target of gun foes. While it prohibits the sale of nearly 200 specific weapons, it wouldn't affect more than 900 other guns currently on the market, and any one of them could be used effectively by someone intent on committing mass mayhem.

Unless we're willing to blow up the Second Amendment and go door-to-door confiscating every privately owned gun, passing feel-good gun control laws is pointless.

But that doesn't mean there's nothing we can do. Gun owners have a powerful incentive to address gun abuse. Their rights are on the line.

Every gun I own is locked in a safe. Trigger locks are available for a couple of bucks each, and usually come free with a gun purchase. Use them. Parents know if their children are troubled or prone to violent outbreaks. Keep the guns out of their reach.

Personal responsibility should go hand in hand with gun ownership. Passed your concealed pistol class and got your license to carry? Great. But don't leave your gun in the car or a purse for thieves to grab.

Gun makers should also read the handwriting on the wall. Feeding the lust for ever-more deadly weaponry may produce profits today, but risks killing their business in the long run.

Same goes for the entertainment industry. The First Amendment can fall as easily as the Second, and there's a growing call to "do something" about bloody movies, music and video games. Lanza reportedly was a devotee of one of the more gory games. Who knows if that's where he got his inspiration?

There's no room for censorship laws, but there should be some self-imposed boundaries of taste and common sense.

Hollywood is not loath to use its art to crusade. Why not aid the cause of creating a less violent society by toning down the grisly and graphic imagery? Haven't we pushed the envelope about as far as it can go?

These are things we ought to be able to talk about. And we can, if we set aside opportunism and political agendas and bore down to what might head off the next Newtown.

June 13, 2013

Obama breaks trust in government

Defenders of the data mining conducted by the National Security Agency say that the tracking of Americans' phone calls and even emails is an essential weapon in the war on terror.

The Obama administration claims the widespread and apparently indiscriminate sweeping of private communications has already thwarted one terror attack, although it won't provide details.

Many of my fellow conservatives, as much as they'd like to stick President Barack Obama with another embarrassing scandal, agree such surveillance is necessary in a world where sophisticated terror networks are constantly plotting America's destruction.

I disagree for the same reason I opposed much of the Patriot Act to begin with—there's no sense protecting our civil liberties from terrorists only to forfeit them to our own government.

But even if a case can be made for such intrusive monitoring of the citizenry, it only works if the people have complete trust that this enormous expansion of power of the government over the individual won't be abused.

Knowing what we now know about the Obama administration's misuse of other powers entrusted to it—quite likely for its own political gain—that trust is completely shot.

Who can have faith that an administration whose Internal Revenue Service targeted Obama's political opponents for harassment won't also use the NSA's surveillance power to gather crucial information on its enemies?

How can we be certain that an administration whose Justice Department secretly seized the phone records of the Associated Press and did a deep dive through the personal communications of a respected television journalist won't use its security arm to listen in on other reporters chasing stories it doesn't want told?

This administration sees no limit on its presidential powers. It bends the Constitution to get and do what it wants.

So why wouldn't we worry that it might collude with its Silicon Valley sycophants to gather embarrassing tidbits on the political opposition?

Imagine the damage that could be done if a major search engine, whose executives are unabashed supporters of Obama, teamed with the administration to manipulate its rankings in such a way as to prioritize stories that touted the president's agenda or marginalized his opponents.

Such an alliance could become the most potent propaganda machine the world has ever seen.

Yeah, I know, I'm delving into the world of black helicopters here, and before you know it I'll be calling in conspiracy theories to late night radio talk shows.

But once a trust is broken, as it is now in America, no abuse of power scenario is too far-fetched to consider.

June 19, 2013

It's time we abolish the IRS

Why would anyone give a federal agency caught in an outrageous abuse of its considerable power even more authority to meddle in the lives of Americans?

There's no justifiable reason. But that's what the federal government is about to do with the Internal Revenue Service.

In a still-unfolding scandal, the IRS has been caught red-handed targeting conservative political groups for special scrutiny in what seems obvious was an attempt to aid the re-election bid of President Barack Obama.

The agency harassed a variety of groups and individuals linked to conservative and Republican political causes, including those with the words "tea party" and "patriot" in their names.

The IRS dragnet inadvertently picked off some non-political groups as well, including Oakland County Judge Michael Warren's "Patriot Week" organization, whose mission is to promote teaching the Constitution to school children. What sort of agency of the United States government finds something sinister in patriotism?

The IRS does. And that's more than enough reason to jettison plans to make it the enforcement arm of Obamacare. The new health care law gives the tax agency 46 new powers and 1,200 new agents to make sure everyone who is supposed to buy an insurance policy buys one. It will also collect the 18 new taxes that will support the program.

That's way too much responsibility for an institution America no longer trusts. It will make the IRS not only the most feared agent of the federal government, but also the most powerful. An agency that has proven itself willing to manipulate the levers of government to achieve a political end should not be rewarded, it should be punished.

The most fitting punishment would be to disband the IRS. And junk the income tax, too.

Mike Huckabee, former governor of Arkansas and now a TV talk show host, is urging Congress to replace the income tax with a national sales tax. You'd pay tax on the money you spend instead of the money you earn.

That would eliminate the need for an IRS that audits tax returns, hands out nonprofit status and enforces a tax code that is egregiously complex and unfair.

If the national sales tax isn't the answer, then a similar outcome might be achieved by drastically lowering current income tax rates in exchange for eliminating all deductions and credits.

With no reason to examine returns, the IRS could be much smaller. Without auditing power, it'd be less intimidating.

There's still the issue of how to enforce Obamacare, which was declared constitutional by the U.S. Supreme Court only because its requirement that everyone buy an insurance policy is considered a tax, not a purchase mandate.

Resolving that may require a rethinking and rewriting of Obamacare. There's very little downside in that.

If, in one stroke, we can eliminate the hated and abusive IRS and revamp an entitlement that seems destined to complete the bankrupting of America, what's the downside? ⚞

Chapter 18

Newspapers

May 7, 2000

New editor is product of community, the *News*

My uncle was the head deacon of a small church in the hill country of southern Kentucky. When the worshipers decided to boot a less than inspiring preacher, it fell to Uncle Baker to draft the letter of discharge.

He took the task seriously, struggling through the night to find just the right words to convey the flock's displeasure. After crumpling a ream of paper, he finally gave up and penned this simple sentence:

"We the undersigned members of New Sulfur Baptist Church would druther have your vacancy than your presence."

Not all that eloquent, but hard to miss the point.

I'm a fan of that sort of directness, and it's what you can expect from these pages as I assume leadership of the *Detroit News* editorial page staff. I'm very much a product of this newspaper and this community, and am wholly committed to both. You can expect to see that reflected here as well.

I've been with the *News* 24 years, starting as a copy boy on my 21st birthday, at a time when one of the morning duties of that job was to roust drunken reporters and editors from various cubbyholes of the newsroom and send them home for a shave and coffee.

As a City Hall reporter covering the Coleman Young administration, I was an eyewitness to the devastating impact of divisiveness, abandonment and racial politics. Every week, it seemed, the lights went out in another office building, hotel or factory. That's why I rejoiced at Opening Day in Comerica

Park, and why I tend to err on the side of optimism when it comes to Detroit's recovery.

My family came here from Kentucky, looking for jobs created by the auto industry. To pay my way through Schoolcraft College and Wayne State University, I worked full-time in a small auto parts factory in northwest Detroit. I remember the long unemployment lines that followed the 1974 oil crisis—I stood in one that wrapped twice around the Michigan Employment Security Commission office in Wayne. Those were terrible days, and nearly everyone wondered with Merle Haggard whether the good times were really over for good.

The impression it left was that poor boardroom decision-making can trigger a chain reaction of suffering, and that horrible things happen when a business allows itself to get fat and uncompetitive.

My tenure as business editor spanned the auto industry's remarkable recovery, a feat accomplished through sacrifice, innovation and courageous leadership. It's an incredible story and a valuable lesson.

From the letters I've received this first week on the job, it's clear many of you are worried about the future of these pages. Mark Silverman, publisher and editor of the *News*, attempted to put those fears to rest last Sunday by stating unequivocally that the *News* will not abandon its traditional philosophy. Some of you believe him, others don't. To that issue, I'll just say:

Watch this space.

I invite you to read us with a critical eye during the next few months, scrutinize our positions and call us to task when appropriate.

A newspaper should not be a mouthpiece for any political party or special interest group. Rather, it should be a powerful and passionate voice for its readers, scolding incompetence, railing against injustice and celebrating the successes of the community.

That's a newspaper's job. And I'm honored that it's now my job to speak on behalf of the newspaper to which I've devoted my career.

≺ ≺ ≺

March 29, 2009

Why your newspaper still matters

Newspapers may go away, but the scoundrels won't.

The opportunists and political grifters will still be around, scheming to move your money into their pockets. The exploiters and manipulators still will be there to prey on the gullible for their own power and profit.

All that will be missing is the barking watchdog to keep them at bay.

This is self-serving, I know. I've been a newspaperman for 33 years and would like to think I have a few more years of newspapering left in me. I've got a personal stake in the health and welfare of the industry.

But for the life of me I can't see how this country can sustain a vigorous, participatory democracy if newspapers disappear. And they're vanishing at a shocking rate.

Last week, Michigan newspaper readers learned the *Ann Arbor News*, one of the state's oldest publications, would quiet its presses in July. Three of its sister papers in the Booth chain, the *Flint Journal*, *Saginaw News* and *Bay City Times*, will only publish three days a week.

The news ought to disturb anyone who buys into the premise that institutions both public and private need an independent monitor to keep them honest. And who wouldn't believe that, considering what the corruption and incompetence of Washington and Wall Street have done to our economy?

If it's not newspapers doing the job, who will? Spend a week with a newspaper reporter and you'll be stunned at how many hours are devoted to mundane meetings of boards, commissions and councils, watching the process of government unfold.

It can be dreary stuff. But every once in a while, there's a nugget tucked into a budget that doesn't seem quite right, or an intriquing tip whispered into an ear, and suddenly the dominos are falling.

Those bases won't get covered without newspapers. Broadcasters don't have the manpower; bloggers lack the credibility.

If you don't believe newspapers are still relevant in a sound bite world, think about this: If it hadn't been for the work of some first-rate reporters, Kwame Kilpatrick would still be sitting atop his corrupt kingdom.

Or consider that disgraced Illinois Gov. Rod Blagojevich feared the prying eyes of newspaper reporters even more than he did the feds, plotting the firing of a *Chicago Tribune* writer who he thought was endangering a pay-off. The *Trib* is among the newspapers in bankruptcy.

There's no federal bailout coming for the newspaper industry, and I doubt we'd take it if it were offered. Better to die than be compromised. We've got to meet this challenge on our own.

Tomorrow, the *Detroit News* joins the *Detroit Free Press* in an initiative to do just that. Our moves will inconvenience some readers. We regret that and wish things didn't have to change.

But if the strategy works, if readers stand by us, we'll be positioned to move newspapers into the 21st century fully loaded with the resources needed to defend the First Amendment.

Again, I'm personally invested in this dice roll. But so are you.

Do you want to rest a pillar of our democracy on a blogger sitting in a basement with a computer and an ax to grind?

January 27, 2013
So much more than a building

One winter I raised a turkey on the roof of the *Detroit News*. Her name was Darryl and her job was to pick winners of NFL games by pecking corn kernels from one tray over another.

Her purchase and care fell to me for reasons I don't recall. Darryl lost interest in football early in the season and turned quite vicious as she fattened up, flailing me whenever I prodded her to prognosticate.

I came to hate that bird and was looking forward to a nice turkey dinner on Super Bowl Sunday. But my editor decided that didn't fit the storyline readers expected, so I had to donate Darryl to a petting zoo. She lasted two days before ending up in someone else's oven.

For me, the *News* building is furnished with memories. I've spent my entire adult life here. I know it the way a farmer knows his fields. I've been in its newsroom for every historical moment of the past four decades, and most of the mundane ones as well. It's where I've met the people who shaped my career and where I bid many of them farewell. I've seen it gutted and restored. I've known it when it was too small to hold all of the people we needed to put out a newspaper and when it became so big for the staff on hand you could hear echoes.

It is what we used to call in the south The Home Place.

And now we're moving away. The announcement last week that we are leaving the building that's housed us since 1917 to seek more efficient quarters elsewhere in Detroit is the right decision from a business viewpoint. With office space such a bargain in Detroit, it makes no sense to own and maintain an aging building that has twice as much floor space as we need.

The overhead is simply too great for a lean operating era.

But it's going to be hard to walk out onto Lafayette Boulevard for the last time. These offices, designed by Albert Kahn, are magnificent and burst with the history of the newspaper and the city. We'll take many of the artifacts with us, I assume, but they won't quite fit somewhere else.

A colleague said it's not the move as much as what it symbolizes that is distressing. She's right. Newspapers all over the country are downsizing because newspapers and their staffs are shrinking.

Working in this industry is like managing Stage 4 cancer. You hope to stay alive until someone discovers a miracle cure. So you bear the side effects of radical treatments and cut away pieces you'd rather keep.

Like this lovely gray lady, with her stained-glass windows and oak-paneled offices and 96 years of memories. It's sad. But if shedding this building buys us more time to figure out how to move journalism profitably from the printing press to the Internet, then I'll leave here happily.

Newspapers aren't about bricks and mortar any more than they are about paper and ink. Ideas and information, watchdog reporting, telling the stories of a time, a place and a people—that's what makes a newspaper. And that's what we'll keep doing, no matter the address on the building.

October 26, 2014
Me and the ghosts, moving on

Lord willing, I'll sit down to work Monday morning for the first time in nearly four decades at a place other than 615 W. Lafayette Blvd.

The *Detroit News* is moving to a new home downtown, and for the past several weeks we've been packing a century's worth of history into orange crates.

Every time I've opened a drawer, memories spilled out. Every corner turned, I've bumped into ghosts of the magnificent misfits who shaped my growing up in that building.

I started here on my 21st birthday, and that first day was prescient. I was led into the newsroom, plopped at a desk against a far wall, and given no further instructions. After a couple of hours, something heavy crashed into the back of my chair and hit the floor beside me.

I looked down at a large, red-faced and quite obviously drunken man struggling to climb to his knees. Reaching for the phone on his desk, he dialed a number and promptly began sobbing. "I'm sorry, baby," he wailed into the receiver. "I've been on an undercover assignment for two days and couldn't call home."

Then he hung up, rubbed his eyes dry and broke into a big smile. Sticking out his hand, he said, "Hi, I'm Jim. Welcome to the *News*."

I called my mother straight off to report, "I think I'm gonna like it here."

And I have. Every single day. My heart always beats a little faster when I round the corner and the *News* building comes into view. Because I know what's inside. When I started here the newspaper war was still raging. We walked through the doors every day with one mission: beat the *Free Press* by any means necessary.

That newsroom ran on adrenaline and whiskey. There were cowboys and con men, scholars and scoundrels, lovers and fighters. I shared a desk with a hooker for six months in the '80s, but that's a bar stool story. Giants walked these floors, too. Amidst the carousing and carrying on some great journalism happened on Lafayette, produced by some damn fine newspapermen.

Too many were idiot savants gifted at that one thing, and otherwise emotionally stunted, too willing to sacrifice family and shred personal relationships to break the Big Story. OK, guilty.

But the chase burns like a fever. And it burned a lot of them out. We had a contract back then with Brighton Hospital, and every so often a drunk would be walked out of the newsroom and into a white van waiting out front.

Some never made it back. Even more were lost to the humorless expectations of corporate journalism that seeped in after the armistice. Imagine our reaction when we learned being drunk in the newsroom was a fire-able offense.

I understand an insurance company is taking over the *News* building, while we're moving into offices better suited to insurance salesmen. Things change, and none more than this business.

But not totally. The last items slipped into my orange crate were a reporter's notebook and a couple of pens, two bourbon glasses and a jug of Makers Mark.

I'm swinging by Lafayette in the morning to see if the ghosts need a lift to the new digs, and I expect they'll be thirsty. ⤛ ⤛ ⤛

February 27, 2014

Keep Obama out of America's newsrooms

Civil libertarians have long called on the government to stay out of our bedrooms. Well, I want the government to stay out of my newsroom.

The Federal Communications Commission hoped to march into television and radio stations—and even newspaper offices, over which it has no jurisdiction—to determine how editorial decisions are made. Its study would have implanted researchers in newsrooms to ask questions about why certain stories are covered and others aren't, and whether bias plays a role in making those calls.

The only correct answer is "none of your business." The First Amendment builds a high wall between America's newsrooms and a government that would control them given the slightest opening.

And this study would have surely cracked open the door.

Fortunately, a backlash, primarily driven by conservative media outlets, forced the FCC to shelf the study while it says it's revising its approach.

House Republicans this week introduced a bill to ban this study and any others like it for good. Congress must do even more to preserve a free press. The Founders weren't concerned with how ideas and information are distributed; they simply wanted to assure the government didn't get between the press and the people.

There must be absolute clarity that the First Amendment extends fully across the information spectrum. All of the same protections granted to print journalists should apply to electronic media outlets.

The best way to assure that is to get rid of the FCC altogether. The agency is obsolete, created at a time when a process was needed to distribute a limited number of airwaves.

Today, thanks to cable, satellite and the Internet, there is no limit to electronic communication outlets, and no need for a government agency that could potentially use its licensing authority to shackle them.

One of the supposed goals of the study was to determine whether all communities are being served by news coverage. It's absurd to think that there are any information deserts in this country. The information industry is vigorous and ubiquitous, and has more than adequately responded to market demand.

This seems to be an attempt by the FCC to reassert itself as the arbiter of media fairness, an inappropriate role that was tossed out with the scrapping of the Fairness Doctrine in 1989.

It would be chilling to have the Obama administration's FCC deciding whether news coverage is fair. Despite his lip service to transparency, this president is hostile to the First Amendment. In addition to spying on the phone calls and emails of reporters, his administration is on a record pace in denying Freedom of Information requests, turning down one-third of those filed.

Why every news outlet in the country wasn't screaming about the study is baffling. It took conservative talk shows, periodicals and Internet sites to derail this intrusion.

No wonder Obama is so eager to silence them. ⚡

About the Author

Nolan Finley began his newspaper career as a copy boy at the *Detroit News* while senior in college. After a brief stint with the *Jackson Citizen Patriot*, he returned to the *News* as a reporter, covering the administration of Mayor Coleman A. Young. He's been the newspaper's City Editor, Business Editor, Politics Editor and Deputy Managing Editor. In 2000 he was named Editorial Page Editor and his columns have appeared in the newspaper ever since. As he wrote in his introductory column, Finley is a product of the *News* and the Detroit community. He graduated from both Schoolcraft College and Wayne State University and in 2012 was inducted into the Michigan Journalism Hall of Fame. He is an outdoorsman, bourbon aficionado and rabid University of Kentucky basketball fan. He is a native of Cumberland County, Ky., where he still maintains a home.